Another Way

Pittsburgh Studies in Comparative and International Education

VOLUME 6

INTRODUCTION TO THE SERIES

The aim of the *Pittsburgh Studies in Comparative and International Education Series* is to produce edited and authored volumes on topics ranging from key international education issues, trends, and reforms to examinations of national education systems, social theories, and development education initiatives. Local, national, regional, and global volumes (single authored and edited collections) constitute the breadth of the series and offer potential contributors a great deal of latitude based on interests and cutting edge research. The series is supported by a strong network of international scholars and development professionals who serve on the Advisory Board and participate in the selection and review process for manuscript development. The volumes are intended to provide not only useful contributions to comparative, international, and development education (CIDE) but also possible supplementary readings for advanced courses for undergraduate and graduate students in CIDE.

Series Editors

John C. WEIDMAN (*Professor Emeritus, University of Pittsburgh, USA*)
W. James JACOB (*Professor, University of Memphis, USA*)

Managing Editors

Xi WANG (*Program Coordinator, Institute for International Studies in Education (IISE), University of Pittsburgh, USA*)
Weiyan XIONG (*Program Coordinator, IISE, University of Pittsburgh, USA*)

International Advisory Board

Dennis BANDA (*University of Zambia, Zambia*)
Regsuren BAT-ERDENE (*Ministry of Education, Culture and Science, Mongolia*)
Siddharth CHANDRA (*Michigan State University, USA*)
Cheng Sheng YAO (*National Chung Cheng University, Taiwan*)
James A. COOK (*Asian Studies Center, University of Pittsburgh, USA*)

Jorge Enrique DELGADO (*IISE, University of Pittsburgh, USA*)
Kathleen M. DEWALT (*Center for Latin American Studies,
University of Pittsburgh, USA*)
Richard DONATO (*IISE, University of Pittsburgh, USA*)
Erwin H. EPSTEIN (*Loyola University Chicago, USA*)
Carl FERTMAN (*IISE, University of Pittsburgh, USA*)
Noreen GARMAN (*IISE, University of Pittsburgh, USA*)
Michael GUNZENHAUSER (*IISE, University of Pittsburgh, USA*)
Michele Ferrier HERYFORD (*Confucius Institute, University of Pittsburgh, USA*)
Ali IBRAHIM (*United Arab Emirates University, UAE*)
Sean KELLY (*IISE, University of Pittsburgh, USA*)
Asif KHAN (*Karakoram International University, Gilgit, Pakistan*)
Lee FENG-JIHU (*National Chung Cheng University, Taiwan*)
Macrina LELEI (*African Studies Program, University of Pittsburgh, USA*)
Alan M. LESGOLD (*IISE, University of Pittsburgh, USA*)
Lin MING DIH (*National Chung Cheng University, Taiwan*)
Maureen W. MCCLURE (*IISE, University of Pittsburgh, USA*)
Nagwa MEGAHEAD (*Ain Shams University, Egypt*)
Rich MILNAR (*Center for Urban Education, University of Pittsburgh, USA*)
Donald E. MORISKY (*University of California, Los Angeles, USA*)
Enrique MU (*Carlow University, USA*)
Christopher B. MUGIMU (*Makerere University, Uganda*)
John MYERS (*Florida State University, USA*)
Erik C. NESS (*Institute of Higher Education, University of Georgia, USA*)
Yusuf K. NSUBUGA (*Ministry of Education and Sports, Uganda*)
Christine ODOUR-OMBAKA (*Maseno University, Kenya*)
Park NAMGI (*Gwangju National University of Education, Korea*)
Louis A. PICARD (*African Studies Program, University of Pittsburgh, USA*)
Allan PITMAN (*University of Western Ontario, Canada*)
Simona POPA (*UNESCO International Bureau of Education, Switzerland*)
Maureen K. PORTER (*IISE, University of Pittsburgh, USA*)
RUSWAN (*IAIN Walisongo, Indonesia*)
SUPARNO (*State University of Malang, Indonesia*)
Stewart E. SUTIN (*IISE, University of Pittsburgh, USA*)
Cynthia A. TANANIS (*IISE, University of Pittsburgh, USA*)
Mayumi TERANO (*Institute of Education, University of London, UK*)
Charlene TROVATO (*IISE, University of Pittsburgh, USA*)

Institute for International Studies in Education
School of Education (University of Pittsburgh)
4115 Wesley W. Posvar Hall, Pittsburgh, PA 15260, USA

The titles published in this series are listed at *brill.com/pscie*

Another Way

Decentralization, Democratization and the Global Politics of Community-Based Schooling

Edited by

Rebecca Clothey and Kai Heidemann

BRILL
SENSE

LEIDEN | BOSTON

All chapters in this book have undergone peer review.

The Library of Congress Cataloging-in-Publication Data is available online at
http://catalog.loc.gov
LC record available at https://lccn.loc.gov/2018039909

ISSN 2542-8675
ISBN 978-90-04-38470-5 (paperback)
ISBN 978-90-04-38472-9 (hardback)
ISBN 978-90-04-38471-2 (e-book)

Copyright 2019 by Koninklijke Brill NV, Leiden, The Netherlands.
Koninklijke Brill NV incorporates the imprints Brill, Brill Hes & De Graaf,
Brill Nijhoff, Brill Rodopi, Brill Sense, Hotei Publishing, mentis Verlag,
Verlag Ferdinand Schöningh and Wilhelm Fink Verlag.
All rights reserved. No part of this publication may be reproduced, translated,
stored in a retrieval system, or transmitted in any form or by any means, electronic,
mechanical, photocopying, recording or otherwise, without prior written
permission from the publisher.
Authorization to photocopy items for internal or personal use is granted by
Koninklijke Brill NV provided that the appropriate fees are paid directly to The
Copyright Clearance Center, 222 Rosewood Drive, Suite 910, Danvers, MA 01923,
USA. Fees are subject to change.

This book is printed on acid-free paper and produced in a sustainable manner.

CONTENTS

Foreword: Community Organizing and Educational Justice – From Local Struggles to a Global Movement ... ix
Mark R. Warren

Acknowledgements ... xiii

List of Acronyms ... xv

Notes on Contributors ... xvii

Series Editors Introduction ... xix

1. Introduction: Community-Based Schooling and the Intersectional Politics of Decentralization and Democratization ... 1
   Kai Heidemann and Rebecca Clothey

2. Social Movement-Led Democratic Governance of Public Education: The Case of the Brazilian Landless Workers Movement ... 11
   Rebecca Tarlau

3. Crisis, Protest and Democratization 'From Below': The Rise of a Community-Based Schooling Movement in Argentina ... 31
   Kai Heidemann

4. Accountability through Community-Based Management? Implications from the Local Level Implementation in El Salvador of a Globally-Popular Model ... 47
   D. Brent Edwards Jr.

5. Decentralization, Centralization and Minority Education in Hungary ... 65
   Andria D. Timmer

6. Decentralization and Education in Tanzania: The Role of Community Schools and Education for the Poor ... 83
   Serena Koissaba

7. Between State and Society: Community Schools in Zambia ... 97
   Richard Bamattre

8. Building a Community-Based Charter School in the United States ... 115
   Rebecca Clothey and Deanna Hill

CONTENTS

9. An Alternative Education Model in Urumqi 129
   Rebecca Clothey

10. School of Feminism in Beijing: Embodied Resistance and "Weak" Education in Twenty-First-Century China 145
    Weiling Deng

Index 157

MARK R. WARREN

FOREWORD

*Community Organizing and Educational Justice –
From Local Struggles to a Global Movement*

Another Way is a timely and important book for scholars and activists who care about the future of education in communities that are struggling from economic marginalization and social and political exclusion. The trends that shape public education are increasingly international, both from the elite and grassroots levels. Many elites have advanced a global agenda of neoliberalism that promotes privatization and decentralization of public education and sometimes austerity measures. Resistance comes in the continual efforts of oppressed or marginalized communities to confront power and inequities in which the struggle over control of education plays a central role. We know more about the neoliberal agenda than we do about grassroots resistance. This volume offers us the opportunity to begin to learn from a diverse set of grassroots efforts to promote community-based education across the globe. Speaking as a scholar of community organizing and education in the United States, we North Americans tend to be woefully ignorant of education movements outside of our country. This volume promises to provoke and stimulate important conversations within the education research community and the broader educational justice movement.

The focus of *Another Way* on community-based education and community schools is highly important and instructive. The editors have assembled an impressive array of careful studies. From them we learn that decentralization can serve in some cases to create opportunities for community control of education, creating schools that are more responsive to community cultures, histories and traditions. If these schools serve marginalized students better, they can be a force for equity and inclusion. On the other hand, decentralization can also serve the movement to privatize education and decrease state funding of education, leading to greater inequities and new forms of exclusion. The chapters in this volume offer careful analyses of the rich array of patterns that exist between these poles including some that seem to contribute simultaneously to both results: increasing local democracy while decreasing the resources available for public education, which of course undermines the foundations for a healthy democracy.

The struggle for the direction of public education is a struggle over power: who will have the power to determine whether decentralization moves towards equity or towards exclusion? In this context, local community mobilization is not sufficient to create the power necessary when privatizing forces are not only well financed but organized nationally and internationally. Community school movements will likely be more successful if and when they can become part of larger social movements which can create the power needed to set educational policy.

This is not to say that localized efforts to create small-scale models of community education are not important. They may well be necessary for a community's survival, as in cases of indigenous communities who need to find ways outside of state controlled institutions to teach their own language, history and cultural traditions. Local organizing efforts are also the places where grassroots people can begin to participate in democratic struggles, so they provide an essential foundation to broader national efforts (Warren et al. 2011).

The danger for cooptation of community movements, however, is ever present. For example, charter schools began in the United States with the promise of local responsiveness and creative innovation. Many were started by community-based organizations looking for alternatives to traditional forms of public education that were failing their children in large numbers. Twenty years later, the U.S. charter movement finds itself dominated by corporate networks bent on the transformation of education from public to private control. Cities like Chicago, Philadelphia and New York, among many others, have experienced large numbers of school closures in black and brown communities and the opening of charter networks and "schools of choice." Under the guise of "choice," some of the schools serve the new urban gentrifiers and thus become a force for the displacement and dispossession of communities of color. Wealthy funders like the Broad, Gates and Walton Family foundations have poured millions into charter schools. As it turns out, both the Republican administration of George W. Bush and the Democratic administration of Barack Obama have supported this trend towards privatization of public education.

The past few years have witnessed a dramatic change in community organizing efforts at education reform as they have increasing sought to combine forces into national alliances to combat the well-financed and politically-connected corporate reform movement behind charters and choice. These national alliances – like the Journey for Justice Alliance and the Alliance to Reclaim Our Schools – sometimes target federal policy but they mainly serve as venues for local struggles to connect, support each other, share resources, and publicize victories to inspire the larger movement. In other words, while centering their work locally, they seek to "nationalize" their local struggles and marshal greater resources and power to their efforts (Warren 2014).

Several of the essays in this volume, however, alert us to the fact that the forces of neoliberalism are increasingly organized at the global level, through institutions like the World Bank and a rapidly growing set of international educational nonprofits and businesses. Yet, we see that community-based efforts remain local, while at best linking at the national level. It would be interesting to know if community-based movements are beginning to seek connections across countries. There are some early signs in the United States, for instance, that groups are beginning to move in this direction, involving both discourse and technology. More and more the American educational justice movement is adopting a discourse drawn from the international human rights movement: that black and brown children and their families have a fundamental right to education, which includes the right of families to participate in the education of children. National alliances like the Dignity in Schools Campaign denounce harsh and racially inequitable school discipline policy as a violation of children's human rights. Meanwhile, community-based movements in the United States are also calling for building sustainable community schools as an alternative to closing and privatizing schools. Adopting human rights and community schools discourses provides a vehicle for connection to struggles employing similar frameworks and demands in other countries.

Meanwhile, social media has provided a platform to publicize local struggles across the globe more quickly and easily. When black parents went on a hunger strike in 2015 to stop the closing of their local high school on the south side of Chicago, they utilized Facebook and twitter and received support from people in many countries. #FightForDyett and associated hashtags trended heavily for five straight days, receiving nearly 100,000 tweets. People from around the United States and the globe posted pictures of themselves holding supportive signs and contributed food and money, while video tributes came in from France, Johannesburg, and Quito, helping to build a broader base of power that eventually forced the Mayor to back down.

In the end, the chapters in this volume, and the community struggles they examine, remind us that education is not simply one public service that communities might try to control or make more responsive to their needs. Education is the key to community development and the liberation of peoples. The Freirean tradition of popular education, the Alinsky tradition of community organizing, and the American civil rights movement's freedom schools are all examples of movements that understood that education was part and parcel of the struggle for liberation. John Dewey, from a somewhat different perspective, understood that education provided the foundation for a healthy and equitable democracy. In order to free themselves, people must learn the knowledge and skills to analyze the world around them understand the root causes of oppression, adopt effective strategies for change and develop the critical consciousness to support social movements.

Sociologists of education have long understood the duality of public schools as both sites of social control and potential sites of resistance or liberation. Schools lie at the epicenter of the struggle over the future of the next generation. Will our young people become cogs in the machine of global capitalism and state sponsored systems of domination, or will they be full human beings capable of determining their own fate and the future of their communities? The essays in this book remind us that the struggle for the soul of public education is at once a local, national and global struggle.

REFERENCES

Warren, Mark R., Karen L. Mapp and the Community Organizing and School Reform Project. (2011). *A Match on Dry Grass: Community Organizing as a Catalyst for School Reform*, New York: Oxford University Press.
Warren, Mark R. (2014). "Transforming Public Education: The Need for an Educational Justice Movement," *New England Journal of Public Policy* 26(1):1–16.

ACKNOWLEDGEMENTS

As the editors of this volume we would like to express our thanks to all the contributing authors who joined us and to thank them for taking the time to undertake multiple drafts and carefully craft each chapter. Thanks also go out to Ms. Dorothee Hoffman at Maastricht University for her very detailed and watchful editorial comments on each of the chapters. We are also grateful to W. James Jacob and John Weidman, the editors of the *Pittsburgh Studies in Comparative and International Education Series*, for supporting our project and providing the useful feedback needed to carry it forward to publication.

LIST OF ACRONYMS

ACE	Community Education Association
AEGS	Associacíon de la Educación de Gestión Social
BEST	Basic Education Statistics for Tanzania
CBM	Community-Based Management
CBPR	Community-Based Participatory Research
CMO	Charter Management Organization
EDUCO	Education with Community Participation
EMO	Education Management Organization
ERIP	Education Reform Implementation Project
FECEABA	Federación de Cooperativas y Entidades Afines de Enseñanza
FEDECABA	Federación de Cooperativas Autogestionadas de Buenos Aires
FMLN	Farabundo Martí Liberation Front
FWCW	United Nations Fourth World Conference on Women
IMF	International Monetary Fund
INGO	International Non-Governmental Organization
KLIK	Klebelsberg Institution Maintenance Center
MINED	Ministry of Education
MMD	Movement for Multiparty Democracy
MST	Brazilian Landless Workers Movement
NGA	Network of Glocal Activism
NGO	Non-Governmental Organization
PCSC	Parent Community School Committee
PISA	Program for International Student Assessment
PRONERA	Program for Education in Areas of Agrarian Reform
PSB	Brazilian Socialist Party
ROCS	Reformed Open Community Schools
RTEI	Right to Education Index
SFB	School of Feminism in Beijing
SHAPE	Self-Help Action Plan for Education
SIDA	Swedish International Development Cooperation Agency
SPARK	Skills, Participation, Access to Relevant Knowledge
SUTEBA	Sindicato Unificado de Trabajadores de la Educación de Buenos Aires
TRC	Teacher Resource Training Center
URT	United Republic of Tanzania
VOS	Vendor Operated School
ZOCS	Zambia Open Community Schools
ZCSS	Zambia Community Schools Secretariat

NOTES ON CONTRIBUTORS

Richard Bamattre is a PhD Candidate in Education at the University of Minnesota. His research interests include political sociology of education, alternative schools and homeschooling, and program evaluation. His dissertation is a mixed methods study on the national policy and current educational outcomes of community schools in Zambia.

Rebecca Clothey is Associate Professor of Education at Drexel University (Philadelphia, PA, USA) with a joint appointment as Director of Global Studies in the Department of Global Studies and Modern Languages in the College of Arts and Sciences. Her research explores education policy, ethnicity, and community driven education initiatives in China, the US, and Turkey. She has published on these topics in such journals as *Comparative Education Review, Compare, Higher Education Policy*, and *Asian Ethnicity*. She has received funding for her research from Fulbright, the Spencer Foundation, the Foreign Language and Area Studies Fellowship, and the American Research Institute in Turkey, among others.

Weiling Deng is a PhD candidate in the Education Department of UCLA, with a specialization in comparative and international education. She is currently working on her dissertation that critically addresses the innovation and limitation of the contemporary grassroots Chinese feminist movement against the backdrop of globalization and neoliberalism. Besides feminist theories and gender studies in relation to the philosophy and politics of education, her academic interests also expand to cultural anthropology, critical media literacy, social movements, urban humanities, youth cultures, and modern Chinese history.

D. Brent Edwards Jr. is Assistant Professor of theory and methodology in the study of education at the College of Education, University of Hawai'i at Mānoa, Department of Educational Foundations. His research interests include political economy of education reform; decentralization; community-based management and global education policies.

Kai Heidemann is Assistant Professor of Sociology at Maastricht University. His research explores the nexus of social movements and education policy with emphasis on community-driven education reform initiatives in Europe and Latin America. His work has been published in academic journals such as *Mobilization, Sociological Focus* and *The European Journal of Cultural and Political Sociology*.

NOTES ON CONTRIBUTORS

Deanna Hill, J.D., Ph.D., is Assistant Clinical Professor of Education at Drexel University (Philadelphia, PA, USA). Her research focuses on education law and policy, the politics of education, and race and gender in education. Before earning a PhD in education, Dr. Hill practiced law in the state of Texas.

Serena Koissaba is a doctoral student in education policy, organization and leadership at the University of Illinois at Urbana-Champaign. Her research interests examine the influence of racial thought on public education policy, particularly in small rural and urban schools. She has worked in international education for 17 years with a particular interest in providing educational access to children from vulnerable populations.

Rebecca Tarlau is Assistant Professor of education and labor and employment relations at The Pennsylvania State University. Rebecca's research agenda has three broad areas of focus: (1) theories of the state and state-society relations; (2) social movements, critical pedagogy, and learning; (3) Latin American education and development. Her scholarship engages in debates in the fields of political sociology, international and comparative education, social movements, critical pedagogy, global and transnational sociology, and social theory.

Andria D. Timmer is Assistant Professor of anthropology at Christopher Newport University. In her research she explores the manner in which nongovernmental and humanitarian organizations seek to provide aid both in times of disaster and to perpetually underserved populations. Her book *Educating the Hungarian Roma* describes efforts of NGOs to desegregate the education system. Currently, she is conducting ethnographic research on the efforts of NGOs in Hungary to fight for the rights and visibility of refugees in the country.

Mark R. Warren is Professor of public policy and public affairs at the University of Massachusetts Boston. Mark studies and works with community and youth organizing groups seeking to promote equity and justice in education, community development and American democratic life. Mark is the author of several books, including *Lift Us Up! Don't Push Us Out! Voices from the Frontlines of the Educational Justice Movement* and *A Match on Dry Grass: Community Organizing as a Catalyst for School Reform*. Mark is co-chair of the Urban Research-Based Action Network (URBAN), a national network of scholars and community activists in the U.S. designed to promote collaborations that produce research that advances racial equity and social justice. He is a John Simon Guggenheim Memorial Fellow and has won many other prestigious awards and fellowships.

JOHN C. WEIDMAN AND W. JAMES JACOB

SERIES EDITORS INTRODUCTION

We are pleased to introduce the next volume in the *Pittsburgh Studies in Comparative and International Education* book series, which is published and distributed by Brill Sense. The issues that will be highlighted in this book series range from key international education issues, trends, and reforms to examinations of national education systems, social and educational theories, and development education initiatives. Local, national, regional, and global volumes (single authored and edited collections) are anticipated in order to offer potential contributors a great deal of latitude based on interests and cutting edge research.

The *PSCIE* series is supported by a strong network of international scholars and development professionals who serve on the International Advisory Board and participate in the selection and review process for manuscript development. Working with our International Advisory Board, periodic calls will be issued for contributions to this series from among the most influential associations and organizations in international studies in education, including the Comparative and International Education Society, World Council of Comparative Education Societies, and UNESCO.

In future volumes in the *PSCIE* series, we encourage the generation of exceptional CIDE scholarship from researchers, policy makers, and practitioners from around the world. We hope this volume will encourage prospective authors and editors to submit manuscript proposals to the *PSCIE* series about their current research and project interests.

KAI HEIDEMANN AND REBECCA CLOTHEY

1. INTRODUCTION

*Community-Based Schooling and the Intersectional Politics
of Decentralization and Democratization*

The case studies compiled in this book offer a tapestry of comparative insights on how community-based schooling initiatives have been shaped by transnational processes of institutional decentralization. In particular, the stories woven into each chapter shed light on the development of community-based schools in eight nations: Argentina, Brazil, China, El Salvador, Hungary, Tanzania, the United States and Zambia. Although there is no single model or universal approach to community-based schooling emphasized in this book, a 'community-based school' is defined in general terms as an alternative type of formal education program that is deeply rooted within, responsive to and oriented toward the political, economic, cultural and historical realities of the social environment within which a given school and its constituents are situated (Smith and Sobel 2010). Community-based schooling initiatives typically operate in ways which seek to position local citizens as both the architects and benefactors of educational programs. As David Corson (1999, p. 10) writes: "community-based education begins with people and their immediate reality. Above all it allows them to become meaningfully involved in shaping their own futures through the schools and other agencies in their community." Community-based schools have often emerged when educational stake-holders, notably teachers and parents, articulate strong disillusionment with the logics and outcomes of 'mainstream' educational practices. This disenchantment often stems from deep-seated grievances based on experiences of systematic exclusion and disenfranchisement from decision-making processes. This is at least partially why the democratic principles underlying community-based education can have such a strong appeal to members of historically marginalized social groups, such as ethnic minorities and the poor. Regardless of their point of origins, community-based schools are thus typically brought to life by collective desires for change and a concerted commitment to craft another way.

Community-based schools can operate as public, semi-public or private entities. Indeed, as shown by each chapter of this book, community-based schools often occupy an ambiguous and thus contentious institutional niche within national educational systems which challenge traditional boundaries between the 'public' and 'private' sectors. Despite considerable cross-national variations in how such schools are legally or formally classified, however, the underlying motives and convictions which often trigger the creation of community-based schools are nicely captured by Christine Villani and Douglas Atkins (2000, p. 121):

> Community-based education is centered on the student's ability to recognize and support the needs of the surrounding community. In this way, students become accountable for providing values which stem from their freedom to express, develop, and solve the inherent problems or concerns they have for their community. Over the long-term use of this ideal model, the entire community will become involved in the process, thereby making the educational process cyclical and continuously propelled. Reciprocal relationships based on these ideals will be promoted and fostered by all. Students and teachers are the fuel that generates community-based education. Parents, community leaders, administrators, school board members, and citizens are an integral part in the development, production, implementation, and assessment of community-based education. This cohesive interplay is designed to foster trust and belief in fellow human beings. It also creates collaborative efforts between school and community to solve various problems.

This book is driven by a desire to understand the patterns and particularities which characterize community-based schooling initiatives from a global comparative perspective. Attention is placed on the diverse issues, identities and interests which have fueled the development of community-based schooling initiatives in Europe, Africa, Asia and the Americas. Concern is also given across the book to understanding the conditions from which community-based schools have emerged and the variety of (intended and unintended) outcomes which have been generated by distinctive community-based schooling projects. As the editors of this book we feel that despite considerable variation in where they exist, what they look like or even how they operate, community-based schools are a truly discernable global phenomenon which merit systemic investigation and theorization by comparative education scholars as well as by anthropologists, political scientists, sociologists and other researchers concerned with issues of educational change and reform.

In addition to the nuanced insights and quandaries raised about community-based schooling in each of the individual chapters, there are two central themes which span the entire book: democratization and decentralization.

DEMOCRATIZATION

On the one hand, a primary concern which unifies the chapters in the book pertains to the relationship between community-based schooling and broader-level processes of educational democratization. Throughout the book the notion of 'democratization' is employed in rather broad terms to refer to increased forms of direct community participation in processes of educational decision-making at the local level (Grugel 2002). Stated otherwise, democratization is about making educational programs subject to increasing public influence and control so as to try and make local schools work in ways that explicitly reflect and respond to the realities of students, their families and the surrounding society. Of course, democratization is not a zero-sum situation characterized by an absence or presence. Rather, democratization is a question of gradations and degrees. As James Manor (1999, p. 9) notes: "Community contributions which provide people with no voice cannot be regarded as democratic, but when some form of supervision or influence is permitted, they have some democratic content." The community-based schools under discussion in this book all generally speak to issues of educational democratization in some way. Nevertheless, the particular manner in which democratization has been perceived let alone pursued or achieved varies significantly from case to case. While some cases demonstrate efforts to realize very strong and explicit degrees of educational democratization, others give evidence to more limited and subtle expressions.

Democratization and community participation in schools has long been a hot topic of discussion among educational scholars, policy-makers, and practitioners (Demirbolat 2012). While concern for community influence and engagement may seem most consistently evident in the policy discourses of liberal democratic nations with histories of universal public education, such concerns are also clearly evident in other national settings, such as China, Cuba, Venezuela and Iran (Griffiths and Millei 2013). Although not everyone agrees as to how exactly community participation should best develop, most discussions seem to reflect agreement on the general merits of providing local families and citizens with increased forms of access, voice and influence in the education system. Strengthening community participation in education is typically promoted as essential to the building of schools which are more egalitarian and inclusive in their design as well as more capable of reaching targeted academic outcomes (Bray 2003; Evans and Hiatt-Michael 2016). A basic conviction at work here is that by positioning members of the local community as central stake-holders in the educational system, the structure and content of schooling programs will be more closely aligned with the tangible needs and realities of students and their families. Such an alignment renders schooling more relevant and meaningful to students which can, in turn, bolster the prospects for enhanced forms of student engagement and achievement in the long and short term. The phenomenon of community-based schooling represents an ideal context to explore the complex sets of struggles, strategies and successes surrounding processes of educational democratization.

DECENTRALIZATION

A second central concern driving this book is a desire to interrogate the ways in which a global politics of decentralization 'from above' can generate opportunities for the construction of community-based schools 'from below'. In this light, the book seeks to scrutinize some of the novel institutional configurations emerging in local settings as a result of the shifting perspectives and paradigms which have transpired through global trends in educational planning and policy-making over the past several decades. Of concern here is the capacity of decentralization policies to variously engender and enable as well as obstruct and/or complicate the development of community-based schooling initiatives (Bray 2007). In simplest terms, the politics of decentralization circulate around questions of who exactly gets to shape essential decisions about educational systems, such as the funding, structure, content and/or purposes of schools. In this book, 'decentralization' is employed rather broadly to refer to territorialized transfers of power in the governance of educational systems which move 'downward' from a relatively singular node of centralized authority toward multiple (semi-) autonomous nodes located at the sub-national and/or local levels of political decision-making (McGinn and Welsh 1999). As with processes of democratization, decentralization is not a zero-sum game, but rather a question of degrees of intensity which can play out along multiple domains of educational policy-making, such as funding, teacher accreditation or curricular content (Weidman and DePietro-Jurand 2011). While some domains may experience high degrees of decentralization (e.g. funding schemas) others may undergo very limited degrees of decentralization (e.g. curricula and assessments). Moreover, educational decentralization is typically an uneven and irregular process that can take years to both unfold and reverse course. The ways in which decentralization policies are implemented typically reflect the particular social and political interests at play within a given nation at a specific historical juncture. In this book, particular attention is placed on understanding the extent to which decentralization policies have engendered novel mechanisms and institutional pathways for educational reform which can either enable or constrain the formation of open and collaborative alignments between local schools and communities.

In each of the individual explorations of community-based schooling situated within this book, it is revealing to see how broad historical trends toward the decentralization of national education systems around the world have played a decisive role in creating a macro-institutional context from which community-based schooling initiatives have emerged and expanded. In this light, one might thus initially suggest that decentralization policies have promoted processes of educational democratization by stimulating the growth of community-based schools. However, the politics of decentralization are not monolithic and have generally played out in very complex and heterogeneous ways. Indeed, decentralization has become one of the biggest sources of heated debate and conflict in educational systems around the world (Bray 2007). On the one hand, increased decentralization is often touted by some as essential to assuring robust levels of community representation, inclusion and participation in the educational system. As Manor (1999, p. 1) writes: "Advocates of pluralist, competitive politics have regarded decentralization as a device for deepening democracy or for prying closed systems open, to give interest groups space in which to organize, compete and otherwise assert themselves." Yet, on the other hand, decentralization policies are also frequently criticized for pushing 'neoliberal' agendas of austerity, marketization and privatization which have next to nothing to do with democratization and the authentic enfranchisement of local citizens (Torres 1998). In fact, decentralization policies in many parts of the world have been strongly correlated with increased forms of ethno-racial segregation and the systematic reproduction of socio-economic inequalities. (Bray 2007; Rofes and Stulberg 2004). While all the chapters in this book show how community-based schooling initiatives have been stimulated by policies of decentralization, they also clearly show that the opportunities generated by the global politics of decentralization are a very mixed bag filled with deep-seated ambiguities, contradictions and dilemmas when it comes to issues of local-level democratization and empowerment. It is thus essential that educational scholars carefully scrutinize the linkages between decentralization and democratization across time and place so as to avoid knee-jerk *a priori* assessments. While it might be easy to say that decentralization has fostered the creation of community-based schools, it is far from easy to claim that decentralization has allowed these kinds of schools to thrive and fully live up to their potential as empowering vehicles of democratization for local communities. As the editors of this collection our goal is neither to praise nor condemn the phenomenon of decentralization outright, but rather to scrutinize some of the (intended and unintended) consequences of decentralization for the creation of community-based schooling programs, most notably the potential of such locally-rooted schools to promote the democratization of public education.

Although decentralization is part of a very influential and widespread educational 'movement' which has been re-shaping the institutional contours of educational systems around the world for the past several decades, it is not a single unitary policy 'package' comprised of clear-cut aims and modes of application. Rather, as noted earlier, decentralization is more of a generalized policy 'logic' which can wear many faces and serve many agendas. Decentralization is thus not an inherently right-wing or left-wing project. As summarized by Manor (1999, p. 1): "[decentralization] appeals to people of the left, the center and the right, and to groups which disagree with each other on a number of other issues." What ultimately gives decentralization a putatively 'conservative' or 'progressive' flavor, are the ways in which particular sets of actors steer and put decentralization to work as a means to achieve certain ends (Mohan and Stokke 2000; Bray 2007; Weidman and DePietro-Jurand 2011). On the one hand, decentralization can offer a path for historically marginalized and subordinate actors to work collectively to combat structural inequalities generated by repressive states and exclusionary markets. On the other hand, however, decentralization can also be utilized by elites so as to whittle down or withdraw the provision of state-based services and resources in the name of economic austerity and efficiency. Hence, for proponents of community-based schooling, the policy logics of educational decentralization may provide an opportune institutional niche for the development of an alternative educational program rooted in democratic principles of local control and management of school, but such logics will not necessarily entail a provision of the material resources needed to effectively run such entities, particularly in economically impoverished and politically marginalized areas.

As each of the chapters reveals, the ways in which decentralization has been implemented in different national settings has provided very distinctive paths for the development of community-based schools and especially for their utilization as more or less influential instruments of 'democratization'. In fact, the cases show how notions of 'democratization' can diverge widely and signify many different things for proponents of community-based schooling located in Europe, Africa, Asia and the Americas. More specifically, the significance and meanings attached to community-based schooling vary widely based upon the social realities and cultural identities of local citizens as well as the politico-economic systems within which they live. This book thus offers some fresh insight into old questions about the contentious and often contradictory relationship between community-driven processes of educational democratization 'from below' on the one hand, and state-based processes of educational decentralization 'from above' on the other.

CHAPTER OVERVIEWS

Each of the chapters of this book provides a case study within a different country context that highlights the interaction of national policy with local level concerns. The first chapter by Rebecca Tarlau looks at how a strategic quest for increased community participation in and control of local schools played a pivotal role in the mobilization of landless peasants seeking recognition and social justice in rural Brazil. Her chapter examines the tensions between community-driven reform and neoliberal practices, or, how decentralization can simultaneously promote citizen participation *and* justify a reduced, minimal state that abandons its role in guaranteeing universal rights. Tarlau explores the case of the Brazilian Landless Workers Movement's (MST) thirty-year attempt to transform public schooling to argue that decentralization does not necessarily lead to more democracy at the local level. However, her chapter also shows that decentralization can offer an *opportunity* for a movement to promote local governance if there is a collective effort by an organized group with a clear vision for how to expand democratic participation. She discusses this as a form of *social movement-led democratic governance*: a social movement's strategic capacity to facilitate communities' participation in state institutions, within contradictory contexts.

Kai Heidemann's chapter also draws from social movement theory to analyze the highly contentious and vocal expressions of democratization which fueled the rise of a community-based schooling movement in Argentina during a time of dramatic national crisis and the diffusion of widespread public protest (Heidemann, Chapter 3). The Argentine case shows how the instabilities generated by a situation of macro-structural rupture during the early 2000s generated empowering opportunities for a diverse network of progressive educators to transform their local schools into community-based schools, forge collaborative organizational alliances between these schools and ultimately seek out a formal institutional status for community-based schooling from the state. Among the insights of the

INTRODUCTION

Argentine case, one particularly interesting aspect lies in the ways that progressive proponents of community-based schooling engaged with a legacy of educational decentralization policies initiated in the 1990s. In particular, these actors tried to detach the logics of decentralization from the 'neoliberal' territories of marketization and privatization so as to convert it into a mechanism for realizing democratic self-determination and empowerment.

Many of the cases in this book show how efforts to democratize education through the vehicle of community-based schooling can be tied to local struggles against entrenched forms of structural inequality and exclusion. In her exploration of community-based schooling amongst the Roma minority in Hungary, for instance, Andria Timmer (Chapter 5) offers an intriguing first-hand look at how a small group of committed civil society actors established an alternative school for Roma youth in the hopes of transcending a legacy of institutionalized ethnic discrimination and segregation. While she argues that community-based education could be a powerful tool to work towards eliminating inequalities, she also demonstrates that community-based education cannot succeed without a corresponding political and public commitment to invest in such efforts.

On the other hand, D. Brent Edwards' chapter explores such a political commitment with a more global look at decentralization policy implementation. In his chapter he looks at how local communities react to a community based management approach centrally imposed by the World Bank through the "Education with Community Participation" (EDUCO) program in El Salvador. As Edwards describes, EDUCO formally transferred the ability to hire and fire teachers to a committee of parents at the community level, with the promise of efficiency, effectiveness, and accountability. Paradoxically, although the language of "democratization and intrinsically-valuable community participation" has been invoked in relation to EDUCO, the program was widely-promoted in terms of its market principles. Edwards finds that a shortcoming of this approach is that it assumes "instrumental relations can be uniformly inscribed in communities regardless of their particular contexts" (Edwards, Chapter 4).

Working in a different context, Richard Bamattre shows how the expansion of community-based schools oriented toward progressive ideals of democratization and the empowerment of rural communities across Zambia have often struggled to realize their aims due to material shortcomings and weak levels of support from the state. Working from a historical perspective, Bamattre shows that amidst a decentralizing yet stagnant public educational system in Zambia in the 1990s, local people built their own schools and staffed them with volunteer teachers. Yet starting from 1991, the government moved towards legitimizing community schools as an official provider of education. These schools were slowly endorsed within a context of liberalization of state services and community participation in education, then positioned as an alternative education system, and finally integrated as a parallel system alongside government schools. Bamattre's case study reflects how states can leverage the rhetoric of decentralization and democratization to sanction the public role of non-state schools, thus moving towards goals of increased educational access, while paradoxically minimizing the active role of national and local government in providing education in remote or poor urban areas.

Serena Koissaba further explores how community schools in poor areas of rural Tanzania negotiate power within a decentralized education system. Specifically, she shows how identity politics and cultural shifts in disenfranchised communities take place through partnerships with a small international non-governmental organization and individual private investors to gain knowledge and resources needed to create a quality and equitable education system for poor children.

Shifting focus from the marginalized poor to the upper middle class, the chapter by Rebecca Clothey and Deanna Hill explores the rhetoric of democratization in the charter school movement in the United States through a case study of one particular bilingual immersion program charter school established by a community of mostly upper middle class White people in an urban environment who did not feel the existing public school options would suit their children's needs. In response to the new charter school laws established in their city in the 1990s, they collaborated to create a new school that they hoped would benefit children across the city. However, though the charter school policy rhetoric promotes 'choice' and opportunity for all, Clothey and Hill's case study demonstrates that without effective social and cultural capital, it is challenging if not impossible for 'all' to benefit from the policy.

The next chapter, by Rebecca Clothey, similarly describes how a community of individuals (in this case ethnic minority Uyghurs in China) see themselves as marginalized from the public school system. They appropriate China's decentralization of education policy to creatively shape empowering non-degree granting community based language schools that promote cultural transmission and employment opportunities within their community. Interestingly, these schools emerge in a notably non-democratic political environment and therefore provide a *subtle* articulation of local empowerment. However, while these language centers do achieve some of the community's aims, on the less positive side, they also reproduce and maintain ethnic segregation in Xinjiang, where the schools are located. Thus while decentralization provides new opportunities for marginalized Uyghurs to assert local control over their curriculum in the only way possible in this context— through private, non-degree granting training centers—decentralization in this case may also serve to marginalize them further.

Working within the same national context, Weiling Deng tells a different story in the final chapter by showing how a community-based education initiative pioneered by feminists in urban Beijing was ultimately shut down by Chinese authorities precisely because of the lack of subtlety regarding its democratic aims and progressive aspirations.

In sum, this book shows that by looking comparatively across cases it is possible to both identify and theorize on the particular ways in which community-based schooling initiatives can (potentially) promote processes of educational democratization as well as the variety of claims, struggles, ambiguities, dilemmas, and disappointments accompanying people's efforts to build alternatives and to envision another way.

REFERENCES

Bray, Mark. (2003). "Community Initiatives in Education: Goals, Dimensions and Linkages with Governments." *Compare: A Journal of Comparative and International Education, 33*(1), 31–45.

Corson, David. (1999). Community-based education for indigenous cultures. In Stephen May, ed., *Indigenous Community-Based Education.* Philadelphia, PA: Multilingual Matters Ltd.

Demirbolat, Ayse. (2012). *The Relationship Between Democracy and Education.* Sharjah: Bentham Science Publishers.

Evans, Michael, & Diana Hiatt-Michael. (2016). *The Power of Community Engagement for Educational Change.* Charlotte, NC: Information Age Publishing.

Gomm, Roger, Martyn Hammersley, & Peter Foster, eds. (2000). *Case Study Method: Key Issues, Key Texts.* Thousand Oaks, CA: Sage Publications.

Grugel, Jean. (2002). *Democratization: A Critical Introduction.* New York, NY: Palgrave Macmillan.

Manor, James. (1999). *The Political Economy of Democratic Decentralization.* Washington, DC: The International Bank for Reconstruction and Development.

Mohan, Giles, & Kristian Stokke. (2000). "Participatory Development and Empowerment: The Dangers of Localism." *Third World Quarterly, 21*(2), 247–268.

Rofes, Eric, & Lisa Stulberg. (2004). *The Emancipatory Promise of Charter Schools: Toward a Progressive Politics of School Choice.* Albany, NY: State University of New York Press.

Torres, Carlos A. (1998) *Democracy, Education and Multiulturalism: Dilemmas of Citizenship in a Global World.* New York, NY: Rowman and Littlefield.

Villani, Christine, & Douglas Atkins. (2000). "Community-Based Education." *School Community Journal, 10*(1), 121–126.

Weidman, John, & Robin DePietro-Juran. (2011). *Decentralization: A Guide to Education Project Design Based on a Comprehensive Literature and Project Review.* Washington, DC: United States Agency for International Development.

REBECCA TARLAU

2. SOCIAL MOVEMENT-LED DEMOCRATIC GOVERNANCE OF PUBLIC EDUCATION

The Case of the Brazilian Landless Workers Movement

It was July 9, 2011, and I was heading to interview Mayor Eduardo Coutinho of the municipality of Água Preta, in the sugar cane region of Pernambuco. This municipality is one of the strong holds of the Brazilian Landless Workers Movement (MST), a large agrarian social movement that occupies land in the region and tries to force the government to redistribute this land to poor landless workers. Over the previous thirty years, MST activists have also developed a range of educational proposals for the public school system that support their broader political and economic struggle. These pedagogies include collective teacher planning, the incorporation of students and parents in the democratic governance of the school, the integration of manual and intellectual labor, and connecting the curriculum to the rural reality of the students and local political struggles. I wanted to interview Eduardo because he was one of the many elected officials throughout the country that was allowing the movement to participate directly in educational governance and incorporate these pedagogies in the schools. Eduardo had recently joined the left-leaning Brazilian Socialist Party (PSB). He was from an elite family that had been in power in the region for decades with different political affiliations. Similarly to other elite families, the Coutinho family's power was derived from their land, as Eduardo's grandfather had been the owner of the largest sugar plantation in the region. Thus, Eduardo's support of the MST seemed at odds with his economic interests.

After miles of driving on almost-impassable muddy roads we pulled up to his plantation, where a group of people was waiting. I was escorted to Eduardo's office and he asked me to have a seat while he "attended to the people outside." The first woman came in and told a story about someone sick in her family, asking if Eduardo could help. Eduardo gave her 50 *reais* [in 2011 US$25], saying to the woman, "It is only a little, but it is from the heart, so you can buy some groceries." Then, two more men came inside. The first told Eduardo that he had walked barefoot for four hours to arrive there. After the two men left the office, Eduardo asked his assistant to give each of the men 30 *reais*. Eduardo turned to me, "I know that it should not happen this way, but I have to help people when I can."[1] In the context of a decentralized political system, where mayors have significant economic and political power, citizens that are aligned with Eduardo look to him for material survival.

After the visitors had left, Eduardo and I jumped into a two-hour interview about municipal politics, the regional economy, and the MST. Eduardo explained, "My relationship with the MST began a year after my election ... I became closer to the movement, I supported MST marches, meetings of *sem terrinha* [little landless children]." Eduardo seemed open to the MST's presence in his municipality, and even supported their participation in the municipal public school system. However, when I pushed him on the issue, asking him why he funded a movement that critiques large land estates, he replied: "I am the mayor, I try to attend to everyone's demands ... I have always had a good dialogue with the MST. Why shouldn't I support a meeting of MST youth? *I attend to the needs of the Evangelical church, the soccer team, a guy who wants to go to the beach. Why not fund a plenary of MST youth?* [emphasis added]" Although Eduardo supports the MST's efforts to increase local democratic participation in the schools – and is able to support them due to the decentralized educational context – these relationships are also clearly part of his strategy for maintaining political power in the municipality.

***

Across Brazil, municipal, state, and federal government officials are devolving educational responsibilities to local MST leaders to develop curricula support teachers, design new educational practices, and facilitate communities' democratic participation in public schools. In many locations like Água Preta, conservative mayors allow this to happen because the benefits of social movement participation seem to outweigh the potential conflicts that might arise if this help is rejected. As another local mayor in Pernambuco explained, "After I took power, the MST became part of the administration – they helped to run the government. They began to make a lot of suggestions about education, and we invited them to participate ... It was very practical. The MST education collective had already been working in the municipality for a long time." For these mayors, the MST's participation in public schools seems to be a "give-away," both avoiding conflicts and helping the schools function more efficiently. The pedagogies the MST implements, which promote collective work practices, democratic participatory governance, and political struggle, do not seem to be immediately threatening.

How do we reconcile this tension between an obvious attempt for co-optation within a decentralized political system, and the possible presence of what has been called empowered participatory governance (Fung and Wright 2003)? In this chapter I argue that decentralization does not necessarily lead to more bottom-up democracy at the local level. To the contrary, given the extreme economic and social inequalities within communities, decentralization often leads to power becoming even more concentrated in the hands of economic and political elites. However, if there is a collective effort by an organized group with a clear vision for how to expand democratic participation, decentralization can also offer an *opportunity* for these movements to claim space within the state to promote local governance.

SOCIAL MOVEMENT-LED DEMOCRATIC GOVERNANCE OF PUBLIC EDUCATION

The following analysis of the MST's attempt to participate in educational governance in two decentralized school systems will illustrate the dynamics of this process.

BACKGROUND AND CHAPTER FOCUS

The MST is one of the largest social movements in Latin America, and has helped over 350,000 poor rural families access land through the tactic of land occupations (Wright and Wolford 2003; Branford and Rocha 2002). In the late 1970s, during the political *abertura* (opening) that led to a return to democracy in Brazil, progressive priests in the Catholic Church following liberation theology (Berryman 1987) were active in both rural and urban areas, proposing alternatives to traditional poverty alleviation programs. These priests began discussions with landless workers in the southern part of Brazil about the possibility of occupying unproductive land estates as a solution to unequal land distribution. In the early 1980s, dozens of rural farmers successfully organized these land occupations, entering large, privately-owned, unproductive farmland and setting up make-shift camps for several years, until the government agreed to give the families the rights to farm this land.

In 1984, leaders of these different land occupations came together to found the MST. Although outside actors played a major role in organizing the original land occupations, the families at the meeting decided that the MST would be an autonomous organization, independent from churches, labor unions, and political parties. The slogan of the newly formed organization was "Land for those who live and work on it." Since 1984, the MST has grown to become a national social movement present in 23 states, with over 1.5 million women, men, and children living in areas of agrarian reform. The MST's land struggle is ongoing, with thousands of people currently living in MST camps, waiting for land rights.[2]

In many MST settlements across the country, especially in the poor Northeast, families continue to face severe challenges after receiving land rights, including lack of irrigation, difficulty in obtaining agricultural credits, and long distances that these farmers have to travel to receive social services such as public health and education. Lack of access to education in the countryside was particularly acute in the 1980s and early 1990s, when schools were so far away and transportation so difficult, that many of the children of the families that were living in MST camps and settlements were out of school. Those youth who did manage to study usually lived with a family member in a local city, often losing their connection to the countryside and abandoning their settlements.

The exodus of youth from the countryside was worrisome to the MST leadership, who wanted to support multi-generational farming communities. However, just as concerning were the cases in which the communities succeeded in demanding a local school in their agrarian reform settlement, but the government sent teachers to those schools who taught the students that the land occupations their parents had participated in were illegal and wrong. Quickly MST leaders realized that access to public education, even within their own settlements, would only serve to divide the

13

settlement families – unless they transformed schools to respect their rural traditions and livelihoods.

Over the past three decades, MST leaders have demanded the right to their communities' democratic participation in educational governance. Activists have drawn on diverse theories to develop a set of pedagogical practices for schools that encourage youth to stay in the countryside, while also fostering activism and collective forms of work. These pedagogies include a focus on student self-governance, the integration of manual and intellectual labor, the creation of an interdisciplinary curriculum that is based on the local reality of rural populations, the promotion of cultural activities, the inclusion of agro-ecological initiatives in schools, and the insertion of students into local political struggles.[3] This combination of pedagogical proposals is in direct contrast to the dominant trend in Brazil towards implementing educational policies that emphasize individualism, meritocracy, managerial efficiency, and preparation for the urban job market. MST activists engage in contentious actions to support their educational ideas, while also facilitating community discussions, organizing teacher trainings, and writing curricula together with state actors.

In this chapter I analyze the politics of the MST's community-driven educational reform efforts, and more specifically, how MST activists engage the decentralized Brazilian state and lead a process of participatory democratic governance in local communities. The Brazilian public school system in is one of the most decentralized systems in the world, with 27 state governments and 5,570 municipal governments that all have autonomy to administer their own schools. This has provided both challenges and opportunities for the MST's educational reform efforts, as in some regions conservative governments reject the movement's educational proposal, while in other locations the movement's participation is embraced. Often, government actors agree to the democratic participation of MST activists not due to ideological alignment with the movement, but because the state itself lacks the capacity to offer a quality education to citizens without additional support. Thus, the neoliberal assault on the state has also created openings for social movement participation, what agrarian scholar Wendy Wolford (2010a) has called "participation by default."

Evelina Dagnino (2007) has discussed the "perverse confluence" of neoliberal and participatory practices, and cautions us to think about how decentralization can simultaneously promote citizen participation *and* justify a reduced, minimal state that abandons its role in guaranteeing universal rights. Drawing on my research with the MST, I argue that communities' involvement in the provision of public education is dependent on their capacity to work with, in, and through local power structures. Therefore, while decentralization does not automatically lead to more local participation and the democratization of public education, it provides ample opportunities for social movements to promote alternative educational goals. This is why it is critical for communities to engage in collective discussions about educational purpose, and cultivate a strong positive proposal for public education, in order to more effectively utilize participatory spaces when they appear. I argue that these processes should be understood as a form of *social movement-led democratic governance*: a social movement's strategic capacity to facilitate communities' participation in state institutions within contradictory contexts. This concept rejects the idea of "democratic governance" as complete co-optation or unconstrained resistance, and instead, analyzes the real consequences of activists' participation in the public sphere.

METHODS

Between 2009 and 2015, I spent 20 months collecting data on MST leaders' attempts to implement their educational proposal in public schools, universities, and other educational programs throughout the country. This research took place in four state school systems (Rio Grande do Sul, São Paulo, Pernambuco, and Ceará), two municipal school systems (Água Preta and Santa Maria da Boa Visa, both located in the state of Pernambuco), and in two federal ministries (Ministry of Education and Ministry of Agrarian Development). In each of these locations I lived in MST communities and participated in school events, teacher trainings, and meetings between MST leaders and government officials. I interviewed 85 MST leaders, 107 government officials, and 35 university professors and other movement activists connected to the MST's educational struggle. In addition, I had hundreds of informal conversations with state and movement actors. In three of the six school systems and one of the two federal agencies where I conducted research, the MST had won the right to participate in the governance of public education, significantly transforming local educational practices. In the other half of these cases, the MST's participation was blocked by the state, or sometimes by the local communities themselves. This background information is significant in order to understand the political, economic, and social conditions that allow a movement to engage in the democratic governance of public education. In this chapter, I draw on my research in the two municipal school systems in state of Pernambuco, Santa Maria da Boa Vista and Água Preta, in order to highlight the dynamics of community-driven education reform. In the municipality of Santa Maria da Boa Vista the MST has been able to democratize the local public school system and participate in educational governance, while in Água Preta the MST's participation has been blocked. I analyze why two similar efforts in community-driven educational reform have had such different results.

CONTRADICTIONS OF DECENTRALIZATION:
DEVOLUTION V. EMPOWERED PARTICIPATORY GOVERNANCE

Since the 1970's, a trend in education has been the decentralization of the school system, and a push for the participation of civil society in strategies for educational development (McGinn and Welsh 1999; Zajda 2004). However, as the chapters in this volume discuss, there is a major tension in the relationship between neoliberal trends towards the devolution and decentralization of state power and grassroots attempts to create "empowered participatory regimes" for marginalized populations (Fung and Wright 2003).

Brazil offers an ideal case to explore these contradictions. After three decades of centralized military rule, the Brazilian Constitution of 1988 devolved much of the federal government's responsibilities to the state and municipal levels (Souza 1996). This has allowed ample opportunities for local democratic participation in state decision-making. However, Dagnino (2007) argues that the Constitution of 1988 represents a "perverse confluence" of two processes. The first process was a redefinition of citizenship that went beyond "formal legal acquisition" and instead became a project of more egalitarian social relations – the right for Brazilian citizens to directly participate in the very definition of the society and political systems in which they were living (p. 552). The second process the Constitution of 1988 represented was a neoliberal project dedicated to promoting a reduced, minimal state, in which citizenship and civil society are redefined in individualistic terms and their relationship to the market and government is that of a consumer/producer. In this latter perspective, Dagnino (2007) argues, "the political meaning of participation has thus been reduced to management, and related concerns with efficiency and 'client satisfaction' have come to replace the political debate on inequality and social justice" (p. 555). This has resulted in the rolling back of many social rights, such as public pension plans, in defense of "development" and "modernization." Social services are increasingly seen by the population as commodities to be purchased, rather than universal rights for all Brazilian citizens. In addition, while NGOs are seen as "ideal partners to assume responsibility handed over by the state," there is a simultaneous criminalization of social movements, such as the MST, that are combative and critique the national government (Dagnino 2007, p. 554).

In the Brazilian public educational sphere, the "perverse confluence" between neoliberal devolution and grassroots democratic governance is especially acute. The Constitution of 1988 devolved complete authority over education to state and municipal governments, while leaving it incredibly ambiguous which powers belong to the state and which belong to the municipality. For example, two public high schools might be located on the same street, but one might be part of the state public school system and the other administrated by the municipal government. This means that thousands of educational bureaucracies are functioning throughout Brazil, with varying levels of state capacity and ideological perspectives. Sometimes this decentralization results in impressive participatory and bottom-up democratic experiments where local communities are invited to help define the goals of the public school system; in other contexts decentralization might mean a local mayor makes all of the decisions concerning public education on behalf of the municipality. Many of these local governments lack financial and material resources and are often incapable of providing quality education.[4] My hope is that this chapter will clarify the contrasting ideological impulses surrounding school participation, and the implications these visions have for the political engagement and educational achievement of marginalized populations, both in Brazil and internationally.

The MST's First Educational Initiatives

The MST first began to participate in public education in the late 1980s, under a military regime that was focused on increasing mechanized agricultural practices, promoting urban industrialization, and offering new educational opportunities in urban centers (Plank 1996). Rural schools were abandoned in light of this project of modernization and industrialization. Even after the 1988 constitution, when municipal governments took control of most rural schools, educational improvement was difficult due to the impoverished contexts – and varying political incentives – of these local governments. Thus, the MST emerged as one of the only proponents of rural education. Activists across the country began partnering with local universities to run literacy campaigns in their communities. In the public school system, the movement demanded a free public school education for all MST youth, as well as adults who never had the opportunity to study. However, the MST also wanted this education to be based in the Brazilian rural reality, so education collectives were set up in each region to defend the philosophical and pedagogical goals that the movement had developed (MST 1996).

These goals included fighting against the notion of schools as a means to prepare students to enter the urban job market. The MST leadership maintained that schools in the countryside should encourage students to be involved in intellectual as well as manual labor, in order to create an intellectual rural workforce. The movement also supports schools that promote cooperative forms of work rather than the specialization of knowledge. Furthermore, the movement defends the students' *auto-gestão* (self-governance) of the public school system, which they see as form of democratic, bottom-up participation. This means that youth are encouraged to be involved in every aspect of administering the school, from debates about curriculum content to decisions about disciplinary actions in the school. Additionally, schools should help students understand their political and economic context, such as the history of capitalism and agrarian development, in order to help them participate in transforming these realities.

At the same time, in the early 1990s, international organizations such as UNESCO, UNICEF and the World Bank were becoming dominant voices in global educational debates (Klees, Samoff, and Stromquist 2012; Samoff 1999). These organizations primarily focused on eradicating illiteracy, as part of their mandate to provide universal access to literacy and primary education in high-poverty countries. International program coordinators were often critical of the priorities of national governments, and tried to circumvent corrupt and "inefficient states" by working directly with local organizations and communities. This was part of a larger neoliberal perspective that was becoming dominant in educational discourse, which promoted the devolution of school authority to local governing levels that were considered more efficient and accountable to communities –similar to the 'perverse confluence' Dagnino (2007) describes.

During this period, UNESCO and UNICEF began to directly fund the MST's educational initiatives. These international organizations invested in the MST, despite the movement's political and socialist goals, simply because the activists – in the absence of the state – had organized some of the only educational programs in the countryside. The imperative for meeting literacy targets and increasing school attendance overshadowed ideological differences between program coordinators and movement activists. In 1995, the MST even received a prize in "Education and Participation" from UNICEF for the certification courses the movement had developed for rural teachers. The fact that an internationally respected organization would give such a prestigious educational award to a confrontational social movement was significant, because it gave the MST a public legitimacy that the national government tried to deny.

The concept of social movement-led democratic governance can help us understand the relationships that developed between the MST and UNESCO and UNICEF during the 1990s. During this period, there was a move towards incorporating issues of "participation" and "empowerment" into development practices, what Hart (2001) refers to as "revisionist neoliberalism" (p. 655). This led to the emergence of "civil society" as a site of strategic intervention in development discourse. The MST took advantage of this new focus on the "local" and the desire among development actors to make "civil society" a site of intervention, and requested funding for their educational programs. International program coordinators and state actors decided to cooperate with the MST, precisely because of their new dedication to local civil society participation. Thus, socialist mobilization and neoliberal hegemonic politics became linked together in complex ways. Again, the concept of social movement-led democratic governance allows us to think about how movements strategically engage the state in contradictory contexts, and why neoliberal trends towards decentralization represent an *opportunity* for social movement participation and bottom-up democratic participation.[5]

TWO REGIONAL CASES OF THE MST'S DEMOCRATIC GOVERNANCE OF PUBLIC EDUCATION

In this section I discuss two examples of the MST's participation in educational governance in highly decentralized contexts. In the first case of the municipality of Santa Maria da Boa Vista in the state of Pernambuco, the MST is able to take advantage of the decentralized educational system and convince local political elites to support the movement's educational proposal. In the second case, the municipality of Água Preta, also in Pernambuco, the decentralized educational sphere offered ample opportunities for local participation, but the MST's own internal contradictions have prevented social movement-led democratic governance. This comparison helps to illustrate why decentralization is always a contradictory process, which can simultaneously facilitate the reproduction of unequal economic and political relationships while also representing an opportunity for deepening local democracy.

Social Movement-led Democratic Governance in Santa Maria da Boa Vista

Santa Maria da Boa Vista is a large municipality in the western part of Pernambuco, located next to the state's second biggest urban center, Petrolina. The region has a semi-arid climate, known as the *sertão*, infamous for its poverty and isolation. The political system in this region has traditionally been controlled by a system known as *coronelismo*, whereby a local "strongman" is in charge of all of the political and economic relations in the municipality. In Santa Maria, for example, one family has maintained political power since the municipality's founding in 1872. Rather than disputes over programmatic differences, in Santa Maria family members vie for power based on direct, clientelistic exchange with citizens.[6] As ex-mayor Guablerto Almedia (PMDB 1993–1996) explained, "The economic question is more important than the ideological question. The municipality is a big employer, when you change the person in power you change the employer, this is the center of political party fighting."[7] The public school system is one of the biggest employers in the municipality, and therefore, at the center of many clientelistic exchanges. After every election, the new mayor fires the seventy principals in this system, and places his political allies in these positions. Hundreds of teachers who cannot be fired are also transferred between schools, depending on their political allegiance.[8] Thus, in Santa Maria, the devolution of educational governance to the municipal level directly helps the members of this historically powerful family to maintain their hold on power.

The first MST land occupation in the *sertão* region of Pernambuco took place in Santa Maria in 1995, with two thousand families, on a former fruit plantation that had gone out of business. Within the next ten years, 15 MST settlements were created in Santa Maria. Soon after these initial land occupations, the MST's regional leadership set up an MST "education collective" in Santa Maria – a group of local activists who would be in charge of implementing the MST's educational vision in the municipal context. Statewide MST leaders selected several local citizens who were active in the camps to attend state and national MST education meetings. These were spaces in which activists learned about the pedagogies the MST leadership had developed, and were given the task of returning to Santa Maria to implement these pedagogies in the municipal public schools. For example, local activists learned how to involve the community in collective discussions about education purpose; to help parents re-write the school mission statement; to organize teacher collectives in the schools that could engage in joint classroom planning; to divide students into small groups, which would then take on the responsibility for school governance; to incorporate manual labor tasks into the school system that teach youth the value of work and to identify as part of the working class; and to link the curriculum to the local agrarian context and also engage students in concrete political actions to improve their livelihoods in the settlements.

Initially, the MST leaders in these education collectives tried to pressure the mayors to allow their own members to be the teachers in the public schools located on agrarian reform settlements. However, since municipal jobs are such an important political resource, none of the mayors were willing to cooperate with the movement, even under contentious political pressure. One principal elaborated on her relationship with the mayor: "Leandro says that I am his eyes and ears in the community. I am here to make sure he knows what is happening in the local community."[9] Faced with this constraint, the MST education collective shifted its strategy, and instead, began a long-term campaign of persuading dozens of these teachers – almost all of whom were from the city – to become allies of the movement. This was a labor-intensive, painstaking process that required an enormous investment in relationship building on the part of the activists. Rather than critique municipal politics, these MST leaders had to engage teachers in "non-partisan" discussions about the movement's educational proposal. Teacher collectives, which brought together educators regardless of their political party allegiance, became the flagship of the MST's reform efforts. The movement framed their educational proposal as a form of democratization of the local school system, which politicians of all stripes and colors could support.

Although these teachers were initially scared of the movement, they learned to appreciate the MST's presence in their schools and their willingness to help them with their daily tasks. For example, the MST leaders would help organize activities with the students on a range of topics, from agrarian reform to agroecology, and also encourage parents to come and participate in school events. The MST also invited teachers to attend seminars and week-long teacher trainings organized by the movement. Many of the teachers in this municipality had not been invited to any type of professional development course for years, and enjoyed attending statewide MST teacher-trainings. As one local teacher, Clara,[10] explained, "At first I was scared of the MST … but I went to a training and realized it was not what I thought … they had a different pedagogy we would work with, to improve our teaching … to show that everyone is equal, use Paulo Freire … a pedagogy of liberation."[11] The MST also helped teachers access public universities through a federal program the national MST leadership helped to create in 1998, the Program for Education in Areas of Agrarian Reform (PRONERA) (Martins and Rodrigues 2015; Tarlau 2015a). During my field research in 2011, I met dozens of teachers, most of whom had nothing to do with the MST's land struggle, who obtained college degrees through this MST-federal partnership. This is important because it shows how the MST's fight for more educational access in poor, rural regions of the country was not simply targeted to their own activists, but rather brought benefits to other local community members as well. Furthermore, after these teachers spent four years studying in a PRONERA university degree program, which national MST leaders helped to administer, they would become directly familiar with the movement's educational vision and feel more capable of implementing this pedagogical proposal in their local school contexts.

How have the mayors reacted to the MST's presence in the public schools? The deep divides between different factions of the ruling family has meant that politicians on all sides of these political divides have been willing to support a "non-partisan" educational proposal – if the teachers in their clientelistic network are advocates. Thus, between 1997 and 2011, the MST education collective was able to work with all of the mayors who came to power, obtaining resources for teacher collectives in every school and attaining permission and funding to send teachers to statewide MST teacher trainings. In the mid-2000s the mayors in power even agreed to create a department for "Education of the Countryside" in the municipal Secretary of Education, and put an MST activist in charge of administering the department. This is significant because it meant that the MST could promote its pedagogical proposal in rural schools throughout the municipality, not simply in the few schools on agrarian reform settlements. Given the MST's overall goal of establishing sustainable farming communities throughout Brazil and encouraging youth to stay in the countryside to help to develop these rural communities, the movement had an explicit interest in engaging other rural populations to support this vision.

The MST's ability to lead a process of social movement-led democratic governance in Santa Maria did not happen by replacing the clientelistic system, but rather, by gathering the support of key actors in different clientelistic networks. In other words, the same political family continued to rule the municipality, however, this family was forced to negotiate with and support the MST and local communities' participation in the school system. This process is clearly contradictory, as all of the mayors are large landowners in the region and ideologically opposed to the MST's demand for agrarian reform. Furthermore, the devolution of state power to these municipalities facilitates the reproduction of unequal power relations, as it allows local mayors to control thousands of municipal jobs that they can offer to their political allies. Thus, there is nothing inherently progressive about a decentralized political system – especially in a place with extreme inequality such as Santa Maria. However, the decentralized system has also offered an opportunity to local MST activists in Santa Maria to strategically engage the state to directly participate in a form of democratic, bottom-up educational governance.

Barriers to Social Movement Participation in Água Preta

Água Preta is located on the opposite side of the state of Pernambuco, a two-hour drive from the state's capital, Recife. Água Preta has a different agrarian history, located in an extremely wet and hilly region of the state that is prone to flooding – a perfect climate for sugar cane production. Sugar cane is everywhere, from established plantations to people's backyards and gaps of land next to the highway. However, although many people plant sugar cane in this region, it is the owners of the sugar processing factories that wield power. Unlike Santa Maria, in Água Preta three political families have been in power over the past several decades, all of whom are connected to the sugar cane industry. Nonetheless, the political systems in Água Preta and Santa Maria are similar in that the relationships between citizens and mayors are based on clientelistic exchange.[12]

The MST first arrived in Água Preta in the late 1980s, organizing a land occupation with the help of members of the local rural union movement (Maybury-Lewis 1994). However, it was not until the mid-1990s when the sugar cane industry was in crisis that the MST leadership was able to organize dozens of successful land occupations in the region with unemployed sugar-cane workers. These land occupations led to the creation of more than thirty agrarian reform settlements in the municipality, the largest number in Pernambuco. Due to this history, Água Preta has historically been considered an MST stronghold in the state. This is significant for social movement-led education reform efforts because MST leaders can only convince local mayors to support democratic governance if the movement has activists in these rural communities that want to participate. Thus, given the large number of agrarian reform settlements in Água Preta, the municipality appeared to be the perfect place for the movement's educational reform efforts.

Similarly to Santa Maria, mayors in Água Preta express feelings of "tolerance" towards the MST.[13] For example, ex-Mayor Paulo Barreto (2005–2008) said, "The arrival of MST was good, if the worker wants his own land to grow and produce, he deserves this ... I have no conflicts with the MST ... I always paid for their transportation to events."[14] Mayor Eduardo Coutinho (1997–2004, 2009–2012), who was featured in the opening vignette, also alluded to the need to avoid conflict with the movement, what he referred to as "a good neighbor policy."[15] In the late 1990s and early 2000s, local MST activists convinced mayors from all three political families to let the movement participate in the public school system. This was not an immediate action, but rather, a gradual process of speaking to each new mayor and his secretary of education about the MST's educational reform proposal. In part, it was the MST's ability to bring influential allies to participate in teacher trainings and municipal seminars that convinced these Secretaries of Education of the legitimacy of the MST's democratic participation. For example, Secretary of Education Albertinha (under Eduardo Coutinho's third mandate) recalled a seminar on "Education of the Countryside" that the municipal secretary of education financed in coordination with the MST. Albertinha emphasized several times the presence of Edla Soarez,[16] one of the most important educational officials in the state, who was invited by the MST to participate.[17] While this poor municipality would have difficulty attracting such prominent speakers on its own, the MST's vast network of supporters made this possible.

Despite these political openings, working with the teachers in Água Preta was not an easy task, as almost all of these teachers were from the city center and had serious reservations about the movement. Local MST activist Mariana recalled, "They thought the MST was a bunch of thieves ... the teachers were very scared of us."[18] Mariana and the other members of the MST education collective had to find creative ways to support these teachers in their educational work, such as holding local workshops on pedagogical practices and helping organize parents to support the teachers' work in the schools. These reforms were all linked to the MST's vision of democratizing the schools. For example, the MST organized teachers into collectives that debated which curriculum was relevant for rural communities and how to develop activities that would engage students in the local political context. Students and parents were also encouraged to participate in the democratic governance of the school. Parents were invited to re-write the mission statements of the schools – through an extensive debate about educational purpose. Students were split into small groups that took responsibility for all of the tasks necessary for the school to function, from cleaning the school to facilitating classroom discussion and participating in disciplinary decisions. Over time many of the teachers, who were initially wary of the MST, began to support the MST's proposal for democratic school governance. For example, local teacher Lourdes had been teaching in the same school for over a decade when the MST occupied the surrounding land. She was scared about what would happen: "The MST activists came to have a conversation with us in the school. They said, now this community is going to be a *Sem Terra* [landless] community, and they put a flag up in the school."[19] However, as MST leaders kept visiting the school and inviting her to teacher trainings, Lourdes became an active supporter of the MST's educational proposal.

Some teachers had even more direct participation in the movement, joining regional marches and protests. Local teacher Gabriela recalled a march she participated in with children from her school on an MST settlement:

> We brought sixty kids from the region, and there were 3,000 children at the event ... What impressed me the most was the march on the last day, we walked to the government palace and there were emergency vehicles and cold water, it was very organized ... in the end three children were allowed to go talk to the governor and give him their demands about their schools.[20]

Gabriela was impressed both with the organization of the event, and the power the MST had to pressure the governor to talk to the children. Gabriela was eventually promoted to work in the municipal Secretary of Education, as an open advocate of the MST.

Nonetheless, despite the opportunities for bottom-up, democratic governance in the decentralized public school system in Água Preta, by the mid-2000s the local education collective was encountering difficulties moving forward with the movement's educational project. More specifically, the parents of the students in the schools were becoming less supportive of the movement's educational interventions.

These difficulties were a consequence of a change in the relationship between the MST leadership and the grassroots base living in the agrarian reform settlements in the region. Namely, when left-leaning President Luiz Inácio "Lula" da Silva

(2003–2010) took office, he began subsidizing the sugar cane industry to increase ethanol production. Consequently, sugar prices shot up and people all over the region began growing sugar cane again, including the families living on agrarian reform settlements. During the previous years, the MST had convinced many of the sugar cane workers to diversify their crops through a lot of cultural and political work that attempted to associate sugar cane production with "exploitation" and agro-ecological farming with being a "good" agrarian reform citizen. However, when sugar cane prices skyrocketed, these alternative initiatives were abandoned; deep divisions grew between families who saw sugar as the most viable means of economic survival, and the MST leadership who tried to convince the farmers that this form of economic production was exploitative. Wolford (2010b) documents these conflicts extensively: "Production decisions became a political battlefield. MST leaders argued that planting bananas and subsistence crops signified a higher political consciousness and the settlers came to equate planting sugarcane with going against the movement's wishes" (p. 181).

Over the next decade, these division led to the MST partially withdrawing from this region. This withdrawal directly affected the public schools, because teachers who had previously relied on the MST's pedagogical support were no longer able to maintain the movement's educational proposal in the municipal schools. When I talked to Eduardo Coutinho's Secretary of Education in 2011, Albertinha, she was still supportive of the movement, but alluded to these difficulties:

> When I arrived in the Secretary of Education, the MST came to talk to me about the schools in the countryside ... they had gatherings of *Sem Terrinha* [MST children] and asked for teachers to go as well ... we try to give the MST whatever it wants ... However, something I realized is that even though we are open to this, it is often the community that does not want the MST in the schools.[21]

Albertinha emphasized her support of the MST, but was cognizant of the lack of support for this proposal in many of the agrarian reform settlements. She told a story of some parents who "came here to say they did not want a certain teacher in her school because she was teaching the children to be *sem terra* [landless]."

The teacher that these parents were complaining about was Isabela, one of the original members of the MST education sector in Água Preta. Isabela was hired as a municipal school teacher in 2010 and assigned to work in a settlement school. She began to incorporate some of the MST's educational pedagogies into her classroom. However, after a few weeks the parents – the same parents who had participated in an MST land occupation the decade before – began to criticize Isabela and her teaching method as bringing "the movement" into the school. The frustration that the families felt with the MST's leadership in the settlements had affected their faith in the MST's other campaigns, including the movement's educational reform efforts. The idea of democratizing the schools by demanding that the municipality allow the movement to participate in educational governance no longer seemed relevant, since the movement was hardly a presence in any of the other aspects of the community's daily lives.

Isabela herself was open about these difficulties. She had been part of the regional MST education collective in the late 1990s, left for several years, and returned to the regional leadership in 2008. Isabela said, "When I returned, it was a big shock ... there were very few older leaders who stayed in the region ... in Água Preta I tried to find the education collective, but I could not find it!" Isabela expressed nostalgia for the "good old days" when the education collective was a strong presence in the settlements. She said,

> Right now, if we had a teacher in a settlement school that we did not like, we could not change this because we no longer have the support of our base. With the help of the base, we could have a protest in the city; but we do not have this support. Today, if we wanted to have a protest about municipal education in Água Preta, bringing people to the streets would be difficult.[22]

Isabela admitted that the MST had lost its capacity to "accompany" the settlements in this region, preventing the movement's educational proposal from moving forward.

Local MST activist Felipe mimicked this sentiment: "The biggest challenge in the region today is to work with the base, we are in lots of public organs, but we are forgetting our settlements." Felipe recounted a meeting that he organized about the MST's educational proposal with parents of a settlement school. In particular, Felipe talked about the importance of transforming the traditional top-down relationship between the municipal secretary of education and the community, by demanding the community's right to democratically participate in the governance of their local schools. The meeting went really well and they had planned to organize another meeting. However, Felipe explained, "We were not able to have other meetings. New priorities came up, I was invited to take a national course and I was not able to return to the settlement." According to local leaders, there are settlements in Água Preta that the MST has not visited for several years.

Among teachers, these lost opportunities were evident. When I visited the schools in 2011, teachers did not express resentment of the MST, but rather a longing for the movement's presence. For example, local teacher Alessandra said, "The MST has to be more present, they have to talk to people and open their eyes, because when the MST is not here in the schools no one participates ... I feel alone. A team of people needs to accompany my work."[23] Similarly, while the teacher Lourdes expressed her continual support of the MST in 2011, when I asked about what aspects of the MST's pedagogical proposal she was implementing in her school, she simply responded, "There needs to be more accompaniment, the teachers need more support." In other words, although Lourdes believed in the MST's proposal for democratic educational governance, she was finding it difficult to create spaces for community participation in her school without the MST's help. Although in the past the teachers, students, and parents would meet each year to re-write the school mission statement and discuss the educational goals for the year, these types of democratic spaces were no longer functioning. Thus, the teachers the MST previously won over are not currently opposed to the movement; they just feel incapable of promoting the MST's pedagogies by themselves. Isolated teachers were not capable of implementing a process of participatory governance on their own; an organized social movement was needed to help to lead this democratic process.

***

The critical difference in the success of the MST's educational campaign in Santa Maria da Boa Vista and Água Preta was not the decentralized school system, but rather, the social movement activists' ability to mobilize local communities to participate in a process of educational governance. Thus, this case comparison illustrates that there are ample political opportunities for social movements to make demands on decentralized states, even in low-capacity, clientelistic contexts such as rural Pernambuco. In these contexts, municipal governments often have a high degree of interest in controlling the education system, given that it is one of the most important sources of employment and therefore political control. Nonetheless, in Santa Maria, even with one family holding political power for over a century, mayors were open to the participation of MST activists – if their teacher-allies were also in support. MST leaders were able to "mobilize the state" (Abers and Keck 2009) to implement the movement's educational reform proposal, by organizing teacher-trainings, offering municipal seminars, and obtaining access to university courses. However, taking advantage of this decentralized system first involved a long-term process of mobilizing the *community* around a united vision of democratic school governance.

This comparison also demonstrates that "social movements" and "communities" are dynamic and contradictory entities, and that divides between social movement leaders and their base are a major barrier to a bottom-up process of democratic participation. Even if social movement leaders can mobilize communities to participate in the local school system at one historical moment. The continual support of the community is not inevitable. In Água Preta, the shift in the macro-economic context (rising sugar cane prices) meant that settlement families were no longer willing to follow the MST's leadership concerning appropriate forms of economic production in the Brazilian countryside. This led to the communities to reject the movement's educational reforms as well. The community began to believe more in the top-down initiatives of the state, rather than then the bottom-up democracy supported by the movement. This suggests that for movement-driven education reform to be successful, social movement leaders must have an organic relationship to the communities that they claim to make up their movement. In other words, grassroots policy reform efforts are not possible without the grassroots; a social movement's successful engagement with public education depends on maintaining a supportive and mobilized base.

CONCLUSIONS: TOWARDS A THEORY OF SOCIAL MOVEMENT-LED DEMOCRATIC GOVERNANCE

Over the past two decades in Brazil, there have been countless efforts to deepen democracy through institutionalized forms of decentralized, participatory governance. Dagnino (2007) argues that "[a]s a result, the confrontational relations between the state and civil society have been largely replaced by an investment by social movements in the possibility of joint initiatives and in institutional participation in the newly created participatory spaces" (p. 550). Dagnino (2007) claims that this direct participation of civil society in state decision-making has become one of the most crucial aspects of Brazilian citizenship. In this chapter, I have argued that even in decentralized contexts this bottom-up, democratic participation is not necessarily inevitable; rather, social movements have to seize the opportunities within the decentralized Brazilian state to promote their policy goals.

MST activists' attempt to implement their educational proposal in the public schools is a form of bottom-up, democratic governance, because a fundamental component of the MST's proposal is the inclusion of multiple stakeholders – parents, students, community members, teachers – in the development of the organizational and curricular content of the public school system. The relationships that currently exist between MST activists and state actors had to be built, over time, and sustained through both daily moments of collaboration and protest. However, the MST's effort to implement an alternative educational pedagogy in schools also has a dual purpose. On the one hand, MST activists work with public officials to improve the quality of rural public education and encourage youth to stay in the countryside. On the other hand, these educational initiatives are a direct attempt to establish a new socialist hegemony in Brazil. This dual function of the MST's democratic participation in the public educational sphere makes the case of the MST different than the majority of the literature on participatory governance, which examines pluralistic and individualistic forms of participation. This, of course, also begs the question: is it actually possible for social movements to promote grassroots democratic governance of state institutions before an entire transformation of the state itself?

In this chapter, I have argued that in decentralized state contexts the answer to this question is *yes*; however, this attempt to transform public institutions will always be partial and contradictory. Public schools are both important institutions for the reproduction of hegemonic social relations, and a terrain of resistance. In public schools in MST settlements across Brazil, examples of counterhegemonic pedagogies *are* present in state and municipal public school systems – e.g., students learning agro-ecological farming techniques and critiquing large agribusiness; classrooms named after revolutionary leaders, such as Rosa Luxemburg and Che Guevara; and manual labor being positively integrated into the school curriculum. These examples of resistance to educational norms exist alongside a curriculum that is still urban-centric; mayors that use schools to maintain political power; and bureaucratic hierarchies that go against the MST's vision of schools as democratic spaces. Realizing the emancipatory – yet always contradictory – potential of decentralization is critical for scholars interested in promoting bottom-up democracy in public schools (Apple and Beane 2007), and researchers of participatory governance more generally (Fung and Wright 2003).

The MST's contribution to educational theory and practice is not a new or unusual development. Grassroots social movements have always been at the forefront of developing educational alternatives, which are connected to a vision of popular, participatory democracy. However, more studies are needed about *how* social movements engage states in democratic governance, and if this participation can transform public schools into vehicles for social transformation. Decentralization offers an opportunity for these types of community-driven educational reform efforts, but that these developments are far from inevitable. Thus, rather than advocate for decentralization as a policy panacea in and of itself, scholars and activists should invest their energy in building stronger grassroots movements that demand the right to democratic participation in both decentralized and centralized educational systems, with the goal of implementing educational proposals that are explicitly linked to broader struggles for political and economic equality.

REFERENCES

Abers, Rebecca, & Margaret Keck. (2009). "Mobilizing the State: The Erratic Partner in Brazil's Participatory Water Policy." *Politics & Society, 37*(2), 289–314.

Apple, Michael W., & James Beane. (2007). *Democratic Schools: Lessons in Powerful Education*. Portsmouth, NH: Heinemann.

Auyero, Javier. (2000). *Poor People's Politics: Peronist Survival Networks and the Legacy of Evita*. Durham, NC: Duke University Press.

Berryman, Phillip. (1987). *Liberation Theology: Education at Empire's End*. New York, NY: Pantheon Books.

Branford, Sue, & Jan Rocha. (2002). *Cutting the Wire: The Story of the Landless Movement in Brazil*. London: Latin America Bureau.

Dagnino, Evelina. (2007). "Citizenship: A Perverse Confluence." *Development in Practice, 17*(4–5), 549–556.

Davies, N. (2006). *FUNDEB: A Redenção Da Educação Básica?* Campinas, SP: Autores Associados.

Fung, Archon, & Erik Olin Wright, eds. (2003). *Deepening Democracy: Institutional Innovations in Empowered Participatory Governance*. London: Verso Books.

Hagopin, Frances. (1996). *Traditional Politics and Regime Change in Brazil*. Cambridge: Cambridge University Press.

Hart, Gillian. (2001). "Development Critiques in the 1990s: Culs de Sacs and Promising Paths." *Progress in Human Geography, 25*(4), 649–658. doi:10.1191/030913201682689002

Klees, Steven, Joel Samoff, & Nelly P. Stromquist, eds. (2012). *The World Bank and Education: Critqiues and Alternatives*. Rotterdam, The Netherlands: Sense Publishers.

Lemarchand, Rene. (1972). "Political Clientelism and Ethnicity in Tropical Africa: Competing Solidarities in Nation-Building." *The American Political Science Review, 66*(1), 68–90.

Martins, Maria de Fátima Almeida, & Sonia da Silva Rodrigues, eds. (2015). *PRONERA: Experiências de Gestão de Uma Política Pública*. São Paulo: Compacta Gráfica Editora.

Maybury-Lewis, Biorn. (1994). *The Politics of the Possible: The Brazilian Rural Worker' Trade Union Movement, 1964–1985*. Philadelphia, PA: Temple University Press.

McGinn, Noel F., & Thomas Welsh. (1999). *Decentralization of Education: Why, When, What and How?* Paris: UNESCO.
MST. (1996). *Princípios Da Educação No MST*. Movimento Sem Terra.
Ondetti, Gabriel. (2008). *Land, Protest, and Politics: The Landless Movement and the Struggle for Agrarian Reform in Brazil*. University Park, PA: Pennsylvania State University Press.
Plank, David. (1996). *The Means of Our Salvation: Public Education in Brazil, 1930–1995*. Boulder, CO: Westview Press.
Roniger, Luzcis. (1994). "The Comparative Study of Clientelism and the Changing Nature of Civil Society in the Contemporary World." In Luis Roniger & Ayse Güens-Ayata, eds., *Democracy, Clientelism and Civil Society*. Boulder, CO: Lynne Rienner Publishers.
Samoff, Joel. (1999). "Institutionalizing International Influence." In Robert F. Arnove & Carlos Alberto Torres, eds., *Comparative Education: The Dialectic of the Global and the Local*. Lanham, MD: Rowman & Littlefield.
Souza, Celina. (1996). "Redemocratization and Decentralization in Brazil: The Strength of the Member States." *Development and Change, 27*(3), 529–535.
Tarlau, Rebecca. (2013). "The Social(ist) Pedagogies of the MST: Towards New Relations of Production in the Brazilian Countryside." *Education Policy Analysis Archives, 21*(41), 1–23.
Tarlau, Rebecca. (2015a). "Education of the Countryside at a Crossroads: Rural Social Movements and National Policy Reform in Brazil." *Journal of Peasant Studies, 42*(6), 1157–1177.
Tarlau, Rebecca. (2015b). "How Do New Critical Pedagogies Develop? Educational Innovation, Social Change, and Landless Workers in Brazil." *Teachers College Record, 117*(11), 1–36.
Wolford, Wendy. (2010a). "Participatory Democracy by Default: Land Reform, Social Movements and the State in Brazil." *Journal of Peasant Studies, 37*(1), 91–109.
Wolford, Wendy. (2010b). *This Land Is Ours Now: Social Mobilization and the Meanings of Land in Brazil*. Durham, NC: Duke University Press.
Wright, Angus, & Wendy Wolford. (2003). *To Inherit the Earth: The Landless Movement and the Struggle for a New Brazil*. Oakland, CA: Food First Books.
Zajda, Joseph. (2004). "Introduction." *International Review of Education, 50*(3–4), 199–221.

NOTES

1. Field notes, July 9, 2011.
2. For more extensive histories on the MST's founding and expansion, see: (Branford and Rocha 2002; Ondetti 2008; Wolford 2010b; Wright and Wolford 2003).
3. In previous writings (Tarlau 2013, 2015b) I have explored how the MST developed these pedagogies.
4. This situation improved slightly after 1997, when the federal government implemented a reform that redistributed educational funding based on the number of students in each municipal and state public school system (Davies 2006) This 1997 reform was known as FUNDEF (the Fund for Maintenance and Development of the Fundamental Education and Valorization of Teaching) and redistributed funding for primary education. In 2006, the federal government passed FUNDEB (Fund for the Development of Basic Education and Appreciation of the Teaching Profession), which also redistributed funding for high school education.
5. This does not suggest that anti-capitalist movements can only contest state power in a decentralized context – there have also been many examples of left-wing mobilization during periods of embedded liberalism and welfare capitalism.
6. As scholars have pointed out, clientelism is not a one-time deal, but rather, entails "mutual, relatively long-term compromises based on commitments and some kind of solidarity" (Roniger 1994, p. 5).
7. Interview, May 10, 2011.
8. I was present in Santa Maria for two political transitions between April and June of 2011.
9. Interview May 6, 2011.
10. All names referring to people not holding public office are pseudonyms.

11. Interview, May 10, 2011.
12. Clientelism is an old concept in the political science literature. Lemarchand (1972) defines clientelism "a more or less personalized relationship between actors, or sets of actors, commanding unequal wealth, status or influence, based on conditional loyalties and involving mutually beneficial transactions" (p. 69). The key here is that it is "a reciprocal arrangement," not completely coercive, "where the client derives some benefit from his subordinate role" (Hagopin 1996). Auyero (2000) refers to these clientelist practices as "problem solving through personalized political mediation," or in other words, the means of material survival for the poor.
13. I interviewed all of the mayors in Água Preta since the MST's arrival in 1988.
14. Interview July 6, 2011.
15. Interview July 9, 2011.
16. Edla Soarez was the Secretary of Education of Recife, Pernambuco, several times, and also the president of UNDIME, a national organization of municipal secretaries of education.
17. Interview, July 7, 2015.
18. Interview, February 23, 2011.
19. Interview, July 27, 2011.
20. Interview, July 18, 2011.
21. Interview, July 7, 2011.
22. Interview, June 17, 2011.
23. Interview, July 27, 2011.

KAI HEIDEMANN

3. CRISIS, PROTEST AND DEMOCRATIZATION 'FROM BELOW'

The Rise of a Community-Based Schooling Movement in Argentina

INTRODUCTION

In this chapter I take a look at how the onset of a large-scale national crisis and corresponding wave of widespread social protest influenced the emergence and expansion of a community-based schooling movement in Argentina during the early 2000s. Particular attention is given to how a diverse but unified network of grassroots actors orchestrated the rise of a community-based schooling movement in the urban context of Buenos Aires. Focusing on a particular juncture in Argentine history, I discuss how the severe macro-structural instabilities and pervasive social grievances associated with the climaxing of a major politico-economic crisis during 2001–2002 spilled over into the educational sector and created conditions for the rise of a community-based schooling movement. While community-based schooling was initially a pragmatic way for people to keep local schools running under conditions of severe instability and uncertainty, I explain how and why community-based schooling quickly evolved into a more expansive, cohesive and purposeful 'movement' oriented toward the Argentine state and the promotion of broader reform agendas rooted in progressive principles of educational democratization and social justice. In addition, I consider how the rise of the community-based schooling movement during the early 2000s influenced, and was influenced by, a legacy of decentralization policies implemented during the 1990s.

Drawing on social movement theory (Snow and Soule 2010), the onset of the crisis and protest wave are interpreted as constituting an 'opportunity structure', that is, a moment of rupture whereby the symbolic and material relations of power in a given society become temporarily destabilized and conducive to processes of contestation and collective action from the grassroots of civil society. As William Sewell (2005, p. 25) notes: "In times of structural dislocation, the ordinary routines of social life are open to doubt, the sanctions of existing power relations are uncertain or suspended, and new possibilities are thinkable." One of the key insights provided by the study of 'opportunity structures' lies not merely in the identification of the macro-structural dynamics which fuel social movement actors and campaigns in times of crisis, but in understanding the agentic capacity of actors to effectively transform moments of large-scale instability and uncertainty into tangible and empowering forms of social change. In other words, it is crucial to look at the practices through which people work collectively to develop and deploy strategic stances toward situations of macro-structural rupture and uncertainty (Heidemann 2017).

Building on these theoretical insights, I show that although the national crisis of 2001–2002 produced severe inequalities and anxieties within Argentine society, it also constituted a critical turning point whereby the educational system became actively re-imagined and re-configured 'from below' by networks of organized citizens seeking to overcome entrenched problems of inequality and exclusion through a commitment to community-based schooling. Although this movement lost some social momentum in recent years and its future political status remains somewhat uncertain, I argue that the network of over 400 community-based schools generated during the early 2000s are an undeniable presence in the Argentine educational landscape which confirm that another way is indeed possible.

Data and Methods

My discussion is based on analysis of qualitative case study data collected during three episodes of fieldwork in Buenos Aires during 2014, 2015 and 2016.[1] My analysis focuses on a network of over two dozen schools affiliated with the largest and most influential umbrella organization representing community-based schools in the city and province of Buenos Aires: *La Federación de Cooperativas y Entidades Afines de Enseñanza* (henceforth 'FECEABA'). The primary data used for this chapter include: (i) semi-structured interviews with 14 key informants affiliated with FECEABA and (ii) 29 texts and documents published by FECEABA for purposes of either external public promotion or internal communication. In addition, the data include interviews with 3 educational policy experts in Argentina, 2 state-based policy reports with direct relevance to the '*escuelas de gestión social*' and '*escuelas cooperativas*', and 16 news media articles dealing with the topic of these schools. My discussion is also supplemented by participant-observation in several workshops and meetings organized by schooling communities affiliated with FECEABA. A handful of secondary sources dealing with the history and politico-legal status of community-based schooling in Argentina (Alonsó Bra 2015; Gluz 2013) were also incorporated for additional context and depth. These diverse sets of qualitative data were triangulated and analyzed in accordance with "process-tracing" methods (Beach and Pederson 2013) so as to identify and understand how the growth of community-based schooling in Buenos Aires unfolded in relation to a macro-level structure of opportunity.

Given that the primary aim of my discussion is to explain the initial rise of the community-based schooling movement, a notable limitation of this chapter is its focus on the particular historical timeframe which corresponds with the tumultuous years surrounding the dramatic climax of the national crisis in 2001. In addition, given that my geographical focus is Buenos Aires, it is important to note that my discussion does not speak directly to the realities of community-based schooling initiatives within other parts of Argentina, such as Rio Negro or Santa Fe. This caveat is significant because the Argentine educational system has a relatively decentralized federal structure and the levels of political support for community-based schooling vary across individual provinces (Rivas 2004).

COMMUNITY-BASED SCHOOLING IN ARGENTINA

The community-based schools under consideration in this chapter are generally known in Argentina as '*escuelas de gestión social*' or '*escuelas cooperativas*'.[2] These are alternative but fully-fledged formalized schools which typically stress high levels of community participation and engagement in the name of promoting equality and empowerment as well as academic integrity and success. The 'alternative' qualities of such schools are relative of course, and linked to the ways in which their curricular programs, pedagogic practices and administrative-organizational structures differ from 'mainstream' educational practices and programs. Didactic distinctions, for example, generally stem from the ways in which state-based curricula are adjusted and adapted in the classroom by teachers so as to align with the local identities and experiences of students. Curricular standardization and homogeneity are thus eschewed in favor of contingency, pluralism and adaptation. Organizational distinctions on the other hand are typically based on the use of so-called 'horizontal' decision-making schemas (*horizontalismo*) whereby administrative authority is collectively distributed amongst teachers along with parents and to varying extent students. While the *escuelas de gestión social* and *escuelas cooperativas* have most often emerged from within 'poor' and working class communities in both rural and urban regions of Argentina, they have also periodically arisen in various middle class neighborhoods, such as the Palermo and Villa Crespo districts of Buenos Aires. The participants and proponents of the community-based schooling movement in Argentina are a very heterogeneous population which cannot (and should not) be easily categorized. Nonetheless, the advocates of this movement consist of networks of teachers, parents, grassroots activists and intellectuals who are unified by at least two sets of overlapping commitments which have linkages to 'progressive' or 'leftist' socio-political values: (i) promoting the democratization of public education through enhanced forms of direct community participation and engagement in educational decision-making, and (ii) developing educational programs which will help citizens to combat problems of inequality and exclusion in Argentine society. Many of the ideals and convictions which drive the supporters of community-based schooling are rooted in the 'emancipatory' educational philosophies of radical thinkers such as Paulo Freire, Simón Rodriguez and Celestin Freinet as well as varieties of Marxian social theory. Community-based schools typically have strong linkages to social movements fighting for labor rights, land rights, human rights, women's rights, and indigenous rights as well as issues of environmental sustainability, multiculturalism and democratization. As will be discussed below, the rapid growth of community-based schools in Argentina during the early 2000s is directly linked to the diffusion and rising influence of progressive social movements in the aftermath of a major national crisis.

Community-based schools in Argentina trace their origins to working class populism during the 1940–1950s when socialist and anarcho-syndicalist groups sought to achieve increased forms of self-determination within the educational system (Alonso Brá 2001). Prior to the era of dictatorial rule (1976–1983), there was a small boom of community-based schooling initiatives which surged among networks of left-leaning utopic communitarians and progressive Catholics. Many of these projects disappeared, however, under the repressive climate of militarized bureaucratic authoritarianism. For years there were very few such entities in existence and they largely operated in isolation from one another. At the time of the restoration of liberal democracy in 1983, for instance, there were only a few dozen readily identifiable community-based schools around the nation. These numbers remained largely unchanged throughout the 1990s. However, over the course of the early 2000s the landscape changed dramatically, and by 2012 there were nearly 400 community-based schools in operation nationwide with a total estimated enrollment of at least 45,000 students working with around 1,500 teachers.[3]

The swift rise of *escuelas de gestión social* and *escuelas cooperativas* took place in the early 2000s during a time of great socio-political upheaval and transformation in Argentina. While some of these schools were newly created entities, most were actually pre-existing schools which had orchestrated a purposeful alteration of their pedagogical culture and organizational structure so as to align with democratic and emancipatory principles of community-based education. Amazingly, the emergence of hundreds of community-based schools across Argentina occurred largely within the span of just a few years. In particular, the boom started around late 2002, reached a peak around 2010 and then seems to have fully stagnated by 2012–2013. This brief but intensive growth spurt was characterized by increased forms of interaction and collaboration among diverse groups of actors based in previously disconnected schooling communities.

On the one hand, the alliances and solidarities forged by grassroots supporters of community-based schooling in the early 2000s took shape via the planning of numerous meetings, workshops and conferences centered on promoting communication and collaboration across different schooling communities with overlapping visions and concerns. While such gatherings typically focused on curricular, pedagogical and administrative issues, they also frequently addressed policy issues and targeted state-level authorities. These events often entailed collaboration with and involvement by progressively oriented teachers unions, such as the *Sindicato Unificado de Trabajadores de la Educación de Buenos Aires* (SUTEBA) and labor associations such as the *Federación de Cooperativas Autogestionadas de Buenos Aires* (FEDECABA). Key concerns among the pioneering proponents of community-based schooling in Argentina often centered on issues of educational self-determination and the development of educational programs which could help citizens to battle entrenched problems of socio-economic inequality and political marginalization as well as local difficulties with issues, such as gang violence, teen pregnancy, drug abuse, unemployment and environmental contamination. Increased forms of sustained interaction among community-based schooling advocates during the early 2000s resulted in the founding of several umbrella associations dedicated to promoting the unanimity and development of community-based schooling at both the provincial and national levels, such as FECEABA (*Federación de Cooperativas y Entidades Afines de Enseñanza*) and AEGS (*Associacíon de la Educación de Gestión Social*).

In addition to increased forms of interaction and collaboration at the grassroots of society, another key dimension of the growth of community-based schooling during the early 2000s was its increased politicization. In brief, as proponents of these schools increasingly interacted and collaborated they began to make collective claims upon local, provincial and national authorities for increased forms of state-level recognition and support. Such claim-making was especially evident after the election of Nestór Kirchner to the Argentine presidency in May 2003. This event was particularly crucial because the Kirchner government induced a leftward shift in public policy-making which generated newfound forms of political legitimacy and leverage to a host of progressive social movements and labor unions within which many proponents of community-based schooling were integrated.[4] Evidence of political claim-making amongst proponents of community-based schooling after 2003 can be found in formal petitioning of state-level authorities to attain a fully-fledged 'public' status for all of the *escuelas de gestión social o cooperativa* operating in provinces around the nation. Although such demands were never fully achieved on a national level, they partially paid off in late 2006 when the Argentine Ministry of National Education formally recognized the heterogeneous niche of *escuelas de gestión social o cooperativa* as an "integral" component of the national education system (Ley de Educación 2006, #26.206, Titulo II, Capitulo I, Articulo 13). While this was a significant initial victory in terms of legitimation, the ambiguous wording and weak application of the policy coupled with the semi-decentralized structure of the national education system ultimately meant that the new law did not guarantee any concrete national schema for comprehensive state-level funding for community-based schools. Rather, any and all final decisions about which schools could get state-based funding let alone how much financing they could receive were ultimately left to provincial authorities.

While a handful of provinces such as Rio Negro, Chubut and Santa Fe did ultimately recognize the *escuelas de gestión social* as fully-fledged public entities and established comprehensive streams of financial support, most provinces have decided to treat them as privately managed schools eligible for public subsidies, such as in the city and province of Buenos Aires. A major aim of the contemporary community-based schooling movement in Argentina in the post-Kirchner era has been to break away from this indeterminate politico-legal classification so as to achieve a nationwide public status for all community-based schools. Particularly central to this agenda are the acquisition of total financing and the development of distinctive teacher training programs in universities.

What explains the emergence and rapid expansion of the community-based schooling movement in Argentina during the early 2000s? As noted from the onset of this chapter, the growth of community-based schooling was intimately linked to the onset of a major national crisis. By looking more closely at the macro-structural dynamics surrounding this unique historical moment, it is possible to understand how the societal rupture which accompanied the climaxing of the crisis in 2001–2002 crisis generated a momentary structure of opportunity which both encouraged and empowered a previously fragmented network of grassroots actors to collaborate in the development of a community-based schooling movement.

MACRO-STRUCTURAL DYNAMICS: CRISIS AS OPPORTUNITY

At the turn of the 21st century the Argentine economy entered into a downward spiral that peaked in late 2001 with the collapse of the financial system and national bankruptcy (Epstein and Pion-Berlin 2006; Grimson and Kessler 2005; Teubal 2004). Although the origins of the crisis can be located in the 1980s, it was over the course of the 1990s that a situation of widespread economic malaise intensified and produced devastating effects on Argentine society and citizens. Poverty, unemployment, crime, inflation, insecurity, and generalized instability skyrocketed to historically unprecedented levels. An especially notable feature of the crisis was the rapid impoverishment and decimation of a once large and prosperous middle class. As the crisis reached its dramatic crescendo in December 2001, widespread popular discontent culminated into a wave of mass protests across the country. The largest and most dramatic of these protests took shape in the capital city of Buenos Aires where tens of thousands of citizens from diverse walks of life spilled onto the streets banging on pots and pans in what became known as '*el cacerolazo*'. Merging with pre-existing networks of social movements and labor unions, large groups of citizens seized the public sphere in order to voice their grievances and frustrations toward the politicians and power-brokers whom they held as directly responsible for both creating and mismanaging the crisis (Dinerstein 2002). When the government imposed a curfew and sent militarized police forces to quell the 'public disorder' in December 2001, many citizens became further enraged and even more committed to the protests.

An infamous rallying slogan that emerged from the wave of public contention sweeping across Argentina at the close of 2001 infamously declared: *Que se vayan todos!*/All of the out! At the heart of this slogan was a collective desire among disaffected sectors of the citizenry to reset the political system, cleanse the state of corruption and revitalize Argentine democracy. Among the main concerns of protestors, for instance, was a perceived hijacking of the Argentine state by self-interested groups of elites who were accused of putting profit and greed above the public good (see Dinerstein 2015; Sitrin 2014; Svampa 2008). The term 'neoliberalism' became widely used in this context as a pejorative label to identify an enduring legacy of policy agendas which had been pursued by political authorities working in tandem with transnational development agencies during the 1980–1990s, most notably the 'structural adjustment programs' promoted by the World Bank and International Monetary Fund. The privatization of public services and resources along with the imposition of austerity measures by the government were especially central to many people's grievances because they felt that such policies had unjustly empowered small cadres of wealthy elites while dispossessing everyday citizens of basic rights, resources and opportunities.

The high levels of public contention across diverse sectors of the Argentine citizenry along with many people's commitment to collective action and protest in the face of a national crisis were fundamental to the rise of the community-based schooling movement. More specifically, diverse groups of parents and teachers located in areas which had been deeply affected by the crisis began to draw on the effervescent energy of the protests so as to undertake the difficult work of transforming local schools into vehicles of social change and empowerment. One of the first and most essential steps in this transformation, from the standpoint of these actors, was to establish a clear break with the ideas and practices of the past. More specifically, the pioneering advocates of community-based schooling in Argentina began to discursively assemble and articulate collective critiques of the so-called 'neoliberal' policies which had been prioritized during the 1990s. From the progressive political standpoints of these actors, the educational policies of the Menem era were unambiguously blamed for having undermined the inclusive and ultimately humanitarian principles upon which the historical foundations of the Argentine public educational system had been built. A novel set of educational visions and projects was thus deemed necessary so as to correct the wrongs and injustices of the not so distant past. The crisis in this regard provided an opportunity to imagine and build something new. Central to any such re-building process, from the standpoint of these actors, was a realization of increased forms of educational self-determination and robust levels of community participation in the governance of local schools. Amongst the pioneering proponents of the community-based schooling movement, such self-determination and participation were unequivocally equated with a democratization of the educational system and corresponding empowerment of the citizenry. These beliefs are evidenced, for instance, in a speech that was given at a meeting of community-based schooling advocates in Buenos Aires in early 2006:

> In contrast to the neoliberal model of the past with its emphasis on privatization, elitism, competition, individualism and segregation, we are working to promote essential humanitarian values of cooperation, respect for diversity and the safeguarding of our social, cultural and also ecological environments ... Through an authentic commitment to social justice and democracy we are putting the school in the hands of the people, of our communities, and together building a future founded on solidarity, hope and opportunity for youth. (Document #21, unpublished transcript of speech by representative of FECEABA obtained during fieldwork, Buenos Aires, August 2016)

The circulation of these kinds of progressive ideological convictions and narratives was directly correlated to the widespread diffusion of protest and social movement activities in Argentine society at the height of the national crisis in 2001–2002. The crisis would authorize and create a space for such discourses in the educational sector in great part by destabilizing and delegitimizing prevailing policy discourses established during the 1990s. As the economic crisis spilled over into the educational system and created severe material shortages and problems of inequality in many schools, it inspired the cultivation of new visions and narratives about educational justice and opportunity among disparate groups of disaffected actors.

The Crisis Spills Over into the Educational System

Among the institutional sectors that was both devastated and transformed by the tumultuous events accompanying the crisis was the national education system. Once upon a time, Argentina had built an exemplary model of inclusive universal public schooling characterized by some of the highest levels of educational opportunity and achievement in Latin America (Gvirtz, Beech and Oria 2008). However, over the course of the 1990s the national education system underwent significant changes as a consequence of policies implemented by the Menem government, most notably the national reforms of 1993–1994 (Rhoten 2000). Rooted heavily in the utilitarian logics of human capital theories of education (Tan 2014), these reforms were ultimately intended to help make Argentina more economically competitive and integrate more effectively into globalizing markets by boosting the skills and capacities of the national workforce (Rhoten 2000). In brief, these reforms combined a political decentralization of educational governance with neoliberal principles of marketization, privatization and austerity. This is to say that state power was transferred 'downward' to provincial authorities who then worked rhetorically to promote increased 'competition' and choice' in the educational system by (i) actively supporting the development of private schools through subsidization and deregulation while also (ii) imposing new forms of austerity and standardization on public schools. Organized resistance to these policies by many teachers unions and educational associations, however, prevented processes of privatization from reaching the levels of intensity experienced in other Latin American countries, such as Chile (Beech and Barrenechea 2011). Nonetheless, in the years leading up to the national crisis of 2001–2002 the implementation of privatization through the logics of decentralization transformed the Argentine educational landscape significantly (for summaries see Narodowski and Andrada 2001, or Narodowksi and Moschetti 2015).

Although decentralization initiatives were broadly touted by the Menem government as a form of democratization, over time it became clear that local citizens and teachers were not generally empowered by these policies. Rather, the reins of educational decision-making were often placed into the hands of provincial elites, who often had strong ties to the Menem regime and steered policies accordingly (Rivas 2004). Among the most notable transformations wrought by Menem's reforms were (i) widespread cuts to the budgets of many state-run public schools and (ii) an overall increase in the provision of subsidies to private schools as well as (iii) a heightened emphasis on curricular standardization in state-run public schools and (iv) increased allocation of curricular and administrative autonomy to private schools (Pini 2008; Rhoten 2000). In other words, as state-based public schools got less funding and less autonomy, private schools received more funding and more autonomy. As a consequence of these shifts in the priorities of educational policy-making, the realm of private schooling grew tremendously in Argentina during the 1990s (Narodowski and Moschetti 2015). Conversely, the domain of state-run public schooling underwent a dramatic decline in terms of the quality of its services as well as a decrease in student retention and graduation rates. Moreover, the latter half of the 1990s was witness to a large-scale exodus of students who migrated *en masse* from the financially struggling public sector to an increasingly subsidized and autonomous private sector. Interestingly, public schools were being abandoned by the very same demographic which had historically championed the development of a state-run system of universal public education in Argentina: the working and lower middle classes.

As the neoliberal policy agendas of the 1990s began to converge with the collapsing of the Argentine economy and state at the turn of the 21st century, the problems affecting the national educational system quickly went from bad to worse. In short, on the eve of the start of the 2002 school year many schools, both private and public, were sliding into a state of bankruptcy and there was tremendous uncertainty as to how many schools could continue operating. In a growing number of public and private schools alike, many teachers stopped receiving salaries and in some cases schools were shut down entirely. Not surprisingly, the array of escalating social problems occurring in Argentine society as a consequence of the economic crisis, such as hunger, homelessness, substance abuse, violence, crime and delinquency, quickly found their way into classrooms and presented monumental obstacles for the development of effective learning environments (Pini 2008). Dropout rates among students and fatigue among teachers skyrocketed. The frustrations and uncertainties which accompanied these deteriorating and difficult conditions laid the emotional as well as strategic groundwork for the rise of the community-based schooling movement. Through the act of sharing their grievances and anxieties in the present, people began to seek out solutions for the future which drew critical lessons from the past. Taking control of local schools and securing strong levels of community participation and engagement became identified as central tasks, thus bringing community-based schools to life.

My investigations found that the simultaneous growth of private schools and decline in the quality of public schooling had major consequence for the rise of the community-based schooling movement. In particular, the state-sanctioned and supported processes of educational privatization would become a major source of protest among many proponents of community-based schooling. These actors expressed severe skepticism about the moral underpinnings of privatization initiatives and maintained very strong commitments to promoting a revitalization of the historical institution of universal public education. Although highly critical of privatization, these actors were nonetheless supportive of educational decentralization policies in the sense that they believed that the curricular and administrative design of local schools should be explicitly adapted to fit the situational realities of local communities. In this light, decentralization became discursively detached from the pursuit of privatization agendas and re-purposed for the pursuit of democratization. Such convictions became woven into a unifying and founding set of narratives upheld by many proponents of community-based schools over time. As expressed by one supporter whom I interviewed in 2015:

> The integrity of public schools should be protected. What we're doing is placing the school more directly in the hands of the public to ensure this integrity ... This is not privatization, it is democratization. History is on our side here and shows that privatization is not about democracy in the true sense, [privatization] does not put the school in the hands of educators or parents and students ... We do not oppose the state. In fact, we believe strongly in the state. Privatization on the contrary is usually anti-statist and, for this reason prevents the possibility of a true democracy ... [Privatization] has a corrupting effect on education by creating large inequalities, and producing class divisions and competition between the people. This is what we saw in the 90s. We cannot repeat the same mistakes. (Interview#6, Buenos Aires, July 2015)

Such notions were common and widespread in my analysis of interviews and documents/texts produced by community-based schooling organizations. My investigations found that such sentiments about democratization were prevalent among constituents of community-based schools, not only persons in position of leadership or public relations. As noted by one young teaching assistant, for example: "We are not private schools or against the state as in a neoliberal manner. No, I would say that we seek to make the state stronger, more democratic. This is best accomplished by bringing power closer to the people, to the community (Interview #9, Buenos Aires, July 2015). Or, as captured in this excerpt from an interview with a parent: "These are not private schools. Our schools reflect a serious obligation to democracy. The *escuelas de gestión social* are public schools in the fullest sense of what this means, they are schools 'of the people' (Interview # 3, Buenos Aires, August 2014).The circulation of such solidaristic convictions and narratives at the grassroots was made possible in great part by many people's negative assessments and rejection of past policies. In particular, the austerity policies which had deprived many public schools of key funding streams and the material endorsement of privatization initiatives by authorities during the latter 1990s were identified as common sources of injustice and frustration by community-based schooling advocates in the 2000s. Strengthening the institutional and social alignments between local schools and communities was widely equated by these persons with the reclamation and revitalization of public education rather than as a show of support for privatization. Many of the schools I visited in Buenos Aires, for example, made a point of having a sign or statement visible at the entrance which declared affiliation and support for public education, such as "*Amo la educación pública*" or "*Education de gestión social = educación pública.*"

New Social Formations

As the wave of massive public protests began to grow and spread across Argentina in response to the escalating crisis in 2001–2002, many educators along with local parents and students became actively engaged in grassroots processes of collective action and mobilization. While participation in these protests was a way for the members of these educational communities to publicly express their disaffection and grievances in unity with other Argentines, it also became a starting point for them to take educational matters into their own hands by orchestrating their own empowering forms of educational change 'from below'. Indeed, many of the pioneering persons who would bring the community-based schooling movement to life were the very same groups of teachers and parents who became active and politicized during the wave of mass public protests which accompanied the start of the school year in early 2002.

Although the initial intensity of the protest wave lost significant momentum over the course of 2002–2003, the spirit of public contention endured as a motivating and unifying symbol for many aggrieved citizens who were eager to realize empowering forms of socio-political change amidst a climate of uncertainty and instability (Dinerstein 2015). Indeed, many citizens would continue to engage in an array of grassroots dialogues and initiatives aimed at forging new social and political realities from within their very own neighborhoods and communities. At the center of many of these vibrant civic discussions and activities were deep-seated critiques of the so-called 'neoliberal' policy logics which had come to dominate public policy-making during the 1990s and a refusal to accept their return in Argentine politics. Progressive notions of social justice and democratization along with parallel concerns for labor and human rights became foundational tropes for citizens seeking to both understand and transcend the problems generated by the crisis, such as political corruption and economic inequality. In working to transform progressive ideals into realities times of crisis, a variety of new social practices were enacted and brought to life by citizens at the grassroots of civil society (see Sitrin 2014). Among the innovative practices to surface at the dramatic height of the time of the crisis in 2001–2002 were: (i) the establishment of neighborhood assemblies (*asambleas bariales*) based on highly localized and collaborative or 'horizontal' modes of political decision-making amongst citizens, (ii) the manifestation of workplace occupations (*tomas*) designed to establish cooperative sites of worker-led economic production amongst the unemployed, and (iii) the creation of highly inclusive adult education programs (*talleres de educación popular*) geared toward the dissemination of information and the genesis of strategic forms of public knowledge and learning.[5] Although these three sets of social practices were relatively new for many citizens, they unambiguously traced their origins directly to long-standing legacies of autonomous mobilization and community organizing pioneered by the networks of progressive social movements and labor unions which had been mobilizing and protesting in the shadows of Argentine politics since the 1980s, such as the so-called *piqueteros* movement of the unemployed (Massetti 2009).

The diffusion of these diverse social movement activities into the educational sector would be pivotal in establishing the organizational logics and ideological foundations from which the community-based schooling movement would take root and eventually sprout up across the educational landscape. For example, the direct democratic practices of 'horizontalism' that were introduced to many citizens through the phenomenon of popular assemblies would be incorporated into community-based schooling initiatives as a way to establish collaborative schemas of leadership and decision-making amongst teachers, parents and (in secondary schools) students. The formal founding of some community-based schools as cooperatives (i.e. *escuelas cooperativas*) was a direct outcome of this new kind of social formation taking root within the educational system. In some locations, the radical logic of spatial occupation would become utilized as a way for community-based schooling proponents to take direct ownership of schools which had been forcefully shut down due to a combination of austerity policies and severe economic shortages caused by the crisis. The teachers, parents and students engaged in the occupation of these schools would then work collaboratively to re-purpose them as community-based schools driven by democratic principles of horizontalism and self-determination. The actions of these teachers and parents were often accompanied by seasoned social movement activists and labor union representatives who supplied strategic and legal advice. Finally, the inclusive and emancipatory spirit of popular education workshop played a very central role in the development of the organizational culture of many community-based schools. In working to establish a strong alignment between schools and communities, many community-based schools were turned into sites for adult education and public deliberation. During the evenings or weekends teachers, parents and other community members would congregate in the school to talk through issues of local importance such as by orchestrating feminist workshops on domestic abuse or setting up legal clinics to help families with legal issues.

In sum, as social movement-led processes of change were put in motion at the grassroots of Argentine society during the early 2000s they were taken up within the educational sector in ways which helped to foster new educational configurations and reform agendas. Frequently underlying these collective action efforts was a commitment amongst educators and concerned families to promote stronger and more systematic forms of community participation in local schools. Such convictions were explicitly understood as expressions of democratization and formed in response to the perceived failings of the 'neoliberal' policy agendas prioritized during the 1990s, notably privatization and austerity. As community-based schools began to grow in tandem with social movements across the Argentine landscape, the rise of a new political climate in 2003 would further fuel their expansion.

The Crisis Yields a New Political Climate

As the tide of social protest by citizens merged with a more organized and enduring tide of mobilization by pre-existing social movements and strike actions by labor unions in December 2001–January 2002, it became a powerful force of political change. As a result, the legitimacy of the ruling de la Rúa administration began to breakdown and ultimately collapsed on December 21 2001. A series of several short-lived replacement presidencies would also fall in rapid succession amidst the ongoing protests of subsequent weeks. Calls were quickly made for a round of national elections by panicked members of parliament and a shaky interim government was formed in early 2002 with Eduardo Duhalde as president.[6] After a heated electoral campaign punctuated by sustained strikes and protests, a new government led by the left-wing populist senator Nestór Kirchner eventually formed and took office in 2003. The rhetoric and policy proposals put forth by the new Kirchner administration- at least initially- often channeled many of the very same grievances and claims articulated by the social movements and labor unions which had seized the national stage at the height of the crisis. Although the devastating effects of the economic crisis would still be felt across Argentine society for years to come, the presidential elections of 2003 would mark the beginning of a new brand of leftist political culture known as '*kirchnerismo*' (Biglieri and Perelló 2007). Some key characteristics of *kirchnerismo* entailed (i) sweeping critiques of the neoliberal policy agendas which had dominated the 1980–1990s, (ii) concerted efforts to expand public sector services and (iii) the incorporation of various types of civil society actors into positions of state-based planning and authority. The ascension of this new left-leaning political culture would play a pivotal role in fueling the expansion of the community-based schooling movement in great part by providing the claims and agendas of grassroots proponents with empowering forms of state-level support.

In particular, the ideological-discursive alignment between the new Kirchner regime and pre-existing networks of progressive social movements and labor unions would help to provide increased visibility and legitimacy to community-based schooling proponents and their claims of promoting democratization and social justice in the educational sector. Indeed, the leaders of some of the largest social movement organizations and labor unions would eventually gain positions in the Kirchner government thus acting as strategic brokers between state agencies and civil society groups. Given the severe financial shortages facing the Argentine state much of the institutional support for community-based schooling under the new regime would be rhetorical. Nonetheless, an important expression of tangible support would come in the form of an official legal recognition of community-based schools under Kirchner's national education reforms of 2006, as mentioned earlier. Tucked inside the new policy on national education (*Ley de Educación Naciónal*

#26.206) was a subtle but nonetheless clear recognition of the *escuelas de gestión social* and *escuelas cooperativas* as forming an "integral" part of the national public education system. This brief mention was an important victory in that it validated the legal status of the schools as constituting a small but unique and strategic niche in the educational system. This moment of recognition also represented a victory in the sense that it validated the labor of the grassroots actors who had worked to bring community-based schools to life amidst a context of macro-structural crisis. From the uncertain circumstances of the crisis, these actors had sized an opportunity to forge new realities and in the process changed the institutional contours of the educational system 'from below'.

CONCLUSION

Despite the serious social problems and widespread suffering produced by the climaxing of the Argentine national crisis in 2001, it was nonetheless a critical event which created opportune structural conditions for the rise of the community-based schooling movement. In particular, the genesis of the massive wave of public protest and the diffusion of social movement activities coupled with a corresponding breakdown and renewal of the Argentine state constituted a moment of macro-structural rupture from which new social and political realities could be forged. On the one hand, as the wave of protest spilled over into the educational system, the stake-holders of local schools began to build new solidarities based around the articulation of common grievances about the failed legacy of 'neoliberalism' and a corresponding desire to achieve progressive educational reforms rooted in progressive ideals of democratization and the pursuit of social justice. On the other hand, the leftward turn in Argentine politics that came with the rise of *kirchernismo* in 2003 would provide the grassroots constituents of community-based schooling with empowering forms of discursive visibility and ideological legitimacy in the political arena. Sustained processes of mobilization, networking and organizing by community-based schooling constituents within this new political climate would pay off in 2006 when a new national reform of the education system by the Kirchner government included a formal legal recognition of the *escuelas de gestión social* and *escuelas cooperativas*.

Although community-based schooling would continue to grow in the years following the national reform of 2006, this growth would begin to stall by around 2011–2012. The causes of this stagnation are beyond the aims and scope of this chapter, but are linked to a blend of mutually reinforcing factors, including a systematic lack of tangible support from state-level agencies, and an overall weakening of solidaristic ties and interactions between individual schooling communities. The putatively energizing effects of *kirchnerismo* for the community-based schooling movement, for instance, declined considerably following the ascension of a new center-right government led by Mauricio Macri in 2014. In this new landscape, the status of community-based schools has remained highly ambiguous in political terms and increasingly precarious in financial terms. Although the Macri government has largely refused to recognize the *escuelas de gestión social* as fully-fledged public schools, proponents of community-based schooling have often been encouraged by authorities to adopt the status of private schools. By accepting this status they become eligible for economic subsidies from the state, particularly if they work with students from impoverished communities. While some schools have accepted this arrangement so as to overcome financial problems, many others have refused and chosen to hold their ground in a longer term battle to achieve full recognition as public schools, i.e. *escuelas públicas de gestión social*. Despite a relative loss of energy at the grassroots as well as the uncertainty surrounding their future political status, however, today there are around 450 community-based schools in Argentina. These schools exist as a direct result of the solidarity and perseverance of the grassroots actors who worked to transform a dramatic situation of societal crisis at the turn of the 21st century into an empowering opportunity for educational reform and renewal from the grassroots of Argentine society. Through concerted commitment to collective action these actors re-defined the neoliberal logics of decentralization and converted it, at least momentarily, into a community-driven mechanism of educational democratization and social justice.

REFERENCES

Alonso Brá, Mariana. (2001). *Las escuelas cooperativas: Alternativas de participación y auto-gestión en el sistema educativo? Instituto Internacional de la Planeamiento de Educación*. Buenos Aires: UNESCO.

Alonso Brá, Mariana. (2015). "La Gestión Social Educativa: Un Recorrido Comparativo por la Politica y Administración Educativa." *Question, 1*(47), 24–40.

Beach, Derek, & Rasmus Brun Pedersen. (2013). *Process-Tracing Methods: Foundations and Guidelines*. Ann Arbor, MI: University of Michigan Press.

Beech, Jason, & Ignacio Barrenechea. (2011). "Pro-Market Educational Governance: Is Argentina a Black Swan?" *Critical Studies in Education, 52*(3), 279–293.

Biglieri, Paula, & Gloria Perelló. (2007). *En el Nombre del Pueblo: La Emergencia del Populismo Kirchnerista*. Buenos Aires: UNSAM.

Dinerstein, Ana Cecilia. (2002). "The Battle of Buenos Aires: Crisis, Insurrection and the Invention of Politics in Argentina." *Historical Materialism, 10*(4), 5–38.

Dinerstein, Ana Cecilia. (2015). *The Politics of Autonomy in Latin America: The Art of Organising Hope*. New York, NY: Palgrave Macmillan.

Epstein, Edward, & David Pion-Berlin, eds. (2006). *Broken Promises? The Argentine Crisis and Argentine Democracy*. Plymouth: Lexington Books.

Gluz, Nora. (2013). *Las Luchas por el Derecho a la Educación: Experiencias Educativas de Movimientos Sociales*. Buenos Aires: CLACSO.

Grimson, Alejandro, & Gabriel Kessler. (2005). *On Argentina and the Southern Cone: Neoliberalism and National Imaginations*. New York, NY: Routledge.

Gvirtz, Silvina, Jason Beech, & Angela Oria. (2008). "Schooling in Argentina." In S. Gvirtz & J. Beech, eds., *Going to School in Latin America* (pp.5–34). Westport, CT: Greenwood Press.

Heidemann, K. (2017). "Overcoming Uncertainty: Agency, Stance, and the Rise of Collective Action in Times of Crisis." *Sociological Focus, 50*(4), 1–18.

Lopez Levy, M. (2017). *Argentina under the Kirchners: The Legacy of Leftist Populism* (Latin America Bureau Special Report). Warwickshire: Practical Action Publishing.

Massetti, Astor. (2009). *La Década Piquetera: Acción Colectiva y Protesta Social de los Movimientos Territoriales Urbanos*. Buenos Aires: Nueva Trilce.

Narodowski, Mariano, & Mauro Moschetti. (2015). "The Growth of Private Education in Argentina: Evidence and Explanations." *Compare: A Journal of Comparative and International Education, 45*(1), 47–69.

Narodowski, Mariano, & Myrian Andrada. (2001). "The Privatization of Education in Argentina" *Journal of Educational Policy, 16*(6), 585–595.

Pini, Monica. (2008). *La Escuela Pública que nos Dejaron los Noventa: Discursos y Prácticas*. Buenos Aires: UNSAM.

Rhoten, Diana. (2000). "Education Decentralization in Argentina: A 'Global-Local Conditions of Possibility' Approach to State, Market, and Society Change." *Journal of Education Policy, 15*(6), 593–619.

Rivas, Axel. (2004). *Gobernar la Educación: Estudio Comparado Sobre el Poder y la Eduación en las Provincias Argentinas*. Buenos Aires: Ediciones Granica.

Rosemberg, Diego. (2015). "Ni Estatles, Ni Privadas: Escuelas de Gestión Social." *Le Monde Diplomatique Suplemento. La Educación en Debate, 36*, 1–2.

Sewell, William H. (2005). *Logics of History: Social Theory and Social Transformation*. Chicago, IL: University of Chicago Press.

Sitrin, Marina. (2014). *Everyday Revolutions: Horizontalism and Autonomy in Argentina*. London: Zed Books.

Snow, David, & Sarah Soule. (2010). *A Primer on Social Movements*. New York, NY: W.W. Norton.

Svampa, Maristella. (2008). *Cambios de Época: Movimientos Sociales y Poder Político*. Buenos Aires: CLASCO.

Tan, Emrullad. (2014). "Human Capital Theory: A Holistic Criticism." *Review of Educational Research, 84*(3), 411–445.

Teubal, Miguel. (2004). "Rise and Collapse of Neoliberalism in Argentina: The Role of Economic Groups." *Journal of Developing Societies, 20*(3–4), 173–188.

NOTES

1. This research was made possible in great part thanks to a multi-year research development grant from the Spencer Foundation (Chicago, USA). I am thankful to Jason Beech and Paula Razquin at the Universidad de San Andrés for providing an academic home in Argentina and for helping me realize my fieldwork in Buenos Aires. I am also deeply grateful to Axel Rivas, Mariana Alonso Brá, Roberto Schimkus and Ana Maria Fernandez for opening so many doors and shedding so much light on the phenomenon of community-based schools in Buenos Aires. My gratitude also goes out to my former students Elisa Garote Soto and Sergio Calderon Harker for helping me to analyze and make sense of the data.
2. The primary distinction between these two types of community-based schools is primarily legalistic and based on the fact that *escuelas cooperativas* are formally classified as worker cooperatives which are technically 'owned and operated' by the teaching and administrative staff. This has consequence for labor and tax laws in Argentina.
3. These figures stem from a national survey conducted in 2013 by the *Associación de Educación de Gestión Social*.
4. For information on the politics and policy agendas of the Kirchner governments, see Lopez Levy (2017).
5. For a good summary and discussion (in English) of these various forms of social practice and organizing that emerged in the wake of the crisis, see Dinerstein (2015) or Sitrin (2014).
6. For a basic timeline of the major events surrounding the Argentine crisis, see www.theguardian.com.world/2001/dec/20/argentina1

D. BRENT EDWARDS JR.

4. ACCOUNTABILITY THROUGH COMMUNITY-BASED MANAGEMENT?

Implications from the Local Level Implementation in El Salvador of a Globally-Popular Model

INTRODUCTION

The "Education with Community Participation" (EDUCO) program in El Salvador achieved fame in the late 1990s and 2000s because it formally transferred, among other things, the ability to hire and fire teachers to a committee of parents at the community level. While recent literature has traced the evolution of this program within El Salvador, as well as its trajectory as it entered the international educational agenda and became a "global education policy," an understudied aspect of this program is the community-level experience. After characterizing the history, design, and system-wide results of EDUCO, this chapter turns its attention to the local level by reviewing the literature that exists on EDUCO's implementation, with a focus on community experiences. This literature is difficult to locate, even within El Salvador, and is almost entirely unknown outside the country. It is argued that the studies which make up this literature provide insight into the experience of average communities in the EDUCO program. In the end, beyond presenting new and little-known insights into the community-level reality of the EDUCO program, this chapter reflects on the implications of these insights for (a) the theory and assumptions behind such models of community-level management, (b) the national and global-level politics of the decentralization trends in education that have been predominant since the early 1990s, and (c) the possibility of democratization from below. In addition to the above-mentioned foci, the chapter begins with a brief characterization of community-based management (CBM) and the research that has been conducted on this phenomenon.

COMMUNITY-BASED MANAGEMENT: CHARACTERIZATION AND LITERATURE REVIEW

CBM envisions the involvement of the community in various aspects of education governance at the local level. In practice, this often means that parents work on their own or together with teachers and principals (sometimes called school directors) on such issues as how the school budget is spent, fundraising, curriculum development, the procurement of textbooks, school maintenance and construction, the monitoring and evaluation of teacher performance, and even the hiring and firing of teachers (World Bank 2007). Committees made up of parents, teachers, and principals are the most common vehicle for operationalizing this governance strategy.[1] As noted in the introduction chapter of this volume, CBM has been a very popular governance model since the early 1990s that has been pursued widely in international development. It has been enacted in many countries because of its promise for increasing community participation, improving teacher accountability, engendering greater efficiency, and enhancing education outcomes, among other reasons (Edwards 2012; Edwards and DeMatthews 2014).

In recent years, two rigorous literature reviews have been conducted that were focused on CBM (Westhorp Walker, Rogers, Overbeeke, Ball, and Brice 2014; Carr-Hill, Rolleston, Phereli, and Schendel 2015). As a result of the methodological preferences embedded in their definitions for rigor, these reviews focused overwhelmingly on quantitative studies that examined the impacts of CBM on various outcomes, such as student achievement, pupil retention, teacher attendance, etc. In light of the widespread popularity of CBM, it is noteworthy that Carr-Hill et al. (2015) conclude that they were not able to produce "any robust conclusions on the conditions necessary for positive impact [of CBM]" (p. 8). While there certainly were studies that reported positive impacts of CBM, the results were not consistent across studies, thus confounding efforts to generalize lessons. Westhorp et al. (2014), for their part, conclude that school councils are more likely:

> (a) to hold staff to account, and to be accountable in their own roles, where their role is clear, they have formal authority, and they are adequately resourced to do so; (b) to be held accountable to communities where parents directly elect their representatives on school boards or councils, when those elections are conducted openly and effectively, and when there are sufficient parent representatives to balance the power of other stakeholders; [and] (c) to be effective when significant power differentials do not exist between committee members and social norms do not inhibit the exercise of community power. (p. 4)

It should come as no surprise that school councils function better when their authority is clearly delineated, when they have sufficient resources, when their representatives are elected, and when there are no social norms that prohibit some members (usually women) from participating.

However, what the above points belie is a belief in the technocratic approach to CBM. A shortcoming of the technocratic approach is that it assumes instrumental relations can be uniformly inscribed in communities, regardless of their particular contexts. In contrast with this perspective, studies have pointed to the importance of preexisting social capital when it comes to implementing CBM (Pryor 2005; Gershberg, Meade, and Andersson 2009; Altschuler and Corrales 2012). In other words, and as emphasized in this chapter, community capacity is crucial when it comes to realizing extreme forms of decentralization, such as CBM.

EDUCO'S HISTORY: FROM CIVIL WAR TO GLOBAL EDUCATION POLICY

The origins and trajectory of EDUCO have been addressed in multiple publications (Edwards 2015, 2018, forthcoming; Edwards, Victoria, and Martin 2015). In short, EDUCO emerged first as a pilot program in six communities in 1991 supported by a UNICEF consultant (with the blessing and collaboration of the Salvadoran government). Starting later that year and continuing into the 2000s, EDUCO received significant financial and technical assistance from the World Bank and other international organizations. Over the course of 1991–1995, EDUCO would go from being a pilot program to an office within the Ministry of Education (MINED), to a program that was incorporated across all administrative areas within the MINED, to a national policy. (See below for figures on the program's reach.)

At the outset, EDUCO was an attractive program because it met the constraints that actors at various levels faced. For the MINED, the program was desirable, first, because it helped to expand educational access in rural areas, areas which were hardest hit by the civil war (1980–1992), and, second, because it represented an innovation that would help "modernize" the education sector, as the sector was being pressured to do by the World Bank and the United States Agency for International Development. Third, and as addressed further below, EDUCO was an attractive model because it had the potential to incorporate communities linked with the civil war opposition.

For the World Bank, the program represented an opportunity to experiment with an extreme form of decentralization, wherein teachers would be hired and fired by the community. Doing so was of interest to the World Bank because it knew that this model–if it was successful–would be lucrative, as the World Bank could sell the idea to other countries in need of loans or technical assistance. Contributing to the bankability of this model was the fact that decentralization and community participation were key ideas in the international development industry during the late 1980s and early 1990s (Edwards and DeMatthews 2014).

Teacher's unions were active in the early 1990s, but they did not block the adoption of EDUCO like they had with earlier reform ideas more clearly aligned with privatization, such as vouchers. In part, this was because EDUCO looked and sounded more like community education, which was less threatening. The lack of significant union mobilization was also because EDUCO did not affect existing members. EDUCO only had indirect consequences for teacher's unions in that teachers who worked in EDUCO schools (initially a small number) were prevented by program regulations from joining unions. It was not until the 2000s, after EDUCO had greatly expanded, that teacher's unions engaged in a sustained campaign against the program (SIMEDUCO 2011).

At the local level, it needs to be noted that the EDUCO model was built on years of community experience providing education. In the context of civil war, many communities had to organize to offer informal education to their children, since teachers frequently refused, for reasons of personal security, to travel to or work in non-urban areas. In practice, an individual, often with nothing more than a primary level education, would teach classes in exchange for donations from community members.

But the community experience mentioned above is only part of the picture at the local level. During the 1970s and 1980s, the tradition of popular education was combined with democratic organization in those communities affiliated with or controlled by those groups who opposed the government – with these groups collectively known as the Farabundo Martí Liberation Front (FMLN) (Montgomery 1995, pp. 119–122; Hammond 1998; Alvear 2002; ADES 2003; Cruz 2004).[2] The key point here is that many communities in the northern part of El Salvador, where the FMLN presence was strongest, had many years of experience from the 1970s onward that helped to build social capital. This social capital was facilitated by the Catholic Church, as priests would organize and work with rural communities during the 1970s. This social capital was arguably further strengthened in the 1980s during the civil war, as communities not only mobilized to combat the government and its death squads but also experimented with community level government and cooperatives in multiple areas (e.g., agriculture, fishing, etc.).

Although the FMLN did not win the war, in those portions of the country controlled by FMLN (e.g., Chalatenango, Morazán, Cuscatlán, San Vincente and Usulután) there were, in the words of Montgomery (1995), "outlines of revolutionary local government" (p. 119). Though these local governments took different forms in different areas, "there was a universal effort ... to organize collective or cooperative farms; to introduce literacy classes for civilians and guerrillas and compulsory education for children; and to institute medical care in areas where most people had never seen a doctor" (p. 122). In contrast to liberal democracies, where political participation tends to involve periodic voting, the FMLN placed emphasis on preparing people for "direct participation in daily decision-making and cooperation toward common goals" (p. 126).[3]

Even though many Salvadorans were forced to flee to refugee camps, they continued to organize themselves democratically and to practice popular education (ADES 2003; Edwards and Klees 2012). Thus, when it came to EDUCO, though many FMLN-affiliated communities were resistant to the program (for reasons explained in the next section), they nevertheless had previous experience with community organization and self-governance that had already prepared them for CBM. Of course, this previous experience also confounds claims that attribute higher education outcomes to the EDUCO model, since many of the communities where EDUCO was implemented benefitted from practice with community management that had nothing to do with EDUCO (Edwards and Loucel 2016).

Finally, before proceeding, it should be noted that the implementation of this policy was not in doubt. All the dominant organizational and political actors agreed on this policy choice, and so it was only a matter of time and effort. Going forward from 1991, when the first education loan was approved, the World Bank provided close monitoring of the program as well as guidance at each step in the process. By 1994, thousands of communities had been integrated into the EDUCO program. Concretely, while the program began in 1991 with six communities, 3 years later it had 2,316 teachers and served 74,112 students (Cuéllar-Marchelli 2003a). Ten years later, in 2004, these figures had risen to 7,381 and 378,208, respectively.[4] Approximately 55 % of rural public schools, which make up two-thirds of all schools in El Salvador, would operate under the EDUCO program (Gillies, Crouch, and Flórez 2010).

EDUCO'S DESIGN: NEOLIBERAL COMMUNITY-BASED MANAGEMENT

For all that has been said about EDUCO's history, what still needs to be clarified is the logic of the model and thinking behind the program. The EDUCO program was theorized in terms of its promise for efficiency, effectiveness, and accountability. That is, although the language of democratization and intrinsically-valuable community participation can be – and has been – invoked in relation to EDUCO, the program has become widely-promoted and well-known for its ability to be conceptualized in terms of market principles.

For the first principle, it was suggested that the education system would be more efficient if the central MINED transferred to the community level the responsibility for hiring and firing teachers, the latter of whom would work on one-year contracts that were renewable at the discretion of the school council that hired them. These school councils, which were known as Community Education Associations (or ACEs, for their name in Spanish), were made up of five elected, volunteer parents from the community. (Note that the schools managed by ACEs tended to be small schools without principals, though one of the teachers would by default assume some of the administrative duties typically associated with the principalship.) Not only was this community arrangement seen as inherently more efficient on a system-wide basis (since parents worked on a volunteer basis and since ACEs would mobilize parents to build and maintain the school without compensation), but, in addition, this arrangement was seen as more efficient because the ACEs would manage the school's budget and would, as such, be responsible for purchasing only the educational materials that the school needed, thereby eliminating waste in purchasing.

For the second principle, it was thought that EDUCO's ACEs would promote effectiveness because they would lead to more consistent teacher attendance and improved student test scores. It was assumed that improved teacher attendance and higher test scores would result from the fact that teachers were under the scrutiny of community actors to perform well or else lose their job. While being present more often, teachers would also attempt to teach better to impress parents, with the implication that achievement would also be enhanced.

Clearly, then, the idea of teacher accountability was central. By turning the local community into an accountability lever, the MINED could effect improved outcomes.

The MINED, on the other hand, was responsible for the following: facilitating the creation of the ACEs, training the members of the ACEs in administrative and accounting procedures, setting the minimum criteria for teacher selection by the ACEs, designing and providing curricula, and overall coordination, supervision, and monitoring of the program as it was scaled up (World Bank 1994; Reimers 1997). As can be seen, though ACEs were responsible solely for a handful of administrative tasks, the ACEs were nevertheless the lynchpin of the EDUCO model because of their ability to hire, fire, and monitor teachers, as well as their ability to manage and spend the school budget.

The design of EDUCO also had serious implications for the community model of FMLN – imbued as it was with notions of solidarity and critical consciousness. Indeed, EDUCO transformed the FMLN community model into a neoliberal experiment inscribed with mechanistic notions of teacher monitoring and punishment. To that end, it bears mentioning that FMLN communities were particularly affected by EDUCO, since this program helped the government, in a post-war context, to incorporate and undermine these communities. (Recall that the war ended in January 1992, shortly after EDUCO began in early 1991.) This incorporation and undermining was a result of the fact, first, that FMLN communities were desperate for resources and, second, that the government would only agree to support education in FMLN areas (as in all rural areas) through the EDUCO program. Crucially, not only were they required to join the EDUCO program if they wanted access to government resources, but, by and large, they also had to hire teachers from outside their communities, since their popular education teachers had low levels of education and thus did not have the required credentials. This requirement was a blow to popular education as well as to the broader community vision and project in which it was often embedded.

EDUCO'S RESULTS: MACRO AND MICRO ASSESSMENTS

General Outcomes and System-Wide Considerations

Before diving into a discussion of the studies that examine the community-level operation of EDUCO, two aspects of the evidence on EDUCO should be highlighted. First, it needs to be pointed out that no fewer than nine quantitative studies exist on EDUCO, with seven being carried out by the World Bank. While the World Bank's studies have played a key role in the global promotion of EDUCO – in that they claimed positive benefits, e.g., in terms of student achievement and student retention – critical reviews of their methods and interpretations have shown that their conclusions are unwarranted (Edwards and Loucel 2016; Edwards 2018). Perhaps more damning is the fact that, in those models where the shortcomings (in terms of statistical modeling) of the World Bank's studies have been addressed, EDUCO has actually been associated with lower levels of student achievement (Cuéllar-Marchelli 2003b).[5]

Second, a study by Cuéllar-Marchelli (2003a) has addressed EDUCO from a system-wide perspective that examined the dimensions of access, equity, productive efficiency, and social cohesion. Beyond the effects of EDUCO, this study raises serious doubts about the benefits of EDUCO more broadly. To summarize Cuéllar-Marchelli's work, though EDUCO is attributed with great gains in access, particularly in rural areas where the program was targeted (since these were the areas with highest need, following the destruction of the civil war), there is no way to know if another approach could not have generated the same improvements. On equity, EDUCO is concerning because of the burden that it can impose, considering that the labor contributed by parents was equivalent to work of 805 full-time employees (an amount that equals 28 percent of the work done by the administrative staff of the Ministry of Education). Of course, parental labor is in addition to other equity concerns. The fact that EDUCO operated in communities that were more marginalized and disadvantaged is evident. For example, in that 61 percent of the communities were without electricity and 74 percent were without piped water (compared with 15 and 48 percent for traditional public schools, respectively). Productive efficiency has to do with EDUCO's effects in relation to its costs. Although there is no definitive answer in this area, since evaluations have not taken costs into account, it has been shown that, in terms of costs alone, EDUCO was more expensive for the government (contrary to the rhetoric around the program), because fewer fees were paid by communities (Cuéllar-Marchelli 2003b). On the final dimension, Cuéllar-Marchelli (2003a) not only notes that community participation varies across communities but also concludes that, "while EDUCO purports greater social cohesion, its success depends greatly on existing social cohesion capacity" (p. 162). The point here is that CBM initiatives, such as EDUCO, are unlikely to function properly in practice if community members do not have the ability to work together for the good of the community. This is an important point, as will become more clear in the discussion that follows.

A Focus on the Community Level

The preceding commentary helps to situate findings of the handful of studies that have examined EDUCO more closely. In reporting on these studies, the purpose is to shed light on aspects of EDUCO that have received less attention, aspects relating to the mechanisms and processes that gave life to EDUCO in practice (for, as the conclusion will further clarify, EDUCO was undone starting in 2009). In order to do this, I rely on six qualitative studies, the majority of which have arguably gone unnoticed by scholars and policymakers, both within El Salvador and in the international literature on EDUCO and CBM. I focus primarily on what is a particularly broad study of EDUCO and its mechanisms at the community level. This study was conducted by Ayala (2005) and investigated EDUCO's operation in 23 communities across 10 of the 14 departments of the country. This study is complemented by five other case studies that either looked very narrowly at EDUCO, for example, in one or a few communities (Ávila de Parada and Landaverde de Romero 2007; Desmond 2009; Srygley 2013) or looked very broadly and drew on case study methods that included focus groups, interviews, and consultations with those who worked with EDUCO at various levels, including the community (Gillies et al. 2010; World Bank 2009).[6] It is argued that, taken together, these studies provide a window in to the functioning of EDUCO in "average" communities. Following Ayala (2005), the findings presented here are grouped according to (a) EDUCO's institutional structure, (b) community participation, (c) ACE management, (d) teacher treatment, and (e) pedagogical aspects.

EDUCO's institutional structure. Generally, EDUCO has been characterized as an administrative reform that increased the MINED's bureaucracy. This characterization is ironic, given that one of EDUCO's selling points was its promise of reducing the bureaucracy of the central MINED. Increased administrative dependence was particularly noticeable when it came to the payment of teachers, since they were employed by the ACE but the government took care of the payroll, leading to the development of "convoluted" systems for issuing checks to teachers (Gillies et al. 2010). Moreover, the EDUCO office was found to be small, with limited capacity, and with access to few resources to cover the program. This was apparent in the fact that support personnel were responsible for up to 100 ACEs, many of which were geographically difficult to access, with the result being that some ACEs did not see their support personnel even once per year. In those cases where support staff came to the school, they did so without warning the ACEs ahead of time, with the implication being that the ACEs did not meet with the officials, who would simply review and sign the documents kept by the ACEs. Moreover, there was no communication with the ACEs about the results of the visit and the findings of the official with regard to the performance of the ACE. Lack of support was compounded by lack of training for program personnel at all levels, which only served to worsen the disconnect between the administrative and pedagogical aspects of the program (Ayala 2005; Ávila de Parada and Landaverde de Romero 2007). On this point, it has also been noted that many EDUCO schools were without principals, that many had teachers acting as principals who were not appointed as such; and that those with principals had weak incentives for the principals to support teachers, due to the conflict of authority with the ACE (Gilles et al. 2010, pp. 25–26).

Community participation. Community participation tended to be restricted to those parents who were on the ACEs, except for when grade-level meetings were called by teachers, though this trend depended on the history of the community and the pre-existing social capital (Ávila de Parada and Landaverde de Romero 2007, pp. 93–94). That is, evidence suggests that community participation was more robust (i.e., beyond only ACE members) in some FMLN communities. Surprisingly, Ayala (2005), like Srygley (2013), also found that most community members did not know what EDUCO was (Ayala 2005). For their part, ACE members knew that they were expected to stimulate community participation, but they were not sure how to do that, did not receive training to that end, and were not entirely sure what participation was supposed to mean in practice. As a result, they focused instead on school construction, raising donations, and involving parents in food preparation, cleaning, repairs, fundraising, as well as accompanying the school principal to visit government agencies related to school business (Ayala 2005, p. 11; Gilles et al. 2010, p. 24). Though the government also hoped that teachers would offer literacy classes for parents, this happened inconsistently, was judged to be of low quality, and only occurred when convenient for teachers (i.e., during the day, during the week, such that mothers and not fathers could participate) (Ayala 2005, p. 11).

ACE management. Studies describe ACE members as inexperienced and illiterate (Ávila de Parada and Landaverde de Romero 2007; Desmond 2009). The decisions that were taken frequently fell to the two or three ACE members who were active, though these decisions were also influenced by teachers, often at the request of ACE members, who asked for guidance or assistance (Ayala 2005). While ACE communication was infrequent, casual, and often directed by teachers, ACEs did carry out valuable tasks related to the use of school funds, in addition to school works (e.g., construction, maintenance, reparation), and the acquisition of resources (e.g., computers, TVs, photocopiers, refrigerators, etc.). They also signed teacher checks, made purchases and payments, and sometimes monitored the attendance and the work of teachers (Ayala 2005).

Yet it was found that the majority of ACE members were not familiar with basic documents such as agreements and contracts; moreover, they seemed only to sign required documents in order to keep the school running (Ayala 2005). Perhaps unsurprisingly, given parents' lack of knowledge, ACEs frequently allowed teachers, principals, and technicians from the Ministry of Education to take decisions into their own hands (Ayala 2005; Ávila de Parada and Landaverde de Romero 2007; Gillies et al. 2010). Crucially, even the hiring of teachers was driven by the director of the school, by a teacher, or by someone from the departmental office of the Ministry of Education, the latter of whom would send pre-selected teachers to the ACEs for contracting (Ayala 2005). In the 2000s, out of recognition of the administrative challenges that parents faced, the Ministry of Education created the position of operations agent, who was to help with payroll procedures and the completion of the required reports and forms – related, for example, to income tax payment to the Ministry of Treasury, social security contributions, pension contributions, etc. (Gilles et al. 2010).

Ultimately, ACEs were seen as necessary not because of their ability to hold teachers to account but rather because, "if there is no ACE, there is no school" (Ayala 2005, p. 14). That is, the ACE became a perfunctory entity that neither contributed to accountability nor functioned in the other ways imagined. Indeed, contrary to the theory and rhetoric around EDUCO, Ávila de Parada and Landaverde de Romero (2007) concluded the following: "The weight of 'management' leaves little space for curricular and pedagogical aspects. There exists the need to return to a comprehensive approach, one that puts administrative and financial aspects in the service of teaching and learning, not the other way around" (p. 120). What stands out here is that this is the same critique so often leveled against public schools. As opposed to operating as independent mechanisms, the ACEs failed to function as envisioned, in part because the MINED did not provide training or technical assistance, and, in the case of the latter, where it did, technical assistants tended to complete tasks on behalf of the ACEs, as opposed to working to increase their capacity (Ayala 2005).

Teacher treatment. Of all those involved in EDUCO, teachers were in the most disadvantageous position. For instance, one study found that "parents exercise authority by using threats of cuts in pay or outright firing, while teachers have no right of appeal. Further, if they lose their job, they are also dropped from the pension plan" (World Bank 2009, p. iv). Also on the issue of contracting, Desmond (2009) not only reports that a teacher was let go so that a relative of an ACE member could be hired, but also that teaching positions could be bought "either through one initial payment or through the payment of three or four increments to the school" (p. 20). Though such instances seem to be few and far between, it is hard to judge their frequency with any certainty.

Separately, a few other points should be underscored, points which are not often emphasized in relation to EDUCO. First, given the dynamics reported in previous section, teachers tended to see ACEs as necessary only insofar as they contracted them, authorized their salary payments, and supported them in their activities (Ayala 2005). Second, teachers did not have access to bank loans or mortgages because of the yearly nature of their work contracts (Ayala 2005). Third, teachers did not receive training about the EDUCO program nor about how to encourage community participation (Ayala 2005), although Gillies et al. (2010) report that, as of 2005, EDUCO teachers were incorporated into the professional development system for other teachers (during 1991–1999, there were 1–2 trainings per year for EDUCO teachers for 40 hours each; during 2000–2004, there were no trainings). Fourth, teacher pay was often delayed – sometimes due to processing time of the Ministry of Education and sometimes because a few "ACE committees had paid teachers late to assert their power over the school finances" (Desmond 2009, p. 19). Fifth and finally, there was no grievance mechanism for parents or teachers in EDUCO schools, as they were seen to be their own legal entities outside of the MINED (Gillies et al. 2010, p. 29).

In addition, a few more comments can be made about the largely ignored circumstances in which EDUCO teachers worked. Initially, according to World Bank documents, EDUCO teachers at the preschool level were to be paid $160 per month (World Bank 1991). However, starting in 1995, they began to receive bonuses ($40/month) for working in rural areas (Gillies et al. 2010). With this bonus, EDUCO teachers made, on average, 7 percent more than teachers in traditional schools (Gillies et al. 2010, p. 64). However, it should be noted that EDUCO teachers were not eligible for pay increases associated with years of service, unlike traditional teachers. This was a significant disadvantage, since traditional teachers could, over time, earn 50% more beyond the entry-level salary due to automatic increases every five years (Rodríguez 2003). Additionally, EDUCO teachers were not eligible for any of the other benefits given by the government to traditional public school teachers, such as the official retirement plan, a life insurance policy, and access to the health system for teachers (Cuéllar-Marchelli 2003b), although EDUCO teachers could access health care through the Salvadoran Institute for Social Security (Gillies et al. 2010, p. 27). In 2007, EDUCO teachers began to be paid according to the official MINED pay scale, with their years of service being reflected in their new salaries, but they still did not have the job security afforded to teachers who were members of the MINED career system (Ramírez 2007). As part of the move to the MINED pay scale, "a career ladder was developed for EDUCO teachers so that they could accrue service time and be eligible for category advancement that would enable them to receive salary raises every five years" (Gillies et al. 2010, p. 65). These details highlight the fact that, beyond difficult working conditions at the school and community level, EDUCO teachers were severely disadvantaged vis-à-vis traditional public school teachers – a fact that makes one question the wisdom of assuming that the EDUCO model would make teachers work harder than their counterparts in traditional public schools.

Pedagogical aspects. Despite the assumptions about EDUCO's ability to produce relations of accountability that would make teachers work harder and teach better, no studies have been found that examined the actual teaching practices of EDUCO teachers. Rather, multiple studies mentioned the lack of resources in EDUCO schools, including books, the official curriculum, didactic materials, and recreational material (Ayala 2005; Ávila de Parada and Landaverde de Romero 2007; Desmond 2009)—an issue that is also present in traditional public schools (Cuéllar-Marchelli 2003b).[7] Teaching quality was further undermined by the fact that there were infrequent visits by pedagogical experts from the Ministry of Education (ranging from 1 to 5 visits per year) (Ayala 2005, p. 30; Ávila de Parada and Landaverde de Romero 2007), in addition to the reality of classroom overcrowding (Desmond 2009). On this point, Cuéllar-Marchelli (2003b) found student-teacher ratios of 60 and 50 for EDUCO and traditional public schools, respectively (as of 1998, p. 133). A final challenge to mention here is that 39 percent of EDUCO schools had multiple grades (up to three) in the same classroom, and without adequate resources and technology to respond to the associated challenges (SIMEDUCO 2011).

In light of the obstacles detailed in this and the previous sections of this chapter, it is unsurprising – and, indeed, should be expected – that the EDUCO model would not lead to better education results in terms of student achievement, for example.

If anything, a close examination of the EDUCO program indicates that what is needed is more attention to the socio-cultural and political-economic contexts in which the model is implemented.

DISCUSSION–OR, HOW HAS THIS PROGRAM BEEN AN EXEMPLAR FOR SO LONG?

EDUCO has tended to receive attention on two fronts. First, an incredible amount of time and energy was dedicated by World Bank researchers to showing the impacts of this program. As noted earlier, no fewer than seven quantitative studies were produced during 1994–2005 by this organization, with those studies claiming positive effects in terms of student achievement and student retention. However, as also noted earlier, these studies have been closely scrutinized and improved upon. In the case of the former, it has been shown that we have good reasons to doubt the conclusions offered by World Bank researchers related to improved student test scores. These reasons are grounded in: (a) the limitations of the program's design (since it was targeted to communities that were more poor on average, and thus differed systematically from those communities to which it was compared in the impact evaluations), (b) the study methodologies (since quantitative methods with inherent limitations were employed), (c) and the contexts into which the program was implemented (since many EDUCO programs were already well-versed in community management) (Edwards and Loucel 2016). Moreover, in the case of the latter, where the World Bank's models have been improved upon, results actually indicated that the EDUCO program was associated with a negative effect on student achievement (Cuéllar-Marchelli 2003b).

The second front on which EDUCO has received significant attention is political in nature. A series of publications has unpacked the origins of the EDUCO program and, along with that, the influence of international organizations in the program's trajectory (Edwards 2015, 2018, forthcoming; Edwards, Victoria, and Martin 2015). These publications have also addressed the strategies through which the World Bank and other actors helped to engrain EDUCO in El Salvador and to promote it on the global stage. Examples of these mechanisms include research dissemination, technical assistance, loan conditionalities, communications campaigns, and international conferences and workshops, among other avenues.

However, the present chapter has sought to highlight an area that has arguably received less attention, that is, the local level experience of EDUCO's implementation. As the debate on EDUCO has tended to focus on whether or not it "worked" in terms of its measurable outcomes, many other aspects of the program were overlooked. It is hoped that the close-range examination of EDUCO at the community level contributes something to the larger conversation on this and similar CBM models. One way this chapter tried to make this contribution was by reviewing studies that are largely unknown in El Salvador, let alone in the international literature on this program.

As was shown, EDUCO was found to exhibit serious deficiencies in practice. This was true in terms of its institutional structure, with limited capacity, too few staff to support all the ACEs, and, frequently, no-one to serve as a school director or principal, since leadership responsibilities fell – problematically, as shown – to teachers and to the parents on the school council. In the area of community participation, it was revealed that many community members were not familiar with what the EDUCO program is and that participation was restricted to school works (e.g., construction, maintenance) and resource acquisition (e.g., fundraising and materials).

For the core feature of the EDUCO program – i.e., ACE management – multiple issues arose in practice. For instance, the ACEs tended to be run by only two or three parents (as opposed to the five stipulated in policy). Moreover, ACE members were frequently unfamiliar with the documentation and forms required to run the program. Unsurprisingly, ACEs commonly deferred to teachers, principals (where they existed in EDUCO schools), and/or staff from the Ministry of Education when it came to filling out forms, processing paperwork, and making decisions. Crucially, even decisions around teacher hiring were influenced by the aforementioned actors. It is imperative that this finding be highlighted, because the ability of parents to hire and fire teachers has been *the* aspect of EDUCO most lauded by international development professionals and education reformers. Thus, although the idea of parents hiring and firing teachers is one that easily attracts attention, especially when it is paired with the neoliberal logic that undergirded the international promotion of the program (see the section herein on EDUCO's design), in practice, we see that the idea breaks down. Considering, on one hand, that teacher turnover was reported to be low, and, on the other, that parents' hiring decisions were often guided by teachers, principals, and governmental staff, one is led to conclude that the central mechanism of accountability embedded in the program – and for which it became, and continues to be, so renowned – fundamentally did not work in practice as envisioned.

This finding is all the more unfortunate when one recalls the discriminatory situation of EDUCO teachers and the dismal condition of EDUCO classrooms. Beyond not having job security – due to the one-year nature of their contracts, renewable at the discretion of the ACEs – teachers at times faced biased hiring practices (e.g. nepotism) and unjust treatment, and all without having any recourse, since the EDUCO program was not set up with any complaint resolution or grievance mechanisms. Legally, management started and ended with the ACEs. If one contemplates the hardships faced by teachers together with the typically impoverished state of EDUCO classrooms, it is to be expected that the program would be associated with negative effect on student achievement. Furthermore, in light of the preceding discussion, it is incredible that the EDUCO program has been held up as a global exemplar for so long – given that it suffers from poor implementation and functioning at the local level, that it cannot be said to produce better results, and, for the kicker, that it costs the government more to offer it (Edwards, forthcoming).

CONCLUSION: TOWARDS BROADER NOTIONS OF COMMUNITY-BASED MANAGEMENT

In 2009, the first left-wing Salvadoran president to be elected in the post-war period began the process of undoing EDUCO and converting the schools and teachers to the traditional public school system. Just as El Salvador has reassessed the desirability of this program, so too should the international community. Moreover, scholars and policymakers should extend this reassessment to how we think about CBM more generally. While both EDUCO and the studies discussed in the literature review section speak to the ability of parents to participate in ways that support the school (e.g., school works, food preparation, resource acquisition, etc.), there are many different issues that come into play which prevent the management of schools by parents. These issues include low levels of education, the higher social position of teachers vis-à-vis parents, gender norms, insufficient training and professional development, and lack of specialized support personnel from the government. Of course, these issues are all in addition to the infrequently addressed assumption that communities are unitary and unfragmented and that they have the ability and desire to be involved in teacher and school management.

Yet, the above is not to suggest that we should move away from CBM. Rather, what both EDUCO and previous studies indicate is that we should extend how we think about decentralization, democratization, and community management as well as the ways that community capacity and agency can be heightened as part of the aforementioned processes. While some recent work has highlighted the position of school directors in marginalized communities and the roles that they can play in mobilizing community members to contribute to educational quality (DeMatthews, Edwards, and Rincones 2016), it is argued here that we also need to think about community social capital more broadly. Indeed, not only has previous literature raised the issue of social capital in relation to CBM, but, in the case of EDUCO, one of its hidden dimensions likewise draws our attention to this matter and is a prime area for future research. Put differently, it is argued here that scholars should think beyond the school itself to also examine the processes, policies, conditions, and strategies that can reinforce community capacity building, community empowerment, community well-being, and community social capital more generally. To this end, within (though also beyond) El Salvador, the legacy of liberation theology, popular education, and experimentation with alternative forms of community self-governance in FMLN-affiliated communities become prime issues for further exploration that can expand the conversation around CBM. Beyond tokenistic and mechanistic notions of community participation in school governance, it is essential that scholars seriously entertain more democratic ways of organizing not only schools but also the communities in which they are embedded.[8]

REFERENCES

ADES (Asociación de Desarrollo Económico Social, Santa Marta). (2003). *Una Sistematización de la Educación Popular en el Cantón Santa Marta, Cabañas, El Salvador, 1978–2001.* San Salvador: ADES.

Altschuler, Danieal, & Javier Corrales. (2012). "The Spillover Effects of Participatory Governance: Evidence from Community-Managed Schools in Honduras and Guatemala." *Comparative Political Studies, 45*(5), 636–666.

Alvear, Virginia. (2002). "La educación en Morazán, El Salvador, durante la guerra civil de 1981 a 1992: ¿parte de una estrategia de supervivencia?" (Unpublished doctoral dissertation). Berlin Free University, Berlin.

Ávila de Parada, Alicia, & Milena Landaverde de Romero. (2007). "La gestión educativa y el desempeño de centros escolares de la modalidad Educación con Participación de la Comunidad (EDUCO) en El Salvador" (Unpublished thesis). Universidad Centroamericana, San Salvador.

Ayala, Rafael. (2005). *Evaluación del Programa de Educación con Participación de la Comunidad-EDUCO.* San Salvador: MINED.

Carr-Hill, Roy, Caine Rolleston, Tejendra Phereli, & Rebecca Schendel. (2015). *The Effects of School Based Decision Making on Educational Outcomes in Low and Middle Income Contexts: A Systematic Review, 3ie Grantee Final Review.* London: International Initiative for Impact Evaluation (3ie). Retrieved from http://r4d.dfid.gov.uk/pdf/outputs/SystematicReviews/61233_dfid-funded-decentralisation-review.pdf

Cruz, María. (2004). "Orígenes de la educación popular en Chalatenango: Una innovación educativa." *Estudios Centroamericanos, LIX, 671,* 897–925.

Cuéllar-Marchelli, Helga. (2003a). "Decentralization and Privatization of Education in El Salvador: Assessing the Experience." *International Journal of Educational Development, 23*(2), 45–166.

Cuéllar-Marchelli, Helga. (2003b). "The Cost-Effectiveness of EDUCO and Traditional Public School in Rural El Salvador" (Unpublished dissertation). Teachers College, Columbia University, New York, NY.

DeMatthews, David, D. Brent Edwards Jr., & Rodolfo Rincones. (2016). "Social Justice Leadership and Community Engagement: A Successful Case from Ciudad Juárez, Mexico." *Educational Administration Quarterly, 52*(5), 711–753.

Desmond, Cheryl. (2009). "EDUCO Schools in El Salvador: A Democratic Tree in a Globalized Forest?" *International Education, 38*(2), 7–28.

Edwards Jr., D. Brent. (2010). "Trends in Governance and Decision-Making: A Democratic Analysis with Attention to Application in Education." *Policy Futures in Education, 8*(1), 111–125.

Edwards Jr., D. Brent. (2012). "The Approach of the World Bank to Participation in Development and Education Governance: Trajectories, Frameworks, Results." In Christopher Collins & Alexander Wiseman, eds., *Education Strategy in the Developing World: Understanding the World Bank's Education Policy Revision* (pp. 249–273). Bingley: Emerald.

Edwards Jr., D. Brent. (2015). "Rising from the Ashes: How the Global Education Policy of Community-Based Management was Born from El Salvador's Civil War." *Globalisation, Societies and Education, 13*(3), 411–432.

Edwards Jr., D. Brent. (2018). *The Trajectory of Global Education Policy: Community-Based Management in El Salvador and the Global Reform Agenda.* New York, NY: Palgrave Macmillan.

Edwards Jr., D. Brent. (forthcoming). "School and Community-Based Management as Global Education Policy: History, Trajectory, Geography." In Antoni Verger, Mario Novelli, & Hulya Kosar-Altinyelken, eds., *Global Education Policy and International Development: New Agendas, Issues and Programmes* (2nd ed.). New York, NY: Continuum.

Edwards Jr., D. Brent, & Claudia Loucel. (2016). The EDUCO Program, Impact Evaluations, and the Political Economy of Global Education Reform." *Education Policy Analysis Archives, 24*(49), 1–50. Retrieved from http://dx.doi.org/10.14507/epaa.24.2019

Edwards Jr., D. Brent., & David DeMatthews. (2014). "Historical Trends in Educational Decentralization in the United States and Developing Countries: A Periodization and Comparison in the Post-WWII

Context." *Education Policy Analysis Archives, 22*(40), 1–36. Retrieved from http://dx.doi.org/ 10.14507/epaa.v22n40.2014

Edwards Jr., D. Brent, & Evelyn Ávalos. (2015). *Resistance to, and Adaptation of, the Program for Education with Community Participation in El Salvador: The Experience of Santa Marta and Its Inversion of Neoliberal Reform Logic*. San Salvador: Universidad Centroamericana.

Edwards Jr., D. Brent, Julián Victoria, & Pauline Martin. (2015). "The Geometry of Policy Implementation: Lessons from the Political Economy of Three Education Reforms in El Salvador during, 1990–2005." *International Journal of Educational Development, 44*, 28–41.

Edwards Jr., D. Brent, & Steven Klees. (2012). "Participation in International Development and Education Governance." In Antoni Verger, Mario Novelli, & Hulya Kosar-Altinyelken, eds., *Global Education Policy and International Development: New Agendas, Issues and Programmes* (pp. 55–77). New York, NY: Continuum.

Edwards Jr., D. Brent, & Steven Klees. (2015). "Unpacking Participation in Development and Education Governance: A Framework of Perspectives and Practices." *Prospects, 45*(4), 483–499.

Edwards Jr., D. Brent, Pauline Martin, & Irene Flores. (forthcoming-a). "Education in El Salvador: Past, present, and prospects." In Charles M. Posner, Christope Martin, & Ana Elvir, eds., *Education in México, Central America and the Latin Caribbean*. New York, NY: Continuum.

Edwards Jr., D. Brent, Pauline Martin, & Irene Flores. (forthcoming-b). "Teacher education in El Salvador: Politics, policy, pitfalls." In Charl Wolhuter, ed., *International Handbook of Teacher Education, (2nd ed.)*. Athens: Atrapos.

Gershberg, Alec, Ben Meade, & Sven Andersson. (2009). "Providing Better Education Services to the Poor: Accountability and Context in the Case of Guatemalan Decentralization." *International Journal of Educational Development, 29*, 187–200.

Gillies, John, Luis Crouch, & Ana Flórez. (2010). *Strategic Review of the EDUCO Program*. Washington, DC: USAID. Retrieved from http://www.equip123.net/docs/e2-EDUCO_Strategic_Review.pdf

Hammond, John. (1998). *Fighting to Learn: Popular Education and Guerrilla War in El Salvador*. New Brunswick, NJ: Rutgers University Press.

Lindo, Hector. (1998). *Comunidad, participación y escuelas: EDUCO en El Salvador*. Washington, DC: World Bank.

Meza, Darlyn, José Guzmán, & Lorena de Varela. (2004, May 25–27). *EDUCO: A Community-Managed Education Program in Rural Areas of El Salvador*. Paper presented at Scaling Up Poverty Reduction: A Global Learning Process and Conference, Shanghai.

Montgomery, Tommie. (1995). *Revolution in El Salvador: From Civil Strife to Civil Peace* (2nd ed.). Boulder, CO: Westview.

Pryor, John. (2005). "Can Community Participation Mobilise Social Capital for Improvement of Rural Schooling? A Case Study From Ghana." *Compare, 35*(2), 193–203.

Ramírez, Claudia. (2007, March 24). "EDUCO inició este mess u ingreso al escalafón." *La Prensa Gráfica*.

Reimers, Fernando. (1997). "The Role of the Community in Expanding Educational Opportunities: The EDUCO Schools in El Salvador." In James Lynch, Celia Modgil, & Sohan Modgil, eds., *Equity and Excellence in Education for Development* (Vol. 2, pp. 146–162). London: Cassell.

Rodríguez, Juán. (2003). *Incentivos a escuelas y maestros: La experiencia del 'Plan de Estímulos a la Labor Educativa Institucional' en El Salvador* (Estudio de Caso No. 74). Santiago, CL: Universidad de Chile.

SIMEDUCO. (2011). *Ya no estamos dormidos*. San Salvador: Instituto de Derechos Humanos de la Universidad "José Simeón Cañas."

Srygley, Mairin. (2013). "Education in Rural El Salvador: A Case Study on Value, Quality, and Accountability" (Unpublished thesis). University of Maryland, College Park, MD.

Westhorp, Gil, Bill Walker, Patricia Rogers, Nathan Overbeeke, Daniel Ball, & Graham Brice. (2014). *Enhancing Community Accountability, Empowerment and Education Outcomes in Low- and Middle-Income Countries: A Realist Review*. London: EPPI-Centre, Social Science Research Unit, Institute of Education, University of London. Retrieved from http://r4d.dfid.gov.uk/pdf/outputs/ SystematicReviews/Community-accountability-2014-Westhorp-report.pdf

World Bank. (1991). *Staff Appraisal Report. El Salvador: Social Sector Rehabilitation Project.* Washington, DC: World Bank.

World Bank. (1994). *El Salvador: Community Education Strategy: Decentralized School Management.* Washington, DC: The World Bank.

World Bank. (2007). *Guiding Principles for Implementing School-Based Management Programs.* Washington, DC: World Bank.

World Bank. (2009). *Strengthening Accountability in Social Service Delivery in Central America: The EDUCO School-Based Management Model.* Washington, DC: World Bank.

NOTES

1. While the label of "school-based management" is often used to describe the use of such school councils, the term CBM is used here to emphasize the community involvement aspect.
2. Popular education is an approach to education that is connected with liberation theology and the teachings of the Brazilian educator, Paulo Freire, both of which stress the need to critically interpret the world, to identify sources of oppression, and then to act against them, with an emphasis not on individual sin but rather on systems that benefit certain groups and marginalize others, such as capitalism.
3. See Montgomery (1995, pp. 119–122) for more on the participatory forms of local government attempted by the FMLN.
4. While the EDUCO program was initially only intended as a strategy to provide education at the preschool level and in grades 1–3, it was subsequently expanded in 1994 to cover through grade 6 and then again in 1997 to cover through grade 9 (Meza, Guzmán, and de Varela 2004). After 2005, even some high schools became EDUCO schools (Gillies et al. 2010).
5. See Edwards (2018) for a discussion of Cuéllar-Marchelli (2003b) in contrast with the World Bank's studies.
6. Not discussed here is Lindo (1998), who studied 36 EDUCO communities. The reason for this is that this study was produced for the World Bank and is seen to suffer from a conflict of interest, since the World Bank was also funding the EDUCO program. The difference between Lindo (1998) and World Bank (2009) is that the latter was produced for an internal audience, that is, it was not meant for public dissemination, and thus the content is judged to be less encumbered by a preoccupation with how the commentary contained therein would affect perceptions of the EDUCO program.
7. For more on the education system in El Salvador, see Edwards, Martin and Flores (forthcoming-a/b). For a few points of comparison, consider that 81 percent of traditional public schools had desks compared with 78 percent of EDUCO schools; 41 percent versus 42 percent had math textbooks, and 38 percent versus 32 percent had language texts (Cuéllar-Marchelli 2003b).
8. For a few pieces that attempt to contribute in this area, see ADES (2003), Alvear (2002), Cruz (2004), Edwards (2010), Edwards and Ávalos (2015), Edwards and Klees (2012, 2015), and Hammond (1998).

ANDRIA D. TIMMER

5. DECENTRALIZATION, CENTRALIZATION AND MINORITY EDUCATION IN HUNGARY

INTRODUCTION

In November 2015, faculty at a secondary school in Miskolc, Hungary penned a letter to the government outlining their frustrations with current educational policies. This letter, which was widely disseminated, sparked a nation-wide protest of teachers' unions, students, and parents. In February 2016, waves of public demonstrations throughout the country brought visibility to the concerns of the teachers. Their complaints were many. The writers of the letter gave voice to several issues: (1) Vocational training is prioritized over gymnasium education such that students are shuttled into trades and away from higher education. (2) Similarly, higher education is underappreciated and underfunded. (3) Teachers do not receive a competitive salary and do not receive adequate resources for their classroom. (4) Teachers have lost autonomy and academic freedom due to a top down administered curriculum. (5) Schools are underfinanced. These points, however, were subsidiary to their biggest complaint, the ever increasing nationalization of schools. As the writers proclaimed, "The new centralized system doesn't work" (Doros 2016).[1]

The centralization of education as the focus of the teachers' protest is illuminating and fascinating. Until recently, Hungary was known as having one of the most decentralized education systems in the world. In the late 1980s, decentralization was proposed as the best solution for countering decades of authoritarian rule under the communist regime. While decentralization was not without its critics, until recently centralization was resisted because it was viewed as a return to Hungary's communist past. Despite that, in 2012, right wing populist leader, Prime Minister Viktor Orbán, pushed through amendments to the Public Education Act that quickly centralized education within the country. The general consensus is that this process happened too quickly and, because it was implemented all at once, did not take into account local needs. The new educational policies replaced a highly decentralized, flexible system that was seemingly responsive to local communities with one that is highly centralized, inflexible, poorly funded, and very top down and authoritarian in its approach with little concerns for the needs of local schools and community members (Zoltán, Simon, and Vadász 2015).

It is beyond the scope of this chapter to hash out the current political debates. Orbán's move toward a nationalized education system is part of his larger right wing populist agenda, one that is swiftly, and thus far largely without significant opposition,[2] moving the country from a liberal democracy to an illiberal one, modeled after the likes of Turkey and Russia. The purpose of this chapter is not to consider the merits of centralization or decentralization. I begin with a discussion of the protests because they provide interesting insights into the manner in which control of education can be fiercely debated as well as highlight the tensions now rife in the country of Hungary. As I will explain in the next section, decentralization is a significant part of Hungarian post-Communist identity and the school system as it is known today was built in the years following the end of Sovietism. This system, which the protestors are fighting for a return to, was one built largely on segregation. The education system is deeply divided and those who have been left out of schooling for generations were absent from the demonstrations. By largely silencing their voice, the demonstrators shed light on the value placed in minority education, which is very little. Throughout all the changes in the Hungarian education system, one thing has remained relatively constant – the education system in Hungary does not meet the needs of the largest and least integrated minority group in the country, the Roma.

Bernard Rorke (2016) calls racial segregation in schools "Hungary's worst kept secret." An estimated 45 percent of Roma youth receive their education in segregated classrooms and schools, one of the highest rates among European Union member states. Regardless of the changes in the structure, Roma continue to be educated separately in underfunded classrooms with poor quality instruction. The decentralized system which characterized Hungary from the late 20th to the early 21st century has both hindered and helped in terms of integrated education for the Roma youth. On the one hand, the policy has exacerbated the deep division between Roma and non-Roma in the country. That being said, the decentralized structure has also allowed for the creation of several innovative educational programs that would not exist if not for a high degree of local autonomy.

In this chapter, I will focus on one such innovative education program, a village school that I call Előrelépés Vocational and High School. This secondary school is located in a rural village with a high proportion of Roma. The school, made possible by the post-Communist system, provides Roma youth and adults access to educational recourses otherwise denied them. The same system, however, that made this school possible, has entrenched inequities which ensures the continuation of segregated education. Centralization as it has occurred in Hungary prioritizes nationalist ideologies and this has further exacerbated the Roma/non-Roma divide. It is too soon to tell what the effect of the centralized policies will specifically be on minority education, but it is clear that the needs of the Roma are far from the concern of the current government.

This chapter will largely be an overview of the processes of decentralization and the manner in which it both facilitates minority education and normalizes societal divides. It is not my intention to downplay the current political climate, but it is not possible to understand the current debates without a contextualization of what came before. I will begin with a brief historical synopsis of the significant changes in the education structure. Educational priorities alter as political priorities shift, and therefore this section also provides a political history of Hungary from the last three decades. I will then discuss the segregated education system as exists for the Hungarian Roma, using Előrelépés as a case example to illustrate broader socio-political structures that affect Roma education. I close with a rearticulation of the main argument, which is that the Hungarian body politics has little to no desire to increase access to education for the Roma or to promote their integration into society. The long-held policy of "separate but equal" has never, nor will ever, work.

Data for this chapter comes from ethnographic research conducted in Hungary over the course of 18 months from July 2004 to July 2008 (Timmer 2016). During my time in the country, I conducted interviews with government officials and NGO workers and observed workshops and programs at many innovative educational programs and schools across the country. In addition, I spent five months conducting intensive ethnographic research at Előrelépés[3] Vocational School and Gymnasium located in Edrőfalu, the school that is profiled in this chapter. In addition to collecting data, I also was the English teacher at the school while I was there.

FROM THE MOST DECENTRALIZED TO THE MOST CENTRALIZED

"School education has always been exposed to direct political interference" (Harangi and Tóth 1996, p. 62). The relationship between education and politics is particularly easy to see in Hungary. The history of Hungary is one of occupation, from the Ottomans to the Austrian Hapsburgs to the Soviets, the country has been considered liberated for only relatively short periods of time (Lendvai 2001). The educational system throughout much of this history was administered by a central authority with decisions regarding curriculum, staffing, and pedagogical goals emerging from the top. As the Soviet Era came to a close, Hungary had to restructure itself politically (from state-sponsored socialism to a multi-party parliamentary state), economically (from authoritarianism to market economy), and ideologically (from a closed to an open society). Education, of course, played a vital role in the transition.

The purpose of education during Sovietism was to act as a propaganda machine to create a reliable and productive labor force (Harangi and Tóth 1996, p. 60). In the new democratic society, the purpose of education was to create an empowered, enlightened populace. In order to do this, the architects of the transition made a decision to "increase participatory decision making through the decentralization of education" (Kaufman 1997, p. 26). The movement towards decentralization began with changes to the legislation governing public education in 1985 and intensified throughout the end of the twentieth century. Educational researchers assert, "Perhaps the most significant changes of the 1990s was the continuation of the previously started decentralized process, which resulted in the Hungarian education system becoming one of Europe's most decentralized systems by the middle of the decade" (Halász, Garami, Havas, and Vágó 2001, p. 9).

The movement from authoritarianism to decentralization was not just a change in educational structure, but a change in the roles of individuals within those structures as well. Teachers, for example, who for decades had been beholden to strict authoritarian mandates and were required to follow rules, were now transformed into decision-makers. They were expected to "change their subservient relationships with party-controlled supervisors for collegial, helping roles" (Kaufman 1997, p. 30). While initially regarded with skepticism, Kaufman (1997) argues that decentralization was ultimately successful in Hungary because it was done correctly in that it was done through small, incremental changes which accounted for long-term structural and attitudinal changes. While I was in Hungary doing field research on nongovernmental efforts to desegregate the education system, the decentralized system was widely accepted as the preferred system and any alteration of that was seen to be a return to a communist past.

As a decentralized system, responsibility for education is shared among several levels. At the national level, the 1993 Public Education Act defines the framework within which schooling should operate. This act affords a significant amount of power to the local governments and institutions, but modifications have been made to ensure that there are some national standards and oversights. The law mandates that all schools prepare a strategic document, called a pedagogical program, in which they outline their curricular goals. In this document, they are to mention two things. The first is the National Core Curriculum, which defines common national cultural material and necessary skills and competencies expected in each subject and in each grade. The second is the framework curricula (added to the law in 2000), which defines mandatory subjects to be taught, minimal competencies expected in these subjects, and minimal amount of time dedicated to each subject. However, beyond these guidelines, the framework is quite flexible such that schools are largely free to do what they want as long as they meet basic standards.

The next levels consist of the state and county offices managed by the Ministry of Education and the Ministry of the Interior, respectively. These offices are entrusted with the evaluation duties. Most of the decision-making power, however, resides with local governments and the individual institutions. Local governments outline school budgets, autonomously decide on the establishment or the shutting down of schools, appoint principals, approve the schools' organization and pedagogical operation, enforce financial and legal restrictions, and evaluate schools' operation. "No higher authority including the central government can give direct orders to the local governments" (Halász et al. 2001, p. 9). At the level of the institution, schools act independently, manage their own budgets, decide on the rules of organization and operation of the school, and determine the pedagogical program. In terms of funding, the Ministry of the Interior distributes funds to the local municipalities which then finance school operations through both state and local support. Therefore, the budgets are fairly flexible.

Decentralization was part of the neoliberal turn which occurred in all former Soviet countries in the 1980s and 1990s in order to move them in line with the exigencies of the global capitalist economy. The move from centralized control of education to a system based on local decision-making and institutional autonomy speaks to the dual functions of education. On the one hand, education (re)creates the citizenry a government wants. "Schools," according to Pierre Bourdieu, "impose the legitimate forms of discourse and the idea that discourse should be recognized if and only if it conforms to legitimate norms" (1977, p. 650). In essence, this is the function of schooling under communism wherein which the goals were: (1) to increase literacy, (2) train personnel to work in the production facilities, and (3) remold behavior to support the ideology of the state. Thus, under communism, more people gained access to schooling, but the training they received best prepared them for work in the factories and life in a closed society. It bears mentioning that arguably these could be seen as the goals of any institutionalized education system and indeed, many make the claim that the schooling under the current government in Hungary exists more to maintain the ideology of the rulers that to educate the populace. However, education is also touted for its liberation potential. It is seen as the "primary vehicle by which economically and socially marginalized adults can lift themselves out of poverty and obtain the means to participate fully in their communities (Farkas 2004). Given this dualistic function, it is clear to see that as much as education is a tool of democracy, it is an important tool of authoritarianism as well.

Adam Fabry (2015) argues that the increasing right-wing extremism in Hungary can be interpreted as a counter-hegemonic reaction against "the injustices wrought by neoliberal capitalism." Hungary experienced a rather peaceful transition in the 1990s. Because of this they were upheld as the forerunner in the democratic transition and perceived as doing the best among former Soviet Bloc countries. However, in reality, this smooth transition was facilitated by not attending to the needs of the people. When I was doing my field research in the country, many expected some kind of uprising by people who felt that they had been left out of the system. This began in 2006 when, in reaction to the leaking of a secret recording of then Prime Minister Ferenc Gyurcsány admitting that he had lied to the Hungarian public, demonstrators flooded from around the country to the capital city to call for his ousting. During the next election, the electorate who heretofore felt disenfranchised elected the right-wing party, Fidesz, as the majority party. Viktor Orbán was appointed prime minister.

Bolstered by such on outpouring of populist support, Prime Minister Viktor Orbán quickly moved to restructure the political system in such a way that dismantled the work of the socialist party, the party which had been responsible for engineering the transition. Since 2010, media has been tightly controlled and the nation has upheld itself as the protectorate of the rest of Europe by staunchly denying entry to any outsider, including asylum seekers fleeing the violence in Syria and Afghanistan. The shift in political ideology can be seen in education as well. Changes made to the Public Education Act in 2012 confirmed in many ways the fears that the country was making a return to authoritarianism. The new measures restructured education by establishing KLIK (Klebelsberg Institution Maintenance Center) as an overseeing body over local districts. Under KLIK, local schools have been faced with excessive administration and the elimination of autonomy. The issues raised by the new system include an overabundance of bureaucracy and lack of institutional autonomy, increased demands on teachers, and a lack of transparency. The report "Role and Functional Change in the World of Public Education" posits "The closure and lack of confidence indicates that the system that has been introduced fails to seek dialogue with public education stakeholders and therefore makes the system unaccountable to society" (Zoltán, Simon, and Vadász 2015). The speed of the roll-out exacerbated many of these issues as changes were implemented quickly and put into place at once. KLIK was dissolved in the summer of 2016 and was replaced with 59 different bodies, but centralization remains in place as the districts have no greater operational autonomy than they did under KLIK. Teachers' salaries have been nominally increased and local educational directors have the ability to provide more pay to teachers who work more. These changes do not address the major concerns of the protestors, but demonstrations have subsided as they are wont to do.[4]

Many see centralization efforts as part of a large scale effort to dismantle education in Hungary. Since Orbán has been in power, funding has been slowly pulled from the education sector and spending on education is at the lowest it has been since 1990 (Veres 2017). Furthermore, the curricular focus has shifted from those skills or competencies that can be seen as essential (such as computer skills, reading, writing, mathematics, natural science, and languages) to non-essential skills such as ethics. In other words, skills that would make one a good Hungarian national are prioritized over those that would help one become an intellectually engaged global citizen. As part of this shift, vocational and technical training have been favored over university preparatory education. As a result, attendance in tertiary education has stagnated and student performance has declined. The results of the Program for International Student Assessment (PISA), a study conducted by the OECD released in December 2016, showed extremely poor results. Hungarian students showed a sharp decrease in reading comprehension and knowledge of science. While math scores remained the same as 2012, these scores had declined fairly dramatically since 2009 (OECD 2016).

Interestingly, and somewhat ironically, the concerns that have arisen among educators and parents due to policy changes under Orbán's government mirror those that the Roma have long faced. In the next section, I will characterize the manner in which the Roma have been historically and systematically excluded from the education system. There segregation exists to maintain social division and there is no large scale movement to integrate the Roma, a group of people Edward Said claimed are "the only group about which anything could be said without challenge or demurral" (Nicolae 2006, p. 137).

SEGREGATED EDUCATION

It is not an overstatement to claim that the Roma are the most discriminated against group in Europe. Since their arrival in Europe about one thousand years ago they have been legally prohibited from settling, enslaved, and, during World War II, targeted for extermination. Currently in Hungary, they face discrimination in terms of housing, health, employment, and education. In brief, they are most likely to live segregated in substandard living conditions, are most likely to suffer health problems with less access to health care resources, are less likely to be able to obtain gainful employment, and, as will be discussed below, more likely to receive substandard, segregated schooling. Far from improving, violent attacks have increased in recent years as the far-right wing party, Jobbik, which takes an unapologetic anti-Gypsy stance, has increased in power and popularity. There is a clear divide in Hungarian society, and this division begins in early childhood when Roma youth are more likely to be educated separately from non-Roma despite recent programs meant to desegregate schooling (Timmer 2016).

New and Merry explained, "Until the Soviet period, the formal schooling of Roma children was rarely a part of anyone's conversation" (2010, p. 393). From their arrival in Europe until the era of Sovietism, the Roma were treated as social pariahs (Crowe 1996; Hancock 1987). The Soviet authority, however, rendered all members of society equal. As such, ethnicity was no longer seen as the basis of differentiation. During this time, Roma experienced unprecedented rates of employment and access to education. I do not mean to imply, however, that the Roma were seen as equals. Rather, they were symbolically framed as social deviants rather than ethnic outcasts since their ethnicity was not officially recognized. While it is true that the Roma may have had more stability during this period, they suffered from the effects of the totalitarian regime as did everyone else while, in addition, they faced continued discrimination and persecution, lost their traditional modes of work, and did not necessarily welcome the forced assimilation (Lucero and Collum 2007). When Sovietism ended, it became clear that ethnic divisions had not been eliminated. The Roma, now most likely to be viewed in terms of their social disadvantage, were the first to lose their employment and, as life moved from rural to urban, the Roma were the most likely to be left in the countryside among the remnants of Sovietism.

A 2004 report by the European Commission, *The Situation of the Roma in an Enlarged European Union*, recognized the "Roma problem" as "among Europe's most pressing human rights and social inclusion priorities" and, since the end of Communism, "an area in which the governments of new Member States must focus policy attention" (European Commission 2004, p. 6). The end of Communism brought heightened attention to the Roma because inclusion of the former Soviet Bloc countries into the European Union[5] increased the total Roma population in the EU to approximately ten million. Education was the mechanism through which the Roma as "foreign elements" could be assimilated and so was touted as a solution to the Roma "problem" (Timmer 2016). The Roma Education Fund was established and several nongovernment organizations were formed to provide educational resources to the Roma. The government framed the Roma as "disadvantaged minorities" and increased normative funding for schools that provided education to disadvantaged minorities. Ironically, however, when these "foreign elements" were inserted into the schools, they came to be perceived as a threat to the health of the nation (New and Merry 2010, p. 396). This is the paradox of Roma education. On the one hand, increased access to education should presumably result in the creation of a Roma class more employable and more "integratable" into Hungarian social life. On the other hand, because the Roma are discursively constructed as outsiders, despite the fact they have been a part of life in Hungary for several centuries, they are often considered to be intellectually inferior and, by some, unteachable. Thus, while activists fight to increase access to educational resources for Roma, many fight to keep them out of the classroom. Two representative comments about the nature of helping the Roma illustrate how they are perceived in Hungarian society:

> [Hungarians] want to stay as far away from [the Roma] as possible because they steal, they're dirty, and smell. They don't want to work. Hungarians don't like them because Hungarians want to work. Gypsies have to change their mentality. They can change but it will take a long time – at least a generation.

> Discrimination is still very bad in Hungary. There are still those who think the Roma should be killed off and don't understand why anyone would want to help them. For example, we are building a house and Gypsies stole some of the building materials. My husband said, "And you are helping them!" I said that I was helping them so that in 50 years they wouldn't be stealing. They would be working or going to school.[6]

The result is that Roma education is a political and humanitarian priority in Hungary, but not one that is embraced by the Hungarian public. Thus, education remains largely segregated. There are four basic forms of segregation. The most egregious form involves sending children perceived to be Roma to schools for the mentally handicapped, the so-called "special schools." Despite recent case rulings[7] which insist that states have an obligation to undo a history of racial segregation "the government of Hungary has failed to properly address the issue of misdiagnosis and placement of highly disproportionate number of Romani children in special schools" (Rorke 2016). A second type of segregation is the creation of "Gypsy ghetto schools," schools with a highly disproportionate number of students identified as Roma. The socio-economic transformation that began at the end of the socialist era created a new pattern of social exclusion: the regional ghetto, defined as small villages with a population that consists almost entirely of unemployed Roma (Virág 2006). This regional segregation leads to an increase in schools with a large proportion of Roma students. A third form of segregation is the creation of Roma classes within schools, remedial classes called "catch up classes" where students never "catch up" (Farkas and Heizer 1996). Instead, these classes became holding areas for Roma students and substandard teachers. The final form of segregation is segregation in the classroom, which occurs when Roma students are placed in predominantly non-Roma classrooms and report being required to sit in the back of the class, not being called on by the teachers, and having low expectations placed on them.

By leaving administrative decisions including staffing and salaries to the purview of the institution, decentralization serves to facilitate the four above mentioned forms of segregation. Although the state sets an integration normative to encourage schools to provide equal access to education for disadvantaged students, there is little oversight concerning how funds are distributed. This leads to the common practice of combining the rosters of two functionally distinct schools. Institutions, which under the decentralized system maintain a high degree of autonomy concerning their student body, face pressure from the parents to keep Roma and non-Roma schools distinct. Thus, although they may be one school on paper, they are two schools in practice. Under the system devised in the 1990s, Hungarian parents have freedom of choice. That means they are able to send their children to any school they wish regardless of district, provided they can coordinate transportation to and from the school. Thus, it was well-known that as the Roma population of a school rises, non-Roma parents will begin to pull their children out and send them to a non-Roma school. One of my informants, a lawyer who fought for integration, explained that this phenomenon should not be seen as discrimination. "It isn't right to accuse Hungarian parents of racism," he argued. Because the ultimate control rests with the schools, there is no public measure of school success. He continues,

> Without this, how do parents measure the quality of a school? They can only talk to other people. Since everyone knows that Gypsy children and poor children do not go on to secondary school and do not do well in schooling, parents do not want to send their children there. It is not irrational; they are making a decision based on rational thinking. So, it is not a decision made out of racism.

Civil rights lawyers have used strategic litigation as a tool to desegregate the education system and they have been somewhat successful. The lawyer quoted above asserts that strategic litigation is the best tool to fight unethical segregation. He explains, "It is true that the local governments have too much autonomy and are too independent, but they can be blamed and sued, and we will win the cases." He is correct; they have sued local school districts and they have won, but the decentralized system has prohibited rulings from being enforced. As Bernard Rorke (2016) explains, those trying segregation cases in the courts have "been hugely successful in winning judgments against segregators. However, securing justice has proven to be more elusive." Securing justice has been so difficult because of a lack of political will and a lack of national oversight. For example, the 2007 case of D.H. and Others v. the Czech Republic (New and Merry 2010) set a precedent that school segregation and other procedural obstacles to access reduces freedom from discrimination and diminishes parents' ability to make choices about their children's futures. The ruling, however, has not demonstrably diminished segregation. As long as the Roma are still seen as "foreign elements," local administrators will not willingly open their doors. Rather than attempt to eliminate segregated schools, local governments typically argue that they are working to improve the "bad" schools, those schools with high proportions of disadvantaged pupils. The activist stance, however, is that the schools should be eradicated, but to date, this has not happened. Even with clear wins in the courts, there is no system of oversight and no incentive to follow the rulings of the court cases.

There is a long history of societal segregation of the Roma and non-Roma in Hungary. Roma live segregated in poor living conditions, are the recipients of high levels of discrimination, and, as a result, do not receive the same access to quality education as their non-Roma counterparts. They receive poorer education at every level. They are less likely to attend preschool, are often segregated into schools for the "mentally disabled" or classes for the learning disabled in primary school, are less likely to attend secondary school, and, if they do, more likely to be tracked into the technical or vocational education tracks, thereby prohibiting them from continuing on to higher education. They are far less likely to attend and complete tertiary education. Despite the existence of a number of education programs (both government-sponsored and non-governmental), segregation appears to be increasing largely due to a lack of any efforts to desegregate society. When hatred for the Roma is still so prevalent within the public at large, the decentralized education system comes to be the vehicle through which separation is maintained. In short, decentralization serves to further entrench and manifest societal divisions in the schooling system. This, however, is not the entire story. Some intrepid activists have been able to thwart the system to use decentralization to their advantage. In the next section I will discuss the village school model, an innovative education program made possible by the high degree of decentralized schooling.

Előrelépés: A Village School

"Village school" is a descriptor. There is not actually a government or non-government sponsored model for village schools. Rather, I use this designator to describe schools that have been established in rural areas with the expressed purpose of providing education for those who have limited access to quality education resources. I am particularly concerned with village secondary schools in Roma villages, high schools that offer the possibility of a diploma[8] to students and are established in a rural village, specifically a village with a high proportion of residents classified as disadvantaged either because of the economic status, their minority status, or both. The student population of these schools largely identifies as Roma, but the school does not identify as a "Roma school." Rather, village schools are simply established by educational activists in areas where they can serve those youth that are in most need of educational resources. Because "village school" is a description, rather than a codified program, it is difficult to say how many there are, but they are still quite rare. I visited two village high schools and one soon-to-be-open school.

The Hungarian countryside, as is common in many nations, is relatively underdeveloped. During Communism, rural areas were epicenters for industry, but with the end of the Communist area, rural regions changed dramatically. As Katalin Kovács explains,

> Differentiation has been highly uneven: in the richest parts, the countryside has been transformed into suburban spaces reshaped by middle-class urban migrants, whilst in the peripheries, weak economies and scare employment opportunities impede development and undermine the wellbeing of the population. In the worst cases, the absence of resources coupled with ethnic segregation as a consequence of selective migration have resulted in a drain of human resources from the area, including both Roma and non-Roma people. (2012, p. 108)

While there have been efforts to reinvigorate these declining areas with, for example, rural development programs and micro-grants to support nongovernment activism in rural areas, the closure of rural schools has been an ongoing conversation in Hungary. Closure of rural schools would disproportionately affect the poor and the ethnic minorities. Rural areas have become increasingly more ethnically segregated due to selective migration and the high birth rate among Roma. The result is "ethnically pure or almost pure, segregated settlements" with vulnerability compounded by "poor transportation and limited access to public services as well as jobs" (Kovács 2012, p. 110). Due to an unequal distribution of financial and human resources, education in rural villages has also been decidedly poor. Add to this the deep-seated prejudice against Roma, and it is possible to understand how excluded from education Roma youth have been. Village schools attempt to intervene to build rural regions and inspire Roma community empowerment by establishing quality schools, which ostensibly offer education on par with that available to non-Roma youth.

Village schools are particularly innovative for two reasons. The first reason is geographic. Because of where they are located, the schools bring education to those who need it most. It is rare to find a secondary school in a rural area and especially uncommon to find a gymnasium, a secondary school that offers a diploma. After completing primary school, youth who live in rural areas typically must be bused to the nearest town to continue their education. It is for this reason that impoverished and marginalized children, those most likely to be living in rural areas, drop out of school at a fairly substantial rate after eighth grade. A school in the village ensures that they can continue their education. The second reason is that village schools endeavor to offer a high-quality education. When they do attend secondary school, Roma tend to attend those schools that offer only vocational or technical training. As such, they are not able to attend university and not able to break into higher paid and higher prestige employment. Poor education exacerbates the cycle of poverty (Westcott 2005). Village schools offer school leaving examinations which prepare the pupils for university education and thus potentially break the poverty cycle.

I conducted ethnographic field work at one village school, Előrelépés Vocational School and Gymnasium, located in Erdőfalu, a small, rural village with a high proportion of Roma residents. The school was founded by the Buddhist church in 2004. The founders of the school were members of the church and were associated with the Buddhist college in Budapest. The reason for the connection to the Buddhist church was twofold. The first reason is a practical one. As a religious school, Előrelépés has certain freedoms in curriculum development and fundraising unavailable to public schools. The second is ideological. The founders see a Buddhist perspective as a tool to use to fight oppression and systemic inequality. They draw upon the example of Dr. Ambedkar, a Dalit in India who was educated in London and New York as a lawyer but, as an untouchable, still experienced high levels of discrimination at home. As one of the most symbolic parts of his fights against untouchability, he and thousands of his followers converted to Buddhism in 1956. This was a powerful story, for the founders were moved by the tale of resistance, uprising and change.

The village of Erdőfalu was selected specifically because of its ethnic makeup. The intention behind the school, like all village schools, is to provide a high-school diploma to disadvantaged, primarily Roma, youth. Students receive culturally sensitive education by qualified teachers. This school was established by a small group of individuals who had experience with Roma education and had initiated many different programs before establishing this school and, through trial and error, had decided that the village school model was the best to increase access to education for the Roma youth. Three individuals were particularly important in establishing the school. Miklós was one of the most important people in Roma education. He had been involved in the establishment of almost all of the innovative educational program for Roma initiated in the early 2000s. This school was his effort to try a new model and reach a new population of Roma youth. He was joined by a former student, a Roma who had greatly benefitted from these educational programs and had converted to Buddhism himself after visiting India, seeing the situation of the Dalits, and subsequently learning about the work of Dr. Ambedkar. Finally, Viktor did not have experience with Roma education but was associated with the Buddhist college.

Without decentralization from above, this school would not exist. The founders and the subsequent administration have been able to run their school as they wish because of a system that allows for institutional autonomy. This is evident in terms of the level of education they provide, funding, and staffing decisions.

In the European education system, secondary school is tracked. Students are placed into one of three tracks: students in the gymnasium track receive an academic training and receive a diploma which allows them to go on to university for higher education; those in the vocational track receive training in a vocation with some emphasis on academic subjects and can go onto a technical college; finally, those in the lowest track receive technical training with no opportunity to continue on to tertiary education. As is to be expected, the Roma are overwhelmingly and disproportionately tracked into the technical track. Előrelépés is a gymnasium and thus provides disadvantaged students with the opportunity to take their school-leaving exams and receive a diploma that will allow them to continue their education at university. Students also receive a vocational education and a vocational degree so they graduate with two diplomas, but what is truly unique about Előrelépés is its focus on academic training for Roma.

There is little support for gymnasium education for Roma. The reasons for this are largely systematic. Roma children are less likely to attend nursery school and then are less prepared for primary school than their majority counterparts. Furthermore, Roma families, who are more likely to be living in rural, segregated settlements, lack access to quality schools and resources. Discriminatory practices within education highlighted above compound the disadvantaged. Thus, Roma are more likely to drop out of school before completing 8th grade and if they do continue on to secondary school, they are not viewed as capable of completing gymnasium education. Előrelépés cares little for the performance of their students prior to coming to the school. Those who have not completed their 8th grade education, begin with a remedial year. Students repeat grades and classes as many times as needed. They are not expected to progress from year to year in the same way that students with more opportunities do. Adults, who had not had the opportunity to continue their education, can also take classes in the evening in order to complete their school-leaving exams and receive their diplomas.

Before Előrelépés, youth from Erdőfalu had few educational opportunities. They attended nursery school through fifth grade in the village. Most then went on to finish their primary school at the Catholic school in a nearby town. From there they had three options: (1) they could attend the high school in the neighboring town, (2) they could conclude their education, or (3) they could attend one of the dormitory programs in the closest city. The dormitory programs provided room and board for Roma students so that they could attend gymnasiums in the city. Richard, for example, followed this route. He attended elementary school in Erdőfalu, then went to the Catholic School, then to one of the dormitory programs. When we met, he was a university student, working for a government agency, and running his own humanitarian nongovernmental organization.

Very few, if any, of Richard's peers followed the same route. Richard was a "highly motivated" and "talented" student, whom educational activists courted to be a part of their programs (Timmer 2010). Most students from Erdőfalu discontinued their education or went on to receive substandard technical or vocational training. The founders of Előrelépés rejected the idea that disadvantaged students needed to be taken out of their home environment and instead focused on community development. Here community development refers to the increased educational potential for community members with the idea that this will in time lead to a more empowered and employable population. Thus, they endeavored to provide quality education to all students regardless of ability, not just those who were "highly motivated." Anita is an example of a student who benefitted from Előrelépés. A young woman in her twenties, she had been placed into a school for the mentally disabled as a child. Now as an adult, she attended night classes at the school and was working with a lawyer to seek retribution for wrongful label of "mentally disabled" on the basis that such labeling had closed off many of her life opportunities. Although I have not been able to reconnect with her to determine the outcome of her case, last I spoke with her, she was committed to her studies and intended to complete gymnasium and apply to university.

Decentralization also ensured that this school had the ability to be funded. As mentioned previously, funds were provided to local municipalities which then had some discretion in how to distribute them. Előrelépés receives some money from the state, but would not be able to remain open with that money alone. In part they are dependent on an integration normative that provides additional funds for those students who meet the federal definition of disadvantaged or severely disadvantaged. All of Előrelépés students qualified as disadvantaged. Finally, Előrelépés, is technically a religious-run school since it was opened by the Buddhist church and thus has additional funds earmarked for religious schools. The school has to meet certain standards but is held more accountable to the church than to the central government in Budapest. As such, the school is able to fund their priorities.

Finally, decentralization gives the institution autonomy in terms of curriculum and staffing. Although the school must have a pedagogical program and must adhere to certain competencies, under decentralization they have a certain amount of freedom in course offerings. This means they can offer classes and exams in Roma history and language. Furthermore, the institution is ultimately responsible for hiring decisions. This is particularly important because Roma youth in segregated classrooms do not generally receive quality instructors. Commonly, teachers in such classrooms did not receive quality pedagogical training or perhaps did not complete their education. Előrelépés is able to hire teachers who want to work with Roma youth. The teachers they hire may not be the best by certain standards, but have the desire to work with disadvantaged students and work towards a more integrated society. There is quite a bit of turnover at the school as there are very specific challenges that teachers do not find at other schools. Therefore, the school needed to be able to look "outside of the box" for individuals who were willing and able to teach in their unique school. This included hiring foreigners, such as myself, to teach English or reaching out to humanitarian–minded people with little to no teaching experience.

As I mentioned previously, the flexibility is afforded the school due to decentralization from above. However, arguably, the strength of the school is the decentralization from below in that its goal is to increase the capacity for local citizens to participate in and shape the educational system. In many ways, Előrelépés meets the definition of a community-based school. The whole purpose of establishing a school in a rural, largely Roma village is to make an investment, in terms of educational resources, in a community rather than in an individual student. "Community-based education," according to Villani and Atkins (2000, pp. 40–41),

> is centered on the student's ability to recognize and support the needs of the surrounding community. In this way, students become accountable for providing values which stem from their freedom to express, develop, and solve the inherent problems or concerns they have for their community. Over

the long-term use of the ideal model, the entire community will become involved in the process, thereby making the educational process cyclical and continuously propelled.

This is what the founders would like to see occur. The teachers recognize that their job is twofold: they must normalize schooling for the community while teaching basic competencies. The hope is that years down the road, Roma education, from kindergarten to tertiary school, will be accepted and attendance and completion excepted among both Roma and non-Roma. In some regards, it is possible to see this occurring in the short term. Parents who themselves had not had the opportunity to complete eighth grade impress upon their children the need to complete secondary school. Young girls in the village are waiting longer to get married and start a family. These incremental changes could add up, but I am cynical. I am cynical because little has been done to change the broader society in which the Roma live. For example, early during my field research I was able to participate in a community-based participatory research (CBPR) program. CBPR is a collaborative approach to research that involves the "subjects" of a study as equal partners. I concluded, however, that CBPR is unlikely to be successful because the interventionists, due to structural patterns of inequality, could not see themselves as being on an equal playing field with their beneficiaries. I argue,

> Despite their best intentions, NGOs working in Hungary fail to make great inroads in addressing the needs of their Roma beneficiaries. Rather than breaking down prejudices in society, they maintain a divide between Hungarian and Gypsy and engage in the production of rhetoric that highlights the "Differentness" of the Roma and their incompatibility with the non-Roma Hungarian majority. (Timmer 2013, p. 308)

In order to be successful, Előrelépés needs to have a certain amount of freedom and flexibility to design a school that meets the specific needs of a group of young people who have been left out of the education system for so long. Előrelépés continues to function and grow. Every year more students receive their vocational and gymnasium diplomas. Although few have continued on to university, the school has made education a real possibility for all the youth in the village. There are many educational interventions that exist for the Hungarian Roma, but I argue that the village school model has the potential to be the most effective in providing accessible schooling for the Roma (Timmer 2016). All youth (and adults who want it) have access to the school regardless of "talent" or "motivation." They receive instruction that they can relate to by teachers who want to be teaching them and thus school becomes of place of belonging rather than a place of exclusion. That being said, it should not be argued that the village school is unambiguously good. The village schools educate a sizable number of Roma, but have not led to a large increase in university enrollment of Roma students or increased employment opportunities. Thus, while producing a tangible increase in number of educated Roma, the school has done little in the way of integrating society. Előrelépés is an example of positive segregation. Unlike negative segregation, positive segregation is intended to be culturally sensitive and based on the choice of the participants. However, it is still segregation. An investment in programs such as Előrelépés perpetuates segregation and inequality. Ethnic discrimination against the Roma is deeply embedded in society and there is no nationwide effort to increase tolerance. In lack of efforts to mitigate the divide between Roma and non-Roma, a school such as Előrelépés will only continue to further entrench societal prejudice.

CONCLUSION: SEPARATE AND UNEQUAL

The doctrine in Hungary is "separate but equal" or "benevolent segregation" (Rorke 2016). This ideology is based on the notion that Roma and non-Roma Hungarians are too different to live together peacefully and is maintained by a society that is very clearly divided. However, it has been made abundantly clear that separate is not equal. Roma suffer high levels discrimination, isolation, and marginalization. The division between Roma and non-Roma begins in nursery school and it compounds over the course of one's life. The educational policies of decentralization acted upon the inherent desires of most Hungarians to stay separate. Active minded individuals had the opportunity to establish innovative education programs that provide accessible, quality schooling to the Roma who had been left out of the education system. The village schools have had some success, but in the absence of any societal political will to integrate society, Roma, regardless of how educated, will not be able to find their place in society.

It is difficult to say what happens next for Előrelépés and this is largely because it is difficult to posit what the future of education will be in Hungary. According to recent reports, significantly more money is expected to be funneled towards education in Hungary next year and, according to a ministerial official working on curriculum reform, teachers are expected to have more freedom in determining competencies. The government, however, is not likely to return to decentralization; rather, in keeping in line with the direction this government has taken, they are likely to continue to exert top-down pressure on teachers and administrators. The efforts of the government to close Central European University[9] are a prime example of the heavy hand Orbán is willing to use to control the national rhetoric. Similarly, the government, which has courted the far-right openly anti-Semitic and anti-Roma party of Jobbik and has put forth recent legislation to hinder non-governmental and humanitarian action,[10] has worked to impede, rather than foster, support for Roma.

I do not predict that Előrelépés will close. I have made the argument that Előrelépés would not have been possible without decentralization, but now that it is an established school, it has greater ability to weather political shifts. When I last visited in 2015, the school had expanded with more classrooms, more permanent teaching faculty, and a newly built gym. I have also argued that the school has many drawbacks and falls short of reaching its aim. This is not to say that it is a broken model. Rather, the shortcomings of Előrelépés come more from the lack of a political and public will than any feature of the school itself. If there was a greater effort to invest in more programs like Előrelépés and a more concentrated effort to address structural violence, community-based education could be a powerful tool to work towards eliminating inequalities. As is, however, the future looks bleak both for the Roma and for those who are working to improve their lives.

REFERENCES

Bourdieu, Pierre. (1977). "The Economics of Linguistic Exchange." *Social Science Information, 16*(6), 645–668.

Crowe, David M. (1996). *A History of the Gypsies of Eastern Europe and Russia*. New York, NY: St. Martin's Press.

Doros, Judit. (2016). "Káosz és Apátia a Tanáriban [Chaos and Apathy among Teachers]." *Népszabadság*. Retrieved January 2, 2017, from http://nol.hu/belfold/kaosz-es-apatia-a-tanariban-1583201

European Commission. (2004). "*The Situation of Roma in an Enlarged European Union*." Luxembourg: Office for the Official Publications of the European Communities.

Fabry, Adam. (2015). The Far-right as a Counter-Hegemonic Bloc to Neoliberalism? The Case of Jobbik. *LeftEast*. Retrieved September 25, 2015, from http://www.criticatac.ro/lefteast/the-far-right-as-a-counter-hegemonic-bloc-to-neoliberalism-the-case-of-jobbik-2/

Farkas, Lilla. (2004). *Education, Education, and More Education*. European Union Monitoring and Advocacy Program. Retrieved from http://www.eumap.org/journal/features/2004/minority_education/edmore/

Farkas, Zsuzsa Sziágyi, & Antal Heizer. (1996). *Report of the Situation of the Gypsy Community in Hungary*. Budapest: State Secretary for Minority Affairs.

Halász, Gábor, Erika Garami, Péter Havas, & Irén Vágó. (2001). *The Development of the Hungarian Education System*. Budapest: National Institute for Public Education.

Hancock, Ian. (1987). *The Pariah Syndrome: An Account of Gypsy Slavery and Persecution*. Ann Arbor, MI: Karoma Press.

Harangi, László, & János Sz. Tóth. (1996). "Hungary." *International Review of Education, 42*(1–3), 59–74.

Kaufman, Cathy. (1997). "Educational Decentralization in Communist and Post-Communist Hungary." *International Review of Education, 43*(1), 25–41.

Kovács, Katalin. (2012). "Rescuing a Small Village School in the Context of Rural Change in Hungary." *Journal of Rural Studies, 28*, 108–117. doi:10.1016/j.jrurstud.2012.01.020

Lendvai, Paul. (2003). *The Hungarians: A Thousand Years of Victory in Defeat* (A. Major, Trans.). Princeton, NJ: Princeton University Press.

Lucero, Florinda, & Jill Collum. (2007). "The Roma: During and after Communism." *Topical Research Digest: Human Rights in Russia and the Former Soviet Republics*, 98–106. Retrieved from https://www.du.edu/korbel/hrhw/researchdigest/russia/roma.pdf

New, William S., & Michael S Merry. (2010). "Solving the 'Gypsy Problem': D.H. and Others v. the Czech Republic." *Comparative Education Review, 54*(3), 393–414.

Nicolae, Valeriu. (2006). "Words That Kill." *Index on Censorship, 35*(1), 137–141.

OECD. (2016). *Education at a Glance, 2016: OECD Indicators*. Paris: OECD Publishing.

Rorke, Bernard. (2016). "Segregation in Hungary: The long road to infringement." *European Roman Rights Centre Blog*. Retrieved from http://www.errc.org/blog/segregation-in-hungary-the-long-road-to-infringement/106

Timmer, Andria D. (2010). "Constructing the 'Needy Subject': NGO Discourses of the Roma." *PoLAR: Political and Legal Anthropology Review, 33*(2), 264–281.

Timmer, Andria D. (2013). "Working with 'Problem Populations': Participatory Interventions for the Roma in Hungary." *Human Organization, 72*(4), 302–311. doi:0018-7259/13/040302-1051.50/1

A. D. TIMMER

Timmer, Andria D. (2016). *Educating the Hungarian Roma: Nongovernmental Organization and Minority Rights.* Lanham, MD: Lexington Books/Rowman & Littlefield.
Veres, Máté. (2017). "Az Elmúlt Hét Év: Magyarország Számokban 2010–2016 [The Last Seven Years: Hungary in Numbers 2010–2016]." *Új Egyenlőség.* Retrieved January 4, 2017, from http://ujegyenloseg.hu/az-elmult-het-ev-magyarorszag-szamokban-2010-2016/
Villani, Christine J., & Douglas Atkins. (2000). "Community-Based Education." *School Community Journal, 10*(1), 39–44.
Virág, Tünde. (2006). "The Regional Ghetto." *Review of Sociology, 12*(1), 51–70.
Westcott, Emma. (2005). "Equality of Opportunity and Inclusion." *Journal of Education and Teaching, 31*(4), 273–274.
Zoltán, György, Mária Simon, & Viola Vadász. (2015). *Szerep- és Funkcióváltások a Közoktatás Világában* [Changes in Form and Function in the Public Education World]. Budapest: Oktatáskutató és Fejlesztő Intézet. Retrieved from http://ofi.hu/sites/default/files/attachments/1507326_szerep-_es_funkciovaltasok_a_kozoktatas_vilagaban_beliv.pdf

NOTES

1. This letter was reported in the national paper *Népszabadság* (Doros 2016), but an English explanation of the letter can be found on the Hungarian Spectrum blog (http://hungarianspectrum.org/2016/01/16/teachers-revolt-is-brewing-in-hungary/).
2. As of May 2017, this statement is not entirely true. In reaction to the Hungarian government's attempt to close Central European University, the European Commission sent a letter to Prime Minister Viktor Orbán, expressing their concerns regarding the legality of the government's actions. It is, however, beyond the scope of this chapter to address this incident.
3. All people and place names are pseudonyms.
4. As of the writing of this chapter, however, demonstrations have restarted, this time in response to the government's efforts to close Central European University, an international graduate institution in Budapest which, due to its stated commitment to democracy and open society, stands in opposition to the stated goals and purposes of the current administration.
5. In 2004, Hungary in addition to former Soviet Bloc countries of the Czech Republic, Estonia, Latvia, Lithuania, Poland, Slovakia, and Slovenia as well as Cyprus and Malta joined the EU.
6. As of the writing of this chapter, however, demonstrations have restarted, this time in response to the government's efforts to close Central European University, an international graduate institution in Budapest which, due to its stated commitment to democracy and open society, stands in opposition to the stated goals and purposes of the current administration.
7. One example is Horváth and Kiss v. Hungary (2013) tried at the European Court of Human Rights. The two applicants attested that they had been placed in "special" schools for the mentally disabled on the basis of their Roma identity. Ultimately, the court ruled in their favor.
8. Not all secondary schools in Hungary offer a diploma. A diploma (*érettségi*) is necessary for those who want to continue on to university.
9. In April 2017, legislation was passed in the Parliament that placed restrictions on "foreign-backed" institutes of higher education which would effectively make it impossible for Central European University to continue to function. The university was originally founded by Hungarian-American philanthropist George Soros. Students receive a degree that accredited in both Hungary and the United States.
10. This legislation is on its surface meant to prohibit foreign interests from meddling in Hungarian affairs but has in reality greatly hindered the ability of humanitarian organizations to function due to introducing financially prohibitive regulations.

SERENA KOISSABA

6. DECENTRALIZATION AND EDUCATION IN TANZANIA

The Role of Community Schools and Education for the Poor

INTRODUCTION

Decentralization of educational systems in Tanzania has shifted the responsibility of providing services for marginalized students onto the public and the private sector. The power to legitimize the formation of quality and equitable educational programs is still centered at the national level. The design and implementation of schooling can be conducted at the community level, but national regulations for curriculum standards must be adhered to by local communities (Carney and Agergaard 2007). Conceptually, the goal of decentralization was to empower the public to have greater authority to facilitate a partnership with the government over how public services were allocated (Nudzor 2015). The realities at the local levels are that Tanzanians believe that the government is responsible for providing education to the citizens. Decentralization not only shifts some powers and authority to the local level but there is a shift in the responsibility to finance those systems locally. However, alliances between small local communities and small international non-governmental organizations (INGOs) have been valuable in developing and implementing educational programs in disadvantaged areas. Educational campaigns and initiatives administered by large corporations and INGOs receive the most attention within international education development discourses, as scholars and practitioners critique how their work is centered within a human capital trajectory (Moutsios 2010; Tota 2014; Klees 2016; Verger et al. 2016). This chapter will examine how community schooling situated in poor areas negotiates power within a decentralized education system. The findings of this work will show how identity politics and cultural shifts in disenfranchised communities take place through partnerships with a small INGO and individual private investors to gain knowledge and resources needed to create a high-quality and equitable education system for poor children.

Background

Legacy Academy was established in 2007 in response to the current impact of the HIV/AIDS pandemic in Tanzania. Many children in Legacy Ward, a subdivision in the Dodoma region, were left semi-orphaned or completely orphaned as a result of the pandemic. Two hundred and eleven children under the age of five were found to live in Legacy Ward in one of three categories: (1) those that lost both parents and live in difficult conditions with guardians most of whom are elderly, (2) those who have lost one parent and live in difficult circumstances, (3) those having both parents but living in extreme poverty. These children began the first cohort of students at Legacy Academy (Field notes, 06/08/2008). Legacy Academy and Legacy Ward are pseudonyms used in this chapter to describe the community school and community where this study was conducted. Legacy Academy's design and purpose was to be a model for offering educational programs that would positively reach and impact vulnerable children affected by HIV/AIDS and influence the psychosocial dynamics that affect each student. The school motto is "combining education with faith" coupled with the concept that a village raises the child, so with this, Legacy became not only a school but a family in the lives of the pupils who attended. The core commitment of the school's administration was to focus exclusively on desperate children in need of education, food, and affection (Field notes, 06/08/2008). The most important contribution that Legacy Academy can make to its student body is to become a safe public sphere where dominant, oppressive values within their society can be challenged.

COMMUNITY SCHOOLING, EDUCATION POLITICS AND THE POOR

Schools are social institutions, whereby principals and teachers provide an essential link between educational policies and practices globally (Assie-Lumumba 2012). There is a significant amount of emerging literature that refers to the term caring schools to describe the psychosocial mechanics of educational settings that are tasked with educating children with special needs in Africa (Ansell 2008; Williams 2010; Campbell et al. 2014). The perception of the teaching profession in Tanzania, especially in rural areas, is low. National education training policies are terse in outlining the ability of the government to design and fund educational opportunities for its citizens. This mode of intentional segregation divides Tanzanian citizens into subgroups of people who do not receive equal access to educational provisions (Lalvani and Broderick 2015). These policies call for partnerships from various sectors globally to aid the country in its educational development aims. Community schooling in this chapter is defined through the caring school model which describes locally designed and managed schools that offer psychosocial support to at-risk students as a dimension of the school experience (see Campbell et al. 2014). The "community" in this model encompasses all stakeholders who are involved in developing and sustaining the community school. Educational systems are contradictory spaces that have the potential to challenge injustices; instead they regularly "reproduce brutal social stratifications" (Fine and Weiss 2003, p. 3). Education policies are interpretations that are enacted rather than implemented due to school specific factors (e.g. constraints, pressures, and enablers). This is where community schooling can counter power imbalances to provide access to richer knowledge production opportunities within the education profession in Tanzania.

Education Policies and Politics for the Poor

Public education in Tanzania is now subject to privatization and commodification which perpetuates further tiers of discrimination by designating representations of worth to disadvantaged groups. These forms of school preclusions continue to be a catalyst for poverty and social disparities as well as construct a space for othering social groups such as teachers, AIDS orphans, and poor citizens in general (Howarth 2004). Assie-Lumumba (2012) notes that in Africa, the social status of teachers and the teaching profession is low especially at lower levels of the system. Stavros Moutsious (2010) posits that the difference between politics and education politics is based upon specific functions between bureaucratic administrators and citizens. He defines politics as the actions of government leaders and education politics as the activity of citizens, such as parents and teachers, to decide the purpose of pedagogical practices. Policymaking is unlike politics in that it is not centered on political opinion but specialization and expertise to set agendas, using an evidenced-based approach to decision-making (Castoriadis 2002; Colebatch 2002; Moutsios 2010). Schools are conceptualized as spaces where policy is created and enacted. This phenomenon may be difficult to perceive within unstable educational settings because much of the discourse around the topic of the problems of global education policy is focused on the psychosocial interventions of disadvantaged students. The marketization of education policies and practices has led to public management mechanisms of "outcome-driven surveillance" (Moutsios 2010, p. 125) over schools that are regulated at regional levels of government.

Schools can be spaces where students and teachers experience liberation to reconstruct their identities and are motivated to not only challenge but change the social imparities working against them. This is where community schools have the potential to procure their own policies based on the culture, ethos, and situated necessities with the limitations and possibilities found within it. For example, during the first two years of designing and implementing teacher training and curriculum programs at Legacy Academy, school leaders surveyed the teachers at Legacy to get their input and thoughts about their professional challenges.

The teachers at Legacy Academy are comprised of teachers who have been teaching for six months to more than seven years. New teachers need to practice the teaching-learning theories they have acquired from college. They feel that learning to teach is one thing but actually teaching is another. All of the teachers want to learn how to be more confident and competent with their teaching in order to have a positive impact on their students. More experienced teachers are eager to learn from the new teachers about the new teaching methods being taught in teacher's colleges now (Survey summary notes, 8/7/2009).

The survey summary demonstrates that both novice and experienced teachers at Legacy were skeptical about their teaching abilities. The more experienced teachers felt that their training was not sufficient to meet the standards of teaching at Legacy. The expectations for teaching in government schools were lower than those established at Legacy. Tanzania does not have special schools or curriculum to educate students with special needs. The closest model of special schools in Tanzania are for gifted or high academic achieving students. Tanzania's education system is anchored in the ideological structures of the colonial British Empire that was designed to support their economic agenda. National education policies in Tanzania are based on the premise of separate but equal. According to Kitila Mkumbo (2014), private schools in Tanzania are autonomous in their pedagogical practices as well as the vetting of their teachers and students. He notes that only gifted children are allowed entrance into these schools and that their parents' income is a major factor on their eligibility to enroll. There is no formal leadership program for educational leaders in Tanzania. Experienced teachers who show promise of being able to be instructional leaders are placed in leadership roles based on their track record as teachers. Teachers at Legacy noted that Legacy needed "new techniques to introduce assessment for learning in classes [because the government] system puts much emphasis on summative exam[s] rather than on continuous assessment of individuals" (Survey summary notes, 8/7/2009). Measuring and reporting student academic performance was a huge concern to the teachers because teachers are held responsible by the government for school failure or success. Teachers are held accountable for their students' success. Failure is borne by teachers alone. Recently a DO [district officer] in Lake zone Tanzania whipped teachers – in front of students – because the school was the worst performed in national exams (Legacy teacher interview, 8/7/2009).

There is an issue of physical violence against teachers in underprivileged public schools by public and private stakeholders (Ngalawa et al. 2015). Monitoring and evaluation of school performance in community schools relieves teachers of the sole responsibility for school achievement. The entire school community is accountable for school success and areas of improvement are never handled with violence against anyone. This is where profession identity shifts happen. School officials are placed in educational settings that provide an environment where teachers are supported through training and development to serve every student enrolled at school without the pressures of being accountable for aspects of school management that is not a part of their training or line of work.

Building Caring Community Schooling

The leadership at Legacy Academy decided that they would not use titles such as "AIDS orphans" or "street children" when referencing members of the student body. Positive school slogans and mottoes were constructed to restructure how pupils at the school saw themselves. Several children within the school community had physical and mental disabilities. Children at Legacy that had visible disabilities and defects were more likely to drop out of school than others. People may self-exclude themselves because of fear and shame (Grant and Hulme 2008). The school adopted a form of responsible inclusion policy that outlined how these students would be treated. Responsible inclusion for this chapter is defined as the development of a school-based education model that is student-centered and that bases educational placement and service provision on each student's needs (Vaughn and Schumm 1995). Implementing this policy was difficult due to the fact that the teachers at Legacy were barely equipped to teach the national curriculum and were struggling to deal with outcomes of poverty in their own lives.

A few ways the school was able to incorporate the responsible inclusion policy in the school curriculum was to create assessments tailored to the local needs of the kids within the learning space. Teaching aids and materials that promote racism, tribalism and classism were forbidden. Students were allowed to decorate the classrooms with their artwork and literature. Pupils felt a sense of ownership as participants in their educational journey while producing creative expressions that celebrated their national culture and reality in the curriculum. There were difficulties in attempting to design a school for disadvantaged children in rural Legacy Ward that would encompass a space for social renewal and a curriculum that would promote critical consciousness for staff and students. One of the greatest incentives for children to attend school is to help redefine themselves as something other than AIDS orphans (Nicolai and Triplehorn 2003). The real issue concerning equity for all is not fairness but freedom.

One of the significant responsible inclusive policies that was implemented at Legacy was the key worker system. The key worker system is an assessment whereby teachers put their students in small groups in order to observe how they learn during center times. Students do not know they are being observed during times of instruction. Each child has a file called "All About Me" which includes samples of the school work, artwork, reports from parent-teacher conferences, and photos. Teachers are able to acquire evidence of each pupil's performance so that curriculum changes and amendments can be made for students who need them. The contents of the "All About Me" files are used during parent-teacher meetings to showcase the progress of each student. Legacy has small classroom size with a 2 teacher to 30 student ratio maximum. Current government school facilities in Legacy Ward are old abandoned buildings from colonial times. Lead-based paint is chipping from the walls with lead-based plumbing pipes that are still in use today along with rows of old Oxford style benches occupying classrooms. Government schools in Legacy Ward have dirt floors, spray-painted chalk boards, and dimly lit classrooms. When it rains, the floor becomes muddy and children are required to sit in dark, damped overcrowded classrooms. Not only are these schools not clean, safe spaces of productive and healthy learning environments, they are unattractive to students, who are sick and disabled because the school design is a hazard to their well-being. Educators in government schools are tasked with teaching more than 100 students in a single classroom with no additional teaching support staff. This is the reason the key worker system is so important to creating a responsible inclusive environment at Legacy Academy.

Children who struggle with diseases and orphanhood do not need to be placed in an environment of violence and verbal abuse. Legacy does not allow caning as a form of punishment. Teachers were concerned with how issues of discipline would be handled at Legacy Academy in the beginning.

Teachers feel that Tanzanian students have discipline partly because of the African culture – which fosters respect for teachers and elders due in part to the use of corporal punishment. Meanwhile, there seems to be a trend to 'abolish' corporal punishment and there's also 'cultural erosion' and we are concerned about this (Survey summary notes, 8/7/2009).

Students at Legacy Academy have an enormous respect for their teachers. The idea that they had done something to disappoint their teachers was enough to make them correct themselves. Teachers were like surrogate parents to each pupil. They conducted weekly home visits and spent time with those who needed special attention in their studies or home life. The removal of harmful policies like caning can be abolished in schools but school leaders must invest in training their staff on positive alternative ways to discipline young people. A part of becoming a liberated person is to understand how to manage and control one's self.

Who Should Be Leading in Schools?

School leadership training is central to the capacity of building a strong education system (Hutton 2014). This begs the question, who should be leading in schools? Schools are sites where citizens are prepared to be socially responsible, thus this is why it is important to address the inequalities in schools so that current forms of oppression are not perpetuated in future generations (Jenlink 2011). Education leadership situated in schools where social injustice is present must conceive and identify itself as an agent of power and notions of political subjectivities that are active systemically to perpetuate injustice (Jenlink 2014). Nevertheless, principals must be able to address the inequity in education by moving away from reproducing the inequalities spatially to constructing new norms of equality. A study conducted by Kitila Mkumbo (2013) found that teachers' commitment to schools in Tanzania was directly linked to their feelings concerning the leadership within those institutions.

Teachers have lots of constraints, which hinder their teaching and bar evaluation:

- Overcrowded classroom (encouraged lecture method)
- Lack of resources e.g. library, texts and extra books
- They (teachers) do not control the curriculum decisions that affect students' performance
- Exhausting work load, paper work, massive marking leave classroom responsibilities lag behind
- Lack of professional development opportunities to improve their methodology

Because of the various limitations, aspiration and changes adopted by the Ministry of Education do not match with reality e.g. inclusion system, the introduction of new topics such as Gender and ICT: these require induction/training, tools/resources like computers (Survey summary notes, 8/7/2009).

Educators who work in the schools examined in this study behaved like surrogate parents and social workers rather than teachers. This narrative reflects the contention and disconnect between education policy expectations and the local realities in classrooms. Pauline Rose (2009) notes that the role of school committees gained prominence in education policy studies during the 1990s with an aim towards improving schools, especially where educational services were decentralized. Principals, teachers, and paraprofessionals can work through their response to performativity by engaging in their own education reforms to restructure their identities within a system set up to diminish their value and position within the political economy of the nation.

Empowering Educators and Educational Leadership through School-Based Training Centers

Tanzania historically has struggled as a nation to provide high-quality and equitable educational opportunities to its citizens due to its inability to train all teachers adequately, provide sufficient budgetary allocations to public schools, and poor planning and school infrastructure (Mbelle 2008; Masenge 2012; Ngalawa et al. 2015). The link in educational leadership development between policy and practice is "a consequence of contemporary capitalism which continuously advertises change, choice and consumption" (Hartley 2007, p. 84). Hartley continues to posit that the market constructs education policy and practice, where more is expected to be accomplished with less. This is the framework for which the decentralization of education services in Tanzania is based. It is an indication of an unstable education system. Decentralization of education in Tanzania promotes an ideology that holds communities and school administrators responsible for the outcomes of discriminatory national educational policies designed to marginalize and divide them amongst socio-economic lines (Howarth 2004). Cost-sharing efforts with community members have resulted in inequalities in educational opportunities (Komba 2012). In developing countries like Tanzania, community participations are the foundation of modern development policy discourse (Phillips 2013). The devolution of power in education systems creates stress on educational leaders who work in impoverished public schools. Learning facilities in Tanzania resemble prisons with iron bars at each window and overcrowded classrooms. Educational initiatives for the poor need to shift to a learner-centered curriculum that is evaluated by its relevance and its ability to develop critical and analytical thinkers. The national curriculum in Tanzania is not competent enough to educate students to be competitive in the modern world. National exams evaluate educational objectives and assess the progress of learners. The exams should be used more significantly to evaluate and improve the education system. "'Blame' for poor scores on the 2010 and 2011 national exams in Tanzania were attributed to poor teachers, but schools that have an acceptable amount of qualified teachers were also poor" (HakiElimu 2016). School design for those

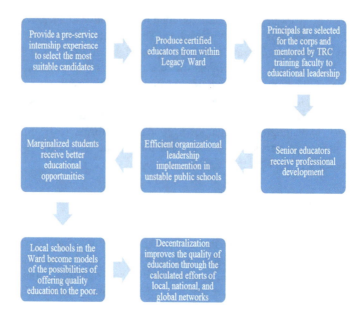

Figure 5.1 The program ontology of the Legacy Ward School for professional and instructional development

living in extreme settings must not focus more on psychosocial intervention over educational service. Nevertheless, the school setting must not become an instrument for oppression. This type of school design leads to dependency that promotes more of the same disenfranchisement.

The school-based teacher resource training center (TRC) in Legacy Ward became an axis where policy and practice converged by establishing local and regional partnerships to legitimize the training and new organizational procedures in village schools. Some of the new administrative changes that were implemented reduced classroom size, new facilities were built, and the school leadership position was restructured to provide more effective school management.

Tony Bush (2009) notes that evaluation models that rely on self-reported evidence with short term development activities are weak and subjective. Our model depends on collaboration from various actors and networks in order to function. The community at Legacy Ward was able to formulate a consensus of what they wanted for their school and the role they should play in the partnership. Selecting candidates from the area made it easy to avoid some of the pitfalls that occur when working with people from outside of the community. Local candidates were already familiar with the local and national languages, they lived within the area so the need for housing was minimal and they were accustomed to living conditions. Most impoverished schools who are impacted by the decentralization of education struggle with the lack of delegated authority from the national government (Chapman et al. 2002).

This was not the case with the community in Legacy Ward. They were equal partners in the planning and implementation of all educational programming as well as set the pace for the timeline of all activities. When international actors are involved, they sometimes want to undertake ambitious projects with short timeframes (Chapman et al. 2002) but all partners agreed that in order to see real change the commitment to the work had to be long-term. This has been the heart of the project's success and sustainability.

INGOS AS PRIVATE INVESTORS: THE TRANSNATIONAL POLITICS OF FINANCING INTERNATIONAL EDUCATION DEVELOPMENT

The current conditions within most public schools in Tanzania are still extremely dire. Compared to Zimbabwe, Chile, Nigeria, and the Philippines on the 2015 Right to Education Index (RTEI) survey, Tanzania scored the lowest on school improvement outcomes. The country continues to fall behind international standards for teaching and learning. The Tanzanian government failed to provide the RTEI survey with the necessary data required from the Basic Education Statistics for Tanzania (BEST) department (HakiElimu 2016). This demonstrates that the national government is not able to keep up with managing the school system in Tanzania. According to the Education and Training Policy in Tanzania (United Republic of Tanzania 2011, p. 4), an appropriate education system is defined below.

A good system of education in any country must be on two fronts: on the qualitative level, to ensure access to education and equity in the distribution and allocation of resources to various segments of the society, and on the qualitative model, to ensure that the country produces the skills needed for rapid social and economic development.

Many countries depend on INGOs to provide educational opportunities to the poorest children, whereas the state by default provides for the masses but excludes the marginalized (Rose 2009). Program cost-effectiveness is evaluated and monitored by donors. The decentralization of power reduces the amount of power of those in the centralized system. Economic power becomes a mechanism of coercion when it is centralized and used to create dependence (Hayek 1944). The state is an independent political power that negotiates interests of labor and economics. When it fails to manage public funds for social costs such as education, the people are taxed until they revolt. The state becomes unable to maintain capital to finance social programs and preserve the legitimacy of capitalism (Carnoy 2014). School districts in poor communities do not see the added financial responsibility to fund educational services as a means of liberation.

Some parents felt that it was inappropriate to be asked to give towards their children's education. Many Tanzanians still feel that it is the government's sole responsibility to fund education and other social services. This is where NGOs can act as brokers of socioeconomic agency. NGOs can introduce the locals to investors both nationally and internationally and offer training and mentoring through the

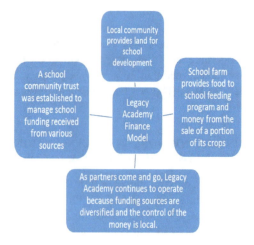

Figure 5.2. Finance model for legacy academy

formation of sustainable initiatives that could provide financial aid and freedom for the socio-economic reconstruction of the community (Koissaba 2015, p. 107).

INGOs operate like para-governments who are "autonomous and powerful agents in transnational policymaking" (Tota 2014, p. 96). The partnership with a small INGO and Legacy Academy is an example of how the phenomenon of community-based schooling works to redistribute power to local poor communities by creating an environment where local school officials can have access to knowledge production and resources through leveraging their networks and financial clout. Historically in Tanzania, child labor and education were juxtaposed in order to help local communities finance educational services as well as produce income for the colonists.

Global networks employ the media to help publicize their campaigns as beneficial to the less fortunate in developing countries to demonstrate their ability to afford political agency to poor populations through their campaigns or activism. Their rhetoric rejects imperialist systems like neoliberalism and capitalism channeled by corporations and international NGOs like the World Bank and the International Monetary Fund (IMF). There is the need to examine the contradictory rationale of systemic reform for institutionalizing educational autonomy.

Decentralization is synonymous with marketization and privatization of public goods (Gobby 2016). This is where the nexus between NGOs and transnational politics collide, forming a complex causal interpretation of purpose, policies, and practices. The United Republic of Tanzania (URT) policy for education and training (2011) ascribes the public sector with the assignment of guiding future development and financial investment of providing education and training within the country. The policy states that its intent is to:

decentralize education and training by empowering regions, districts, communities and educational institutions to manage and administer education and training ... and broaden the base for the financing of education and training through cost sharing measures involving individuals, communities, NGOs, parents and end-users, and through the inclusion of education as an area of investment in the Investment Promotion Act.

The differences in the pilot research model in Legacy as opposed to the old colonial model are that the school farm does not require teachers and students to work but parents and hired farmers do all the work. The children and the school benefit 100% from the food and funds generated from the business. Labor is not emphasized over learning. The aims at child protection interventions should consider how those interventions will impact the child's entire life.

CONCLUSION

A number of countries worldwide are currently undergoing decentralization of educational services. Discourses around the privatization and marketization of schooling are prevalent to decentralization reforms. Not all international education scholars believe this is a bad thing (Anderson-Levitt 2003). Some feel that it is the responsibility of governments to provide public goods such as education and that they must be held accountable to do so. I believe the community school model is vital for creating educational schooling in Tanzania for children who are out of school. Community schools are the link between national policy goals and practice on the ground. Legacy Academy is an example of how a poor rural village can establish and sustain a community school that has high academic standards. Legacy began with local and international partnerships with a small INGO and individual private investors and it continues to operate today with the same base. International educational development schemes do not have to have large donor investments or excessive national government involvement in order to succeed. Actually, small donor partnerships enable more control of resources and curriculum design than they would have if they were to be accountable for larger sums of funding. Legacy Ward was able to shift their cultural perceptions and identities of deficiencies about themselves through the growth of the students and faculty at Legacy Academy.

REFERENCES

Anderson-Levitt, Kathyrn. (2003). *Local Meanings, Global Schooling: Anthropology and World Culture Theory*. New York, NY: Palgrave Macmillan.

Ansell, Nicola. (2008). "Substituting for Families? Schools and Social Reproduction in AIDS-Affected Lesotho." *Antipode, 40*(5), 802–824.

Assie-Lumumba, Ndri T. (2012). "Cultural Foundations of the Idea and Practice of the Teaching Profession in Africa: Indigenous Roots, Colonial Intrusion, and Post-Colonial Reality." *Educational Philosophy and Theory, 44*(S2), 21–36.

Campbell, Catherine, Clare Coultas, Louise Anderson, Elena Broaddus, Morten Skovdal, Connie Nyamukapa, & Simon Gregson. (2014). *Conceptualising Schools as a Source of Social Capital for HIV Affected Children in Southern Africa* (HCD Working Paper Series 6). London: The London School of Economics and Political Science. (Unpublished)

Carney, Stephen, Min Bista, & Jytte Agergaard. (2007). "Empowering the Local Through Education? Exploring Community-Managed School in Nepal." *Oxford Review of Education, 33*(5), 611–628.

Carnoy, M. (2014). *The State and Political Theory.* Princeton, NJ: Princeton University Press.

Castoriadis, Cornelius. (2002). *On Plato's Statesman.* Stanford, CA: Stanford University Press.

Chapman, David, Elizabeth Barcikowski, Michael Sowah, Emma Gyamera, & George Woode. (2002). "Do Communities Know Best? Testing a Premise of Educational Decentralization: Community Members' Perceptions of Their Local Schools in Ghana." *International Journal of Educational Development, 22*, 181–189.

Colebatch, Hal. (2002). *Policy.* London: Open University Press.

Fine, Michelle, & Lois Weiss. (2003). *Silenced Voices and Extraordinary Conversations: Re-Imagining Schools.* New York, NY: Teachers College Press.

Gobby, Brad. (2016). "Putting 'the System' into a School Autonomy Reform: The Case of the Independent Public Schools Program." *Discourse: Studies in the Cultural Politics of Education, 37*(1), 16–29.

Grant, Ursula, & David Hulme. (2008). *Services for the Poorest: From Angst to Action* (Working Paper No. 128). Manchester: Chronic Poverty Research Centre.

HakiElimu. (2016). *Is the Right to Education Fulfilled in Tanzania? Findings of the Right to Education Index 2015* (Hake Brief No. 6). Retrieved from http://www.hakielimu.org

Hartley, David. (2007). "Theory and Practice in the Management of Education." *Journal of Education Policy, 13*(1), 153–162.

Hayek, Friedrich A. (1944). *The Road to Serfdom.* London: Routledge.

Howarth, Caroline. (2004). "Re-Presentation and Resistance in the Context of School Exclusion: Reasons to be Critical." *Journal of Community & Applied Social Psychology, 14*, 356–377.

Hutton, Disraeli M. (2014). "Preparing the Principal to Drive the Goals of Education for All: A Conceptual Case Development Model." *Research in Comparative and International Education, 9*(1), 92–110.

Jenlink, Patrick M. (2011). "Leadership Education Priorities for a Democratic Society." *Scholar-Practitioner Quarterly, 4*(4), 306–308.

Jenlink, Patrick M. (2014). "The Spatial Nature of Justice: A Scholar-Practitioner Perspective." In Ira Bogotch & Carolyn M. Shields, eds., *International Handbook of Educational Leadership and Social (In)Justice.* New York, NY: Springer.

Klees, Steven J. (2016). "Human Capital and Rates of Return: Brilliant Ideas or Ideological Dead Ends?" *Comparative Education Review, 60*(4), 644–672.

Koissaba, Serena. (2015). "Looking Beyond Millennium Development Goals: Funding Quality Education Through Building Local Capacity: A Sample from Tanzania." In N. Andrews, E. N. Khalema, & N. T. Assié-Lumumba, eds., *Millennium Development Goals (MDGs) in Retrospect: Africa's 'Development' Beyond 2015.* London: Springer.

Komba, Aneth A. (2012). "Strategies for Enhancing Equity in Financing Primary Education in Tanzania." *Education Research, 3*(6), 495–501.

Lalvani, Priya, & Alicia Broderick. (2015). "Teacher Education, in Exclusion, and the Implicit Ideology of Separate but Equal: An Invitation to a Dialogue." *Education, Citizenship and Social Justice, 10*(2), 168–183.

Masenge, Ralph W. P. (2012). "The Current Environment of Education in Tanzania: Challenges of Teaching/Learning Mathematics in Tanzania." *Journal of Issues and Practice in Education, 4*(2), 122–134.

Mbelle, Ammon V. Y. (2008). *The Impact of Reforms on the Quality of Primary Education in Tanzania* (Research Report No. 08.1). Dar es Salaam: Research on Poverty Alleviation.

Mkumbo, Kitila A. K. (2013). "Factors Associated with Teachers' Motivation and Commitment to Teach in Tanzania." *Journal of Educational Sciences & Psychology, LXV*, 58–71.

Mkumbo, Kitila A. K. (2014). *Teaching Effectiveness in Primary and Secondary Schools in Tanzania.* Dar es Salaam: HakiElimu.

Moutsios, Stavros. (2010). "Power, Politics and Transnational Policy-Making in Education." *Globalisation, Societies and Education, 8*(1), 121–141.

Ngalawa, Athanas, Elaine Simmt, & Florence Glanfield. (2015). "Exploring the Emergence of Community Support for School and Encouragement of Innovation for Improving Rural School Performance: Lessons Learned at Kitamburo in Tanzania." *Global Education Review, 2*(4), 101–125.

Nicolai, Susan, & Carl Triplehorn. (2003). *The Role of Education in Protecting Children in Conflict* (Humanitarian Practice Network Paper No. 42). London: Overseas Development Institute.

Nudzor, Hope P. (2014). "An Analytical Review of Education Policy-Making and Implementation Processes within the Context of "Decentralized System of Administration" in Ghana." *Sage Open, 4*(2), 215824401453088.

Phillips, Kristin D. (2013). "Dividing the Labor of Development: Education and Participation in Rural Tanzania." *Comparative Education Review, 57*(4), 637–661.

Right to Education Index (RTEI). (2015). *Right to Education Index Report Tanzania.* Retrieved December 10, 2017, from https://www.rtei.org/en/explore/rtei-country/?id=TZ&year=2015

Rose, Pauline. (2009). *NGO Provision of Basic Education: Alternative or Complementary Service Delivery to Support Access to the Excluded?* (Research Monograph No. 3). Sussex: Consortium for Research on Educational Access, Transitions & Equity.

Tota, Pasqua M. (2014). "Filling the Gaps: The Role and Impact of International Non-Governmental Organizations in Education for All." *Globalisation, Societies, and Education, 12*(1), 92–109.

United Republic of Tanzania. (2011). *Education and Training Policy.* Dar es Salaam: Ministry of Education and Culture.

Vaughn, Sharon, & Jeanne Shay Schumm. (1995). "Responsible Inclusion for Students with Learning Disabilities." *Journal of Learning Disabilities, 28*(5), 264–270.

Verger, Antonio, Xavier Bonal, & Adrian Zangajo. (2016). "What are the Role and Impact of Public-Private Partnerships in Education? A Realist Evaluation of the Chilean Education Quasi-Market." *Comparative Education Review, 60*(2), 223–248.

Williams, Samantha E. (2010). *Exploring the Viability of School-Based Support for Vulnerable Children: A Case Study of Two Township Schools in Johannesburg* (Research Monograph No. 46). Retrieved from http://www.create-rpc.org

RICHARD BAMATTRE

7. BETWEEN STATE AND SOCIETY

Community Schools in Zambia

Among African countries seeking to "decenter" government administration and public social services structures, including education, is the Republic of Zambia, a landlocked country with a population of 16 million, with over 4 million enrolled primary and secondary students (Ministry of Education 2016a; The World Bank 2017). Decentralization was presented in the mid-1990s as a practical application of philosophies of democracy and liberalism and was most clearly articulated with the establishment of District Education Boards for 72 districts, which were responsible for financing and staffing government schools. The declared benefits of decentralization matched some of the motivations highlighted by McGinn and Welsh (1999): to minimize government funding and coordination and relieve the national ministry of "much of the burden of day-to-day business," but also to encourage local democracy in the form of community participation and increase the political legitimacy of the education system by promoting "a sense of ownership and responsibility" for schools (Ministry of Education 1996, p. 124).

However, Zambia's decentralizing efforts met a significant challenge in the 1990s and 2000s, with which the Ministry of Education and civil society partners are continuing to grapple. An economic crisis and resulting period of structural adjustment in the previous two decades had led to a fairly stagnant education system, in which the building of schools was nearly frozen and school fees were imposed in government schools. This, combined with a liberalization of education brought by a transition to a multi-party state, and a global emphasis on "education for all" led to a grassroots movement around the country, as communities began building their own primary schools with volunteer teachers. These so-called *community schools* mushroomed in the last fifteen years: 38 of these schools in 1996 had grown to over 3,000 in 2013 (Ministry of Education 2014). Few of these schools have been integrated into the government system by being converted into state schools: instead, community schools have been legitimized by the Zambian state as a separate category of schooling and seen effectively as both non-government and non-private. However, both the cohesiveness and boundaries of this grassroots movement are not clear, although there are links to historical community self-help activities. Along with the growth of these schools emerged a patchwork of civil society organizations and international projects, which have supported these schools and negotiated their relation with the state.

While national policymakers and local districts in the country have struggled to accommodate these schools alongside an established and decentralizing government system of education, community schools in a way represent an extreme version of devolvement on the most local level, where people in communities and villages are responsible for many of the core aspects of education, including building schools, hiring teachers, and supervising teaching and learning. These institutions represent a dramatic shift in how state and society are constructed and imagined in the arena of education, by allowing and even empowering communities to play an increasingly major role in creating and managing their own education provision, a sector previously seen as a belonging to the state.

This chapter seeks to question how community schools and a larger context of decentralization and community democratization are outcomes of sociopolitical changes and how these schools have in turn shaped the construction of the state and society in Zambia by upturning the public nature of state-financed primary education. In short, this chapter aims to explore the historical context and sociopolitical implications of this community school movement, specifically how the government has sought to distinguish, via policy, state and society, and used tactics of governance, particularly calls for community participation, to maintain this division. By maintaining a division between state and society, calling on community involvement and self-help, and emphasizing partnerships with bilateral, international, and local non-government organizations, the Zambian state has been able to assert its authority to define and delegate education provision, while at the same time allowing local people and a variety of NGOs to perform most of the financing and management of these schools. While the government maintains that these schools constitute a "crucial pillar" in resolving access to education (Ministry of Education 2014, p. 14) and thus relies on the "community action" of parent-school committees that run them (1), the extent of the democratic role of these institutions is not clear, and recent policy changes, including a standardized national curriculum, seem to reduce democratic opportunity rather than increase it. While the initiative of local communities has created basic learning institutions for the most marginalized in times of crisis, it is not clear whether these schools operate in parallel to the government system and serve to reproduce existing inequalities.

While there have been numerous community school projects around the world – among them the Save the Children community school model in Africa and Escuela Nueva in Colombia – Zambia is a unique case for two reasons. First, many of the schools seem to have been created by communities themselves out of pragmatic necessity rather than by non-government organizations, although organizations later provided necessary support. Secondly, the sheer scale of community schools makes it a case in point: these schools constitute the second largest provider of education after government schools with more schools and pupils than private schools and traditional church-based schools combined. Almost one-third of all primary schools are community schools, capturing nearly 20 percent of primary student enrollment in the nation, although this data still may underestimate the number of schools, as some continue to operate outside the recognition of the state (Ministry of Education 2014, 2016a).

Along with its main aims, this chapter contributes to an argument for the need for an updated and nuanced theory of the state to understand community-based and so-called alternative primary schools and their relationship with the government. A brief analysis of community schools is followed by an overview of the history of these schools in Zambia with a focus on three critical moments. Then, issues of democratization within these schools are explored, with a conclusion addressing how these schools in Zambia connect with larger opportunities and drawbacks within decentralization and democratization.

THE LOCAL AND COMMUNAL: COMMUNITY SCHOOLS IN SUB-SAHARAN AFRICA

Community and community-based schools are becoming more prominent in both lower, middle, and upper-income countries. However, within Sub-Saharan Africa, there is not a common definition of what a community school is, or what differentiates this type of school from other education institutions, like those operated by the modern bureaucratic state, or private options. A brief definition is that these schools are founded, managed, and supported at the local level, by towns or villages, religious groups, or non-government organizations. Glassman et al. (2007) note that scholars have chosen to define these schools not by what they are, but what they are *not*. Miller-Grandvaux and Yoder (2002) view them as non-governmental, while retaining a connection with public education, either by receiving some public funds or operating as feeder schools, which transfer students to state institutions. Hoppers (2005), adopting a conflict approach, views community schools in the region as emerging from a *de facto* informal sector, for which the state no longer claims direct responsibility. This is distinct from other contexts, particularly in middle or upper-income countries, where community-based schools were created in opposition to an overly bureaucratic or overreaching state or to provide an alternative to human capital approaches to learning (Mwalimu 2010). In Hoppers' analysis of eight countries in Sub-Saharan Africa, community schools rarely offer radical adaptations or transformations to state schools but instead only vary or adapt national curriculum. This suggests the discourse around community schools, that they offer accessible, affordable, and locally relevant education, is more expansive than actual practices, as many schools offer a limited version of the teaching and learning taking place in government schools.

Overall, the literature in Zambia and beyond is rife with ideas for establishing and managing these schools, along with critiques of these approaches. Yet, within a context in which management of public education is a role traditionally attributed to the state, there is little attention paid to how community schools reflect, enhance, or contradict existing theories of the state. A political analysis of community-based education is increasingly pertinent, as literature on these schools, and rhetoric frequently attached to decentralization of education, often has an implicit theory of the state, albeit one in which the state has a remote coordinating or facilitating role. Drawing on theories of state and society (Abrams 1988; Mitchell 1991; Dill 2013) and community participation as a form of governance (Midgley et al. 1986; Mohan and Stokke 2000), this case study examines how community schools have been rationalized and managed, along different strategies, by the Zambian state. Within this case, there will be an effort to draw out and explore a tension present both in decentralization and community-based schooling, identified by Carnoy (1999): the conceptual difference between goals of improving local ownership, quality of learning, and democratic decision-making, and that of reducing public expenditure in education by sharing cost with parents and local communities. The next section traces the history of both community self-help and the emergence of community schools in Zambia in light of socio-political and economic changes.

GRASSROOTS AND GRASS THATCH: THE EMERGENCE AND GROWTH OF COMMUNITY SCHOOLS IN ZAMBIA

In short, community schools emerged in Zambia in the early 1990s due either to a lack of government schools, primarily in rural areas, or school fees and over-enrollment in existing schools in both rural and urban areas. As the growth of these schools became undeniable, they were accepted by the state as a legal form of schooling within a liberalized space for social service provision. However, there is a more nuanced and rich history behind these schools linked to larger social and political movements in Zambia, including the increased role of non-government organizations in working directly with schools and the reliance of the Ministry of Education on bilateral assistance and consultation, stemming from changes in governance in the era of structural adjustment in the 1990s. While the commonly accepted narrative views community schools as only emerging in this decade, the practice of communities building their own schools was common even in eras where the state took symbolic control over the education system. In this section, a brief history of the role of communities in school building both before and after national independence will be followed by an overview of the growth of contemporary community schools and the state's evolving response to them, within three "critical moments." This overview will focus on how communities have been empowered to take on a primary role in these schools, which in turn have been integrated into a decentered governance structure.

Villages Building Schools before and after Independence

There was historical precedent for community schools in pre-independence Zambia, then Northern Rhodesia, a protectorate of the British Empire. So-called "village" or "bush" schools were prominent in the early years of British colonial rule, in the 1920s and 1930s. Most of these were run by missionary societies, staffed by teachers with minimal education and training, and existed alongside "proper schools" or mission station schools, which were the only institutions recognized by the government and able to receive grants-in-aid. In some ways village schools were distinct from contemporary community schools: these institutions were administered by missionary societies in an often strictly centralized way, and the evangelist nature of these societies often led to itinerant teachers moving from village to village to prophesize through education. However, there are some similarities between village and community schools. First, the colonial government was reluctant to directly support these schools, although there were indirect means, including collaboration with societies at large to address issues of quality and training of teachers. Secondly and more importantly, communities and parents were responsible for erecting structures, providing the materials, and supporting the school by paying in kind. Snelson (1990) describes the conditions of schools started by the Paris Evangelical Missionary Society:

> Classes in the village schools were often held in the open air. When a building was erected, this was provided by the local people, who were also responsible for building huts for the teachers. All the early buildings were in pole and mud; they were rarely substantial unless the teacher or missionary directed the building operations. Pupils provided their own equipment. This was no more than a slate, a slate pencil, and, perhaps, a reader. Sometimes small fees were charged; usually they were paid in kind in the form of eggs, a fowl, fish or meal. (pp. 47–48)

While the colonial administration began prioritizing investment in education, particularly after the Second World War, its funding and building of schools were inadequate, and the quality and scope of African education paled in comparison to schools for Europeans. The output of this system was starkly evident at independence.

When Zambia became independent in 1964, the new nation was, according to Kelly (1991), "rich in material and financial resources, but almost destitute in developed human resources" (p. 13). Less than 5% of the population had completed six years of primary school, and illiteracy was 76% for men, and 95% for women (Carmody 2009). Under the presidency of Kenneth Kaunda and the United National Independence Party (UNIP), a focus on "Zambianizing" the nation and the bureaucratic apparatus was undertaken alongside an increasingly radical plan to reform the education system. Departing from a colonial model of partnership with missionary schools, the state declared a "virtual monopoly" over education provision: along with taking over the functions of public local authorities, the government encouraged non-government and missionary organizations to surrender their schools to the state. However, the rhetoric of central government control and progress was not reflected in reality. Kelly (1991) notes that almost all of the schools developed in the decade after independence were built by communities on a self-help basis and were temporary structures, which needed to be replaced. This effort was influenced by strong support for the new state boosted by a campaign by UNIP revolving around work and self-reliance; however, this self-help was more common in rural areas, as urban residents were mostly occupied with wage employment (Mwanakatwe 2013). In fact, local government actors, even later in the Kaunda era in which government had further assumed responsibility for education, encouraged communities to build their own schools, relaying that the state would eventually take over the costs, particularly providing for teachers (Kelly 1991). However, because of the predominant narrative on the role of centralized Zambian state and its efforts to reach universal education, there is little systematic documentation of these self-help efforts in this period, including the extent to which communities managed and ran schools while waiting for the government to take over.

However, both the rhetoric of national ambitions and the structural reality of the government – what Abrams (1988) refers to as the idea and system of the state – met an economic decline in the 1970s. Low copper prices and increasing prices for oil led the mineral-dependent nation into crisis. Within a decade, one of the richest countries in Africa became among the poorest (Andersson et al. 2000). This affected not only the fulfillment of educational goals but the plans themselves: in 1977 a proposal for a radical redesign of the Zambian education system, which sought to universalize education while reducing inequality between state and private schools, was rejected in favor of a more conservative policy. On the side of implementation, education expansion towards universal primary education could not even keep up with population growth, and this crisis led to solutions which sought to manage the catastrophe rather than reform the system to address inequalities, particularly with what Kelly (1991) describes as a bias in development against the rural population. In other words, the response to educational issues became typified by gradual and scattered changes to elements of the entire system, as opposed to more large-scale reform; this theme is present in the government's approach to community schools, which will be explored shortly.

The 1980s were considered a "lost decade" in the history of Zambia, as the devastating economic decline limited government activity, leading to public dissatisfaction with the little visible progress in many sectors. However, there were two policies and projects which planted the seeds of a decentralized and liberalized approach to education. The first was the Education Reform Implementation Project (ERIP), financed by the World Bank, which released a report recommending changes to education, given limited financial resources. Among these were: a focus on primary education, considering the cost inefficiencies of higher levels of schooling; cost-sharing and user fees, including boarding and material fees; pluralism and the encouragement of private and grant-aided schools; and increased support from the local community (Carmody 2009). The second were projects which sought to extend the centralized education system's efforts through community-based or decentralizing efforts: one of these was the Self-Help Action Plan for Education (SHAPE) project, financed by SIDA (Swedish International Development Cooperation Agency), which involved communities in constructing schools, preparing educational materials, and providing in-service training; the second was the creation of Resource Centers within school zones, which were intended to be hubs and meeting places for teachers to reflect on practice and conduct additional training. These centers would later become one of the main spaces where teachers from both government and community schools would formally interact.

The economic crisis and public discontent ultimately led to a political transition from the one-party state to a multiparty democracy in 1991, with the Movement for Multiparty Democracy (MMD) winning the presidency and parliamentary majority. The next sections will look at three key moments from this transition on, in the growth of community schools and the accompanying response from the state: (1) the introduction of multiparty democracy and liberalization of social services, accompanied by a reintroduction of structural adjustment programs; (2) efforts to cater to community schools as a parallel system of education with the creation of a civil society "umbrella" organization and a separate curriculum and teacher training program in the late 1990s, (3) a "balanced" approach from the 2000s which seeks to integrate these schools into a decentralized government system and strike an equilibrium between top-down governance and local control.

Critical Moments in the State's Response to Community Schools

Liberalization and structural adjustment. Similar to the 1980s, the 1990s were equally lost in regard to education: liberalization of education provision saw the increased rise of private schools but also government cuts in spending, declining teaching materials, and poor conditions in schools accompanied by low teacher motivation (Beyani 2013). Cost-sharing was both an emergency response to the economic crisis and an outcome of larger cuts in public expenditure as part of structural adjustment.[1] Policies in the 1990s, drawing on recommendations from the previous decade, sought to transfer material costs (books, pencils, etc.) to parents, leverage boarding fees, expand the role of parent-teacher associations, and further encourage private schools. While communities were already expected to make some contributions to education when feasible, in crisis the government's input declined and, according to policy, "community participation in the provision, management and financing of education should be the rule and not the exception" (Ministry of Education 1992, p. 4). In addition, decentralization was seen as the solution for issues attributed to an overly centralized state, and decentering efforts occurred in conjunction with cost-sharing. District councils were put in charge of fees for education, and parent-teacher associations levied so-called "user fees" to fund day-to-day activities. A lack of building of schools, rampant cost-sharing and cost-cutting measures affected school quality, and the imposition of fees contributed to a reduction in primary school attendance in the 1990s, particularly in rural areas. Those who never attended or dropped out primarily cited costs of education and the long distance to schools (USAID 2005). Rather than increasing access and participation, reforms had decreased the number of children regularly attending school, thus moving backward on universal education goals and setting the stage for the growth of community schools.

There are two narratives about the emergence of contemporary community schools in Zambia: one is an origin story in which a few urban schools led to the establishment of civil society organizations and recognition by the state; the other is the uncharted growth of both urban and remote grassroots rural schools, which operated for a decade outside official record. The first narrative of urban schools, however, is the more commonly accepted history. The concept of community school was credited to Dr. Janice Stevens, who opened a school in the Misisi compound in Lusaka in 1992 (Chondoka 2006). The Misisi Open Community School, along with a few other schools, were the beginning of Zambia Open Community Schools (ZOCS), an organization which continues to directly support schools registered as open schools, but also has advocated for community schools at large.

The alternative story, which explains the fast growth of schools around the country, as a grassroots effort responding to a stagnant, more expensive, and, in some areas, nonexistent education system, has not been adequately explored. DeStefano (2006) cites the HIV/AIDS epidemic as an additional reason for the growth of community schools, as these schools provided a more feasible option for the increasing number of orphans than government schools. These schools were supported early on by a variety of NGOs, including ZOCS, as the "turbulence in the education sector" had prompted both NGOs and communities to independently pursue low-cost options to deliver education to marginalized populations (Frischkorn and Falcolner-Stout 2016, p. 4). While community effort and the bottom-up nature of these schools are lauded and advanced in policy, the voices of the people building these schools are relatively absent.

However, the growth of these schools, mostly at the primary level, is undeniable: in 1996 there were only 38 recognized community schools, constituting only a small proportion of the total schools; in 2005 there were 2,129 community schools, 4,442 government, and 685 private and grant-aided schools (Ministry of Education 2014); by 2015 there were 2,406 community schools, representing almost 30% of all primary schools. There is also a geographic component of these schools: they tended to be set up either in locations with large concentrations of children, sites far from government schools, or in areas with disproportionally high school fees (UNICEF and Ministry of Education 2014).

In general, the 1990s were seen as the decade in which community schools emerged and grew rapidly. On the other hand, sociopolitical conditions related to a change in government gave greater legitimacy to existing community efforts. In the Kaunda era, communities or villages built schools, but this ran against the narrative of central state efforts to engineer solutions to social problems. With multiparty democracy, overlapping themes of liberalization, partnership, community responsibility, and also privatization offered validity to these efforts. Nevertheless, official recognition by the state happened gradually and was negotiated by a variety of state and non-state actors. And most importantly, *how* the state responded to these schools changed considerably over time.

Efforts to Serve a Parallel System. The state response to community schools from 1991 on was heavily influenced by both lobbying from and coordination with civil society organizations. As these schools grew in number, there was an increasing concern about what entity would ultimately coordinate and manage them, as they supplemented the government system by enrolling students and thus increasing access to education but operated beyond its control and outside established standards. This section will look at an attempt to create an "umbrella" organization and efforts to serve community schools as parallel to the government system.

In education policy, there was no mention of these schools until the early 1990s, when they were effectively recognized as operating beyond the state system and considered private schools, at least at the secondary level, where they were expected to charge quite high fees to cover running costs (Ministry of Education 1992). Yet, at this stage the approach of the Ministry of Education was merely exploratory: there was a call to more systematically harness community involvement in response to the education crisis, particularly school building, and to control the quality and supervise community schools but no concrete plans to do such. The first significant effort to address the needs of community schools was taken up by civil society actors, specifically ZOCS. As mentioned, Zambian Open Community Schools (ZOCS) was started in 1992, and it has retained a constant role in supporting and advocating for community schools, to the extent that its history has often been conflated with that of these schools in general. It works directly with schools, providing funding, capacity building for school committees, and training for teachers. While the number of schools associated with ZOCS has grown since its establishment, it only represents a portion of the total schools: in 2003 there were 1,340 community schools, but ZOCS supported 16 mostly around the capital of Lusaka (Carmody 2009); recently the organization supported 520, when the total number was around 3,000 (ZOCS 2017).

Despite its limited role in providing direct assistance to selected schools, one of the main goals of ZOCS is to advocate and lobby for sustainable community schools nationwide. In the late 1990s, ZOCS worked with the government to form the Zambia Community Schools Secretariat (ZCSS), a non-governmental organization funded by UNICEF and others, which was intended to be the only "umbrella organization" for community schools in the country. ZCSS sought to coordinate and manage these schools, while using resources and financial support from the Ministry of Education by working at the national Ministry level and recruiting point people at provincial levels to liaise between the government system and community schools. The secretariat's roles included registering schools by establishing accreditation criteria and collecting data, coordinating with various local and international NGOs working with these schools, and lobbying the government towards channeling resources towards community schools. The organization set up the structure for the democratic core body that manages the school on behalf of the community – the Parent Community School Committee (PCSC). In order to be eligible for any government funding, schools would have to register with both ZCSS and the Ministry of Education; DeStefano (2006) noted how the organization had repeatedly lobbied for a relaxing of the standards for registration, as many schools failed to meet them.

The existence of ZCSS, working parallel to the Ministry of Education, gave credibility to these schools as an important alternative system, which could work in conjunction with the state. Another project which further cast community schools as alternative institutions was SPARK (Skills, Participation, Access to Relevant Knowledge), an abbreviated and practically focused curriculum and teacher training framework. SPARK was developed specifically for community schools under the guidance of UNICEF: it collapsed a seven-year primary curriculum into five years and focused on locally relevant topics, life skills, creative thinking, and problem-solving. The curriculum catered to students who tended to enter education later and leave earlier and emphasized practical skills, including some vocational skills training. Chondoka and Subulwa (2004) note how this curriculum represented a shift in thinking about the purpose of community schools from teaching basic literacy to "mak[ing] the literate child acquire certain practical skills for survival in the community where she/he came from" (p. 13). Yet, while both SPARK and ZCSS sought to address the needs of community-based schools as alternative to the government system, there were tensions in this approach, which emerged in the mid-2000s.

Integrating community schools into a decentralizing system. There were clear challenges in positioning community schools as a parallel and alternative system: in the end, SPARK was supplanted by the national curriculum, and ZCSS was declared defunct, as the state and civil society organizations sought to integrate community schools closer to a decentralized government system. Ultimately, SPARK failed because it represented a further move towards what Cashen et al. (2001) describe as a two-tier and hierarchical system of education, in which community school pupils would be in poor positions to succeed in national Grade 7 exams, and teachers had specific training and credentials which did not translate into employment in the government system. In the end, it was popular voices which contributed to the end of the curriculum: parents were split in their response to SPARK, with educated parents concerned that it would not prepare their children for advancement to Grade 8 and further education. Finally, it was not clear how the curriculum fostered local control: the SPARK manual was relatively inaccessible to teachers and parents, since it was written in English and at an advanced level; in addition, the skills classes intended to connect students with practical vocations were rarely taught or were conducted abstractly without proper materials (Chondoka and Subulwa 2004).

ZCSS had no offices in provinces or districts, and thus existing education officers were established as focal point persons. As this personnel had fulltime positions supporting an already resource-poor government system, relying on them to take up the needs of additional schools was ultimately unsuccessful. In addition, there was lack of coordination and information sharing between private and public partners, and procedures regarding registering schools were "not uniformly followed or interpreted" (Ministry of Education 2007), with some community schools operating for years without the Ministry's knowledge or assistance. Along with these challenges, and other administrative and financial issues, ZCSS was declared defunct in 2007 (Mwalimu 2011), leaving what Frischkorn and Falcouner-Scout (2016) call a "void in national policy and coordination of community schools" (p. 5). Other existing organizations, including ZOCS, directly supported only a portion of the total schools, and the Ministry of Education lacked the resources to directly manage them and has only recently integrated community schools into its processes, including data collection and yearly assessments.

Yet, within this void there was an opportunity to integrate community schools more closely with the decentralized system of government education, although still with some distance. With the demise of ZCSS, there were three programs sponsored by the U.S. Agency for International Development Zambia Mission (USAID/Zambia) supporting community schools. One of these programs (EQUIP2) worked with the Ministry of Education, along with other partners that had supported ZCSS, including ZOCS, Reformed Open Community Schools (ROCS), and CARE International, developed operational guidelines for community schools, which deemed the Ministry responsible for: determining educational needs and demand patterns in establishing schools, grading and registering community schools, and developing procedures for the establishment of these schools. At the same time, they assign communities the core role of managing and financing schools. The guidelines were adopted in 2007 by the Ministry of Education; in addition, all schools were now expected to follow the national curriculum. In 2011, community schools were declared a legal category of schooling, thus making official what had existed de facto for at least a decade, if not more.

The guidelines were "welcomed, albeit cautiously" by various levels of the government system: for some districts, they bolstered support officials already extended to community schools, while others were concerned about maintaining a balance between local control and government support (Chakufyali et al. 2008). In 2016 the operational guidelines were updated through a participatory process facilitated by Time to Learn, a USAID funded program to enhance early grade reading in community schools. Like previous projects, one of the main objectives for Time to Learn was to advocate for increased state support to schools. Along with revising the guidelines, Time to Learn organized a steering committee which in turn conducted two symposia on community schools, drafted an inclusion of community schools in national policy, and lobbied successfully for these schools to be included in the national budget (Falcolner-Stout et al. 2017). The revised guidelines (Ministry of Education 2016b) specify increased government support for community schools, but also confer similar and overlapping responsibility to civil society organizations: the state and civil society, religious, and non-government organizations are responsible for providing infrastructure support, and capacity building for teaching and learning, among others. Teachers, community members, and even learners are increasingly responsibilized to hold their institutions together: learners should "claim [their] right to education by showing interest in learning" and "encourage one another to attend class," while parents, community members, and traditional leaders should support teachers financially or materially as well as mobilize them and offer performance incentives (Ministry of Education 2016b, pp. 20–22). These groups are also given additional roles related to cross-cutting themes found in various education projects and initiatives, such as health and nutrition programs, HIV/AIDS sensitization, and life skills; additionally, there is an emphasis on reading and literacy, connected with the Time to Learn project.

The first operational guidelines noted that at the time there was no need to replace ZCSS coordination, as the guidelines clearly spelled out the roles and responsibilities for both the state and civil society (Chakufyali et al. 2008). However, the updated guidelines in 2016 recommend an umbrella organization separate from the Ministry of Education to manage and coordinate these schools. Until now no such organization exists: instead, there is a patchwork of civil society and NGO organizations and projects targeting community schools, which have sought to strengthen various areas of schools in line with overarching global goals or trends in education development, often overlapping with the state's commitments or providing technical assistance within the Ministry of Education.

Within this current system, a variety of actors seek to balance the responsibility of the state to provide education, along with the democratic value – and cost-efficiency – of local management of schools. However, there are still political debates on whether the government should take over these schools as a whole. This was highlighted in the manifesto of the political party, the Patriotic Front, which ran on a progressive platform in opposition to the MMD government, winning the presidency in 2011. Using strong language to critique the existing system, the original manifesto (Patriotic Front 2011) decried low spending on education, declaring that access to quality education as remaining a "pipedream" for many in the country (p. 3). The party called for the conversion of all community schools into government schools; however, this was backtracked in the most recent manifesto (Patriotic Front 2016), which called only for the "continued upgrading" of some 500 government and community schools which had mud and thatch buildings (pp. 10–11), thus putting on hold any radical plans to overhaul the current parallel system of education.

A parallel approach, which saw government and community schools offering distinct learning opportunities, was supplanted with a balance between state and local involvement in community schools. While this balancing was and continues to be negotiated by non-state actors, specifically NGOs, there are still political tensions around what role the state plays, as well as overlapping and contradictory functions given both to state and civil society actors. State policy in the era of multiparty democracy and liberalization laud the ability of communities to support their own local education systems, drawing on historic ideas of "self-help" but also recasting them in contemporary notions of community participation. However, it is important to understand whether this democratization from below is actually occurring in schools, drawing on studies conducted during the emergence and height of the community school movement.

Limits of Community

While there is a long history of the state calling on community participation to erect school structures in Zambia, contemporary community schools represent an extreme version of both community participation and decentralization. As the previous section explored, the community school is a platform on which a division between state and society can be clearly laid out: a parallel system of education continues to demarcate schools operated by communities and supported to some extent by the state, and those directly managed by the state but reinforced by community involvement. At the same time, education policy points to a cohesive and organized "community" imagined within society by state and civil society policies and programs, and has almost positioned it as the cornerstone of a liberalized and democratic nation. However, it is fruitful to step back and look at how community support for these schools happens. Unlike other community-based schools, which were created to offer an alternative option to existing schools, Zambians built schools out of need, in the absence of existing or affordable government schools, and took on managing and sustaining them seemingly by default. Yet, do communities want to manage schools, and do they have the knowledge and resources to do so? There is evidence from qualitative studies that communities are neither coordinated or knowledgeable enough to properly manage schools, nor would they likely do so in different circumstances.

The first was a study conducted by the University of Zambia on community participation on education, in the midst of the emerging community school movement, commissioned by the World Bank funded Zambia Education Rehabilitation Project (Ngwisha et al. 1995). The findings were starkly contrasted to the policies adopted thereafter: according to the report, most members of the communities interviewed "said they would not like to own schools because they lacked knowledge and resources to do so" (p. 1). Instead, there was a preference to let local experts continue to manage schools, particularly teachers, who themselves saw community participation as compromising their profession, and agreed that communities lacked the capacity to run schools. In addition, the report identified structural issues within education which are rarely the focus of community participation or decentralization efforts: that parents' lack of education may hinder effective school management; hunger of pupils, and the drinking and absenteeism of teachers affect the frequency and quality of learning, along with low salaries and lack of teaching materials; a lack of resources at district level hindered proper supervision of schools. While this study is dated, interviews with district and national officials confirm that these issues are still prominent, even though districts are responsible for monitoring community schools, along with government and other types of schools.

Okitsu (2011) analyzed community participation in both government and community schools and came to similar conclusions: rural parents and communities "frequently lack ability, agency and the spirit of voluntarism," and also saw education as privy to trained professionals (p. ii). In addition, there was a perceived high cost of participation, which many parents felt outweighed the benefits, as volunteering often meant not being able to attend to immediate survival needs. Within enacted forms of participation, there were "micro-power relations" between community members and education professionals, particularly teachers and district officials, which affected how the former could participate in decision making. In addition to these challenges, parents in community schools were tasked with recruiting and sustaining sufficiently qualified teachers, which were difficult to find and even more challenging to remunerate sufficiently to meet their basic living standards. While the Zambia state maintains its education environment is a liberalized and decentralized space of free choice, Okitsu concludes that many parents do not have the geographic or socio-economic resources to exercise this choice, and the center "still holds control over many areas while resources allocated to the local level are grossly inadequate" (p. iii). Both studies speak to notions around community participation: that, despite being empowered within policy, communities encounter real obstacles which hinder their effective involvement in planning, localized curriculum development, and management of schools.

CONCLUSION

The community school movement in Zambia is in stark contrast with rational government projects to engineer society, like Tanzanian efforts at "villagization," analyzed by Scott (1999), in which rural villages were reorganized into cooperative farming units, in order to create self-reliant socialist communities. Instead, the Zambian state's response to community schools developed over time and was guided by lobbying by and support from transnational and national non-government organizations. At first, rural communities built schools, but their initiative ran against the narrative of the central nation-state of the Kaunda era. With the onset of multi-party democracy and liberalization, driven by structural adjustment policies, these schools were in line with global discourses of community participation and cost-sharing, although they were reluctantly recognized by the state. The approach to governing community schools shifted from casting them as a parallel system of alternative education to a cautious balance between local control and state management and coordination, in which schools have been matched along a decentralized public system. However, there is still a significant divide between government and community schools, accompanied by political tensions around the role of the state in supporting education.

The Zambian state has sought to govern community schools at a distance, creating an environment in which willing civil society organizations and bilaterally funded projects can fill in the gap between the state and community-based schools, and citizens are increasingly made responsible for self-provision of education. Following Dill (2013), policies of guidelines, grants to registered institutions, and tactics of registration and inspection outline the political space of education, and the boundaries of power given to community members. However, as this chapter has explored, these boundaries have shifted over time and have been negotiated by both state and non-state actors. The power exercised at the local level is further restrained: first by the expectation that community schools serve as de-facto government schools, following the national curriculum with volunteer teachers and a variety of funding sources; and secondly, by the available knowledge and resources within communities.

Community schools reflect how a contemporary political state can utilize rhetoric both of decentralization and democratization to extend the power of the state into local spaces, particularly remote areas or marginalized populations, areas in which direct governance otherwise would be difficult. The Zambian state was able to gradually take over the community school movement, making the schools official and centering itself in a role that Dale (2007) terms the "coordinator of coordination" (p. 34). By doing so, it has allowed the nation to move significantly towards goals of providing access to education (Ministry of Education 2014), while minimizing the active role of national and regional offices. Currently the national Ministry of Education does not have an office or desk dedicated to community schools and instead relies on civil society organizations, like ZOCS, to lobby for and support schools. The state has increased government funding for these schools, but it is not clear that this amount enables communities to upgrade their infrastructure to meet standards, pay for qualified teachers, or supply teaching and learning materials without imposing undue cost on parents.

The Zambian case is compelling because, out of economic and educational crisis, the resulting outcome has many of the traits lauded by advocates of decentralization and privatization in education: community schools lower costs of infrastructure by having parents construct their own schools, but more importantly also reduce the reoccurring human resource cost by utilizing volunteer teachers. The schools are locally managed and are supported by a variety of sources via public-private partnerships, thus reducing the cost and the active role of the state. Through managing this schools at a distance, the Zambian state has also enacted the principles of its education policy of liberalization (Ministry of Education 1996): it maintained its role as "the custodian of the human rights of all individuals, including their right to education," yet in order to foster democratization has created an "enabling environment" (p. 3), in which private or civil society provision has become a norm rather than exception. However, these schools also serve as a cautionary tale, as an extreme form of decentralization and devolution of providing and financing education: while a bottom-up approach created basic centers for learning in remote areas and for previously marginalized children, it is not clear whether communities can overcome significant obstacles and democratically run quality institutions without continuous support from NGOs and the state. In addition, community schools serve as an example of how decentralization, despite operating with a discourse of democratization, can often reproduce existing inequalities and in the case of Zambia result in parallel yet incommensurate systems of education.

REFERENCES

Abrams, Philip. (1988). "Notes on the Difficulty of Studying the State." *Journal of Historical Sociology, 1*(1), 58–89.
Andersson, Per-Ake, Arne Bigsten, & Hakan Persson. (2000). *Foreign Aid, Debt and Growth in Zambia*. Uppsala: Nordiska Afrikainstitutet.
Beyani, Choolwe. (2013). *Zambia: Effective Delivery of Public Education Services*. Johannesburg: The Open Society Initiative for Southern Africa.
Carmody, Brendan. (2009). *The Evolution of Education in Zambia*. Lusaka: Bookworld Publishers.
Carnoy, Martin. (1999). *Globalisation and Educational Reform: What Planners Need to Know*. Paris: International Institute for Educational Planning/UNESCO.
Cashen, Liz, Greg Elacqua, Edward Gometz, Shumbana Karume, Katya Nadirova, Ema Naito, & Nadja Schmeil. (2001). *Educating Children out of the System: The Community Schools Movement in Zambia*. Lusaka: UNICEF.
Chakufyali, Peggy, Jane Chinobwe, & Judith Oki. (2008). *USAID/Zambia Assistance to Strengthen Ministry of Education Support to Community Schools*. Lusaka: USAID.
Chondoka, Yizenge A. (2006). *Situational Analysis of Community Schools in Central Province of Zambia*. Lusaka: Government Printers.
Chondoka, Yizenge A., & Charles Subulwa. (2004). *Evaluation of the SPARK Curriculum in Community Schools in Zambia, 2000–2004*. Lusaka: UNICEF.
Dale, Roger. (2007). "Globalization and the Rescaling of Educational Governance: A Case of Sociological Ectopia." In Carlos Alberto Torres & António Teodoro, eds., *Critique and Utopia: New Developments in the Sociology of Education in the Twenty-First Century* (pp. 25–42). Lanham, MD: Rowman & Littlefield.
DeStefano, Joseph. (2006). *Meeting EFA: Zambia Community Schools*. Washington, DC: EQUIP2.
Dill, Brian. (2013). *Fixing the African State*. New York, NY: Palgrave Macmillan.
Falcolner-Stout, Zachariah J., Rebecca Frischkorn, & Lynne Miller Franco. (2017). *Time To Learn Endline Evaluation Report*. Rockville, MD: Encompass LLC.
Frischkorn, Rebecca, & Zachariah J. Falcolner-Stout. (2016). *Ensuring Inclusive and Quality Education for All: A Comprehensive Review of Community Schools in Zambia*. Rockville, MD: Encompass LLC.
Glassman, Deborah, Jordan Naidoo, & Fred Wood. (2007). *Community Schools in Africa: Reaching the Unreached*. Boston, MA: Springer US.
Hoppers, Wim. (2005). "Community Schools as an Educational Alternative in Africa: A Critique." *International Review of Education, 51*(2–3), 115–137.
Kelly, Michael J. (1991). *Education in a Declining Economy: The Case of Zambia, 1975–1985*. Washington, DC: Economic Development Institute of the World Bank.
McGinn, Noel F., & Thomas Welsh. (1999). *Decentralization of Education: Why, When, What and How?* Paris: UNESCO.
Midgley, James, Anthony Hall, Margaret Hardimann, & Dhanpual Narine. (1986). *Community Participation, Social Development and the State*. London: Methuen.
Miller-Grandvaux, Yolande, & Karla Yoder. (2002). *A Literature Review of Community Schools in Africa*. Washington, DC: USAID.
Ministry of Education. (1992). *Focus on Learning*. Lusaka: Zambia Ministry of Education.
Ministry of Education. (1996). *Educating Our Future*. Lusaka: Zambia Ministry of Education.
Ministry of Education. (2007). *Operational Guidelines for Community Schools*. Lusaka: Zambia Ministry of Education.
Ministry of Education. (2014). *Education for All 2015 National Review*. Lusaka: Zambia Ministry of Education. Retrieved from http://unesdoc.unesco.org/images/0023/002317/231725e.pdf
Ministry of Education. (2016a). *2015 Educational Statistical Bulletin*. Lusaka: Zambia Ministry of Education.
Ministry of Education. (2016b). *Operational Guidelines for Community Schools*. Lusaka: Zambia Ministry of Education.
Mitchell, Timothy. (1991). "The Limits of the State: Beyond Statist Approaches and Their Critics." *The American Political Science Review, 85*(1), 77–96.

Mohan, Giles, & Kristian Stokke. (2000). "Participatory Development and Empowerment: The Dangers of Localism." *Third World Quarterly, 21*(2), 247–268.

Mwalimu, Michelle Chama. (2010). "Alternative Primary Education and Social Stratification in Resource-Scarce Countries: Theoretical, Substantive, and Methodological Debates." *Educate, 10*(1), 6–18.

Mwalimu, Michelle Chama. (2011). "Access, Quality, and Opportunity: A Case Study of Zambia Open Community Schools (ZOCS)" (PhD dissertation). Michigan State University, East Lansing, MI.

Mwanakatwe, John M. (2013). *The Growth of Education in Zambia Since Independence*. Lusaka: University of Zambia Press.

Ngwisha, John, Chosani Njobvu, & Jolly Kamwanga. (1995). *Education Policy Studies Study on Community Participation*. Lusaka: Zambia Education Rehabilitation Project.

Okitsu, Taeko. (2011). "Policy and Practice of Community Participation in the Governance of Basic Education in Rural Zambia" (PhD thesis). University of Sussex, Brighton. Retrieved from http://core.kmi.open.ac.uk/download/pdf/2710693.pdf

Patriotic Front. (2011). *2011–2016 Manifesto*. Lusaka, Zambia: Patriotic Front, Office of the Secretary General.

Patriotic Front. (2016). *2016–2021 Manifesto*. Lusaka, Zambia: Patriotic Front, Office of the Secretary General.

Scott, James C. (1999). *Seeing Like a State: How Certain Schemes to Improve the Human Condition Have Failed*. New Haven, CT: Yale University Press.

Snelson, Peter. (1990). *Educational Development in Northern Rhodesia 1883–1945* (2nd ed.). Lusaka: Zambia Educational Publishing House.

The World Bank. (2017). *World Bank Open Data*. Retrieved March 20, 2017, from http://data.worldbank.org/

UNICEF, & Ministry of Education. (2014). *Global Initiative on Out-of-School Children, Zambia*. Lusaka: UNICEF/Ministry of Education.

USAID. (2005). *DHS EdData Education Profile: Zambia 1992, 1996, 2001, 2002*. Lusaka: USAID.

ZOCS. (2017). *Zambian Open Community Schools (ZOCS)*. Retrieved June 18, 2017, from http://zocs.kabilibranding.com

---

NOTE

1. The previous Kaunda government had its first structural adjustment program with the International Monetary Fund (IMF) in 1983 but was eventually considered a "non-reformer," as the government adopted seven different programs, none of which were seen to completion (Andersson, Bigsten, and Persson 2000).

REBECCA CLOTHEY AND DEANNA HILL

8. BUILDING A COMMUNITY-BASED CHARTER SCHOOL IN THE UNITED STATES

INTRODUCTION

Ten years ago in a large urban district in the northeast of the United States, a Spanish medium global studies charter school was founded by a group of parents who felt the district schools could not serve their children's needs. Today, the school has grown to a population of 800 students from across 40 zip codes within the city and is considered among the best schools in the city. The school is not a traditional district school, nor is it a private school. Rather, the school is one of more than 6900 public charter schools that serve more than 3.1 million students (roughly 6 percent of the more than 50 million public school students) in the U.S. (National Alliance for Public Charter Schools 2017).

In its mission the school describes itself as a community-based school. As Kai Heidemann and Rebecca Clothey explain in the introduction to this book, community-based schooling initiatives typically operate so as to position citizens as both architects and benefactors. In this case, a group of parents conceived of and created the school, and some sent their children to the school. Further, as a charter school, its very existence was made possible by state law allowing non-governmental actors to start and operate schools for the public. That some scholars have questioned the "public" nature of charter schools (see, e.g., Green, Baker, and Oluwole 2015; Miron and Nelson 2002) is not an uncommon phenomenon for community-based schools. As Heidemann and Clothey (2018) also state in this volume, community-based schools often occupy an "ambiguous and thus contentious institutional niche within national educational systems which challenge traditional boundaries between the 'public' and 'private' sectors" (p. 1).

There is a well-developed body of literature on charter schools. We know a lot about the types of schools and students served (see, e.g., CREDO 2017; Miron et al. 2010, The Civil Rights Project at Harvard University 2010), and there is an ever-expanding body of empirical research on the academic performance of charter school students (see, e.g., CREDO 2015, 2013; Mathematica 2010a, 2010b). While there is research on charter school policy, most studies focus on how policy has impacted the growth and consumer-driven demand for charter schools (Ericson & Silverman 2001; Gill et al. 2006). Few studies consider the supply side of the equation in terms of who creates charter schools and why (but see Cowen, Fleming, and Gofen 2008; Fuller 2000; Rofes and Stulberg 2004). And yet, better understanding school founders and their motivations is key to understanding the policy intervention of charter schools – especially as it relates to providing opportunities not being provided (or not being provided equitably) by the traditional public school system.

The purpose of our study was to better understand how and why one school's founders used charter school policy to develop a community-based school located in the center of the city in which it was eventually situated, and which was designed to provide their diverse community of learners with an intellectually-stimulating curriculum with a bilingual curriculum and global focus. Our primary concern in this project is the intersection at the macro-level of public policy with the micro-level agency and practices of actors who are working to promote the development of community-based schools. Our primary research questions were thus as follows:

1. What motivations drove the group to develop its community-based school?
2. How did policy enable the group to develop its community-based school?
3. What challenges did the group face in developing its community-based school?

These questions aimed to elicit an understanding of the broader policy processes influencing the practices of those actors behind community-based schools, the motivations and agency of the actors, and how individuals were defining 'educational opportunity' on their own terms.

The researchers utilized a case study design as proposed by Robert Yin (2009) as a means by which to understand a complex social and organizational phenomenon. Yin (2009) suggests that case study design is a valuable approach when trying to "contribute to our knowledge of individual, group, organizational, social, political, and related phenomenon" (p. 4). The case study 'triangulates' multiple methods of investigation (Merriam 2009), drawing from school and city policy documents and interviews with stakeholders. The documents include: monthly meeting minutes of the School's Board of Trustees, two School expansion proposals submitted to their school district, School District hearing minutes, and the school's curriculum documents.

Structured open-ended interviews were conducted with founders of the case charter school. All interviewees were recruited using a snowball sample. This served to establish a greater level of trust between the researcher and those being interviewed, as the researchers were introduced to participants only through mutual acquaintances (Creswell 2013). Specifically, the researchers had one acquaintance who was among the original founding school members. That acquaintance introduced the researcher to other founding members, each of whom also provided the contact information for others. In the end we were able to interview nine out of ten founding members. The tenth member chose not to participate in the study.[1]

BACKGROUND: CHARTER SCHOOLS AND CHARTER SCHOOL POLICY

Charter schools have existed for more than a quarter of a century. Minnesota was the first state to pass a charter school law in 1991, and there are now charter school laws in all but six states (Montana, Nebraska, North Dakota, South Dakota, Vermont, and West Virginia). Most states with charter laws passed them in the 1990s. Just eight of the states with charter laws passed them in 2000 or later (Alabama, Iowa, Kentucky, Maine, Maine, Maryland, Tennessee, and Washington). The state in which our site resides was one of the states to pass its charter school law in the mid-1990s.

Many education historians situate the charter school movement within reform efforts that began in the 1960s and 1970s, including site-based management, school choice, privatization, and community schools. However, the term "charter" was first used by educator Ray Budde in a 1974 paper, and it was published in his 1988 book *Education by Charter: Restructuring School Districts* to describe a model district where teachers received charters. According to education historian Diane Ravitch (2016), Budde saw charter schools as freeing teachers. His idea was to allow teams of teachers to receive short-term charters (3–5 years) in which they would have complete autonomy over curriculum and instruction.

Referencing Budde's idea, Albert Shanker, then President of the American Federation of Teachers used the language of the "chartered school" when he gave a speech at the National Press Club where he suggested groups of teachers be given charters to set up new schools within existing schools where they could then innovate. According to Ravitch (2016), Shanker had similar ideas toward the goal of allowing teachers to identify and utilize strategies to engage unmotivated students.

In essence, both Budde and Shanker saw the innovation as freeing teachers from regulations that prevented them from trying and doing things they believed would better serve students. Similarly, Philadelphia, one of the earlier cities with charter schools, started some "schools within schools" that it called "charters" in the 1980s, and early advocates saw charters as a "supply side" reform that would provide "research and development" laboratories for the public school system. Today, charter schools are governed by state laws that provide for some differences from traditional public schools, but also important similarities.

While charter schools are generally considered as public schools, their legal status is complicated because charter schools contain both public and private characteristics (Green, Baker, and Oluwole 2015). Like traditional public schools, they are publicly funded and open to all. However, they differ from traditional public schools in that they operate under a contract (the charter agreement) that captures how they will be organized, managed, and held accountable. They operate free from many of the laws and regulations that apply to traditional public schools, so they have more authority over operational decisions like budget, staffing, curriculum, and instruction. In addition, most charter schools require an application process to enroll.

The charter school movement has its roots in the "early" decentralization efforts of the 1980s. As Kenneth Saltman (2010) explains, the decentralization efforts of the 1980s took the form of administrative decentralization and community control, with administrative decentralization shifting decision-making down to lower units (e.g., principals, teachers) while retaining accountability at the top (e.g., district, local board of education) and community control shifting both decision-making and accountability to the local community. However, despite the potential for more local control of educational decision-making, Bruce Fuller (2000) also points out that charter school policy does not address the underlying causes of educational inequality. Instead, it risks resegregating students along economic and racial lines, as families "choose" charter schools as alternatives to their local district school (Fuller 2000). This takes students out of the district public schools through a process of self-selection.

Charter schools are ultimately responsible for their students' achievement and may be closed for failure to meet agreed upon outcomes. The mix of deregulation and accountability is often referred to as the charter bargain where charters are provided more autonomy or freedom from regulation in exchange for increased accountability. The ultimate consequence for poorly performing charters is revocation or nonrenewal of the charter—resulting in closure. While closure was rare in the earlier years, it has become more common in the last decade (CREDO 2017).

Charters are held accountable to their charter by their authorizers. Authorizers are entities the charter law designates to approve charter applications and provide ongoing oversight for charter operations. Today, there are six types of authorizers: school districts, state education agencies, higher education institutions, not-for-profit organizations, independent chartering boards, and government (e.g., the mayor in Indianapolis, the City Council in DC). Some states allow for multiple authorizers while others give that authority only to local school districts. Most states allow for appeal while more than a handful do not. In the state in which our site is located, the law provides for multiple authorizers, including the school board, two or more school boards, and the state department of education. The law also provides for an appeals process. If the authorizer denies the application, the organization may appeal to a charter school appeals board whose decision is binding on all parties. The charter law provides charter schools with a blanket waiver from most district regulations. The exceptions are regulations that apply specifically to charter schools, as well as civil rights, health and safety, and accountability regulations.

At the time of our study, there were two types of charters in this state: local brick and mortar charters authorized by a single school district, and regional brick and mortar charters authorized by more than one school district. The state provided a funding formula for districts to follow. The funding formula is based on the past years' expenditures but includes a number of deductions. According to state documents, this ends up being, on average, around 70% of the cost per student who remains in the traditional public school (with a range from 52–80%).

Some states limit or cap the number of charters that can be authorized. Some set a total number, some set a number before a certain date, and some set a number per year. According to the National Association of Charter School Authorizers (2015), 90% of all authorizers are school districts, and school districts authorize 53% of all charter schools. The particular northeastern state in which our site is located does not place a cap on the number of charter schools in the state. This is significant because the authorizer may approve as many (or as few) charters as meet the criteria and need not consider factors such as overall number of charters that may be granted.

State laws also tell us who can start charter schools. Some states limit charters to non-profits and/or non-religious entities. Our state is open to charters started by individuals; one or more teachers planning to teach at the proposed charter school; parents or guardians of students planning to attend the charter school; any nonsectarian college, university or museum located in the state; any nonsectarian not-for-profit corporation; any corporation, association or partnership; or any combination thereof.

Two-thirds of charter schools are single, independent, non-profit organizations. Such schools are sometimes referred to as "singletons" or "mom and pops" schools (CREDO 2017). Approximately one-fifth of charter operators operate more than one school. The terminology for these schools varies and is not consistent in the literature. For example, some use Charter Management Organization (CMO) to denote organizations that hold charters for multiple schools, regardless of whether they are for-profit and non-profit entities. Others distinguish non-profit and for-profit status by using CMO for non-profits and Education Management Organization (EMO) to denote for-profit entities. Both CMO and EMO should be distinguished from Vendor Operated Schools (VOSs) where the entities do not hold the charters but provide management services to multiple schools for a period of time on the basis of a contract (CREDO 2017).

Importantly, charter schools are schools of choice. Students are not assigned to them (as they may be assigned to traditional public schools), but must apply to them. Thus, the idea is that parents vote with their feet so that, in a competitive market, demand determines which schools survive (Miron and Nelson 2002). Parents also have more choices, theoretically providing a more democratic process for enrolling in public schools. Yet if more students apply than there are available spaces, then the charter school must select students via a lottery process, which is entirely dependent upon luck. Some states also allow certain preferences (for example, for siblings of children already enrolled), which narrows the number of available spots in any given charter school even further.

The school of this study was one of the first charters in the city. We have not studied charters that emerged later. Additionally, the school preceded the entrance of large EMOs and CMOs into the charter market for the city. The impact of the evolution of the market is beyond the scope of this study.

FINDINGS

Motivations

The charter school of this study was founded by a group of parents with children who would be entering an urban district school in the coming years. This fact bonded the parents who founded this school together and was one of the drivers for initiating their own charter school. Indeed, one of the motivations for starting the charter school of this study, mentioned by all of the people we interviewed, was a negative perception of the school district in which they lived. As one founder put it:

> There were all sorts of scare stories in the media, and I remember specifically seeing that where our house was ... the catchment would have put us into school where I think the published reading scores was that 99% of the children in the school were not reading at grade level. I didn't think too much about what that meant; I just knew that it probably wasn't an option for my kid. So I went into parenting and living in the city assuming that I was going to have to figure something out. (Interview 1)

And another:

> I teach in [this city], and I'm a product of public school in [this city]. That being said, I wasn't really happy with all of the choices ... I didn't feel that the choices were optimal for me and for my kids. So we decided to explore other avenues.... (Interview 7)

Interviewees also expressed dismay at seeing friends with school-aged children leaving the city in favor of the suburbs, and feeling a civic duty to keep parents of school-aged children from leaving the city's school system. The words of several founders illustrate this:

> [W]e actually wanted to create a school that would help to keep people in the city, because we love living in the city and we wanted to live in the city, and we didn't want to keep seeing this happen so partly it was audacious it seems like in a way, you could create something that could actually do that and keep people from moving out of the city. But we also wanted a place for our kids to go, and we also really wanted a public school, we wanted what everything that a public school means. (Interview 2)

Another explained:

> We wanted to be able to create a top quality school to keep families in the city. We observed that a lot of families would be in the city when they are young until their kids grow up to school age and then they'd leave. So one of the reasons was simply to try to create an excellent school that would be a magnet for parents with young kids to stay in the city and improve the community. (Interview 3)

One individual further elaborated that it wasn't only about creating a good public school option that would keep families in the city. They hoped they could improve public education more generally by gathering experts and other people from the community. They viewed charter school law as giving them that opportunity (Interview 3).

Interestingly, while all of the founders shared a dream of creating a "good" school, there was no consensus among the founders about what a "good school" would look like. Several of the founders had a specific goal of creating a school with an emphasis on foreign languages or bilingual education, which was not something offered at the time in their school district. However, there was a lot of dispute among the founders about whether a foreign language education emphasis, and particularly a bilingual or foreign language immersion program (which was also proposed) would be a good idea. Charter schools need students in order to run, and many of the founders did not think that they would be able to attract students with a language immersion program.

Another founder who had worked as a teacher in the school district joined the founders in their vision for a "good" school because he wanted to create a school that was good for teachers. This point is interesting because critiques on charter schools often note that they tend to provide fewer benefits and lower salaries for teachers than traditional district public schools do. They also often prevent teachers from organizing into unions, which is viewed by some as giving teachers less ability to voice their rights within the organization (see e.g., Kahlenberg and Potter 2014; Rofes and Stuhlenberg 2004). This founder was aware of those critiques and included provisions within the original charter (e.g., salary steps) that were specifically designed to attract and retain good teachers (Interview 6).

The founders all agreed it was the possibility of starting a school that was public that brought them together. None of the founders had been interested in starting a school that was not public. As one founder told us: "…we were very committed to the idea … of public education as a concept, so it never occurred to us to start another independent school" (Interview 1). Another remarked that "[t]here was no other way to open a school," and that the idea became possible only after the charter school law passed (Interview 2). Another founder explained that the charter school law gave them the motivation to start a school. In his words:

> Part of the idea was that it would be public education. I think we all felt that part of the motivation was this public spirited thing and we wanted to be like a public school and open to everybody. If it were a private school and everybody had to pay 20 thousand dollars to go it would defeat the purpose of what we were doing. (Interview 3)

These comments reflect democratic ideals shared by these founders as a motivator for starting their charter school.

Challenges

While the founders were highly motivated, opening the school was not without challenges. These included practical challenges as well as some interpersonal challenges within the group dynamic. In some cases, the line between practical and interpersonal was blurred.

For example, just as creating a good school was noted as one of the driving factors, it was also noted as a challenge. This was mainly because the group had different ideas about what a "good" school would look like. Although the founding Board was comprised of predominantly white and upper middle class Americans, one founder described the diversity of their background as an obstacle in coming to consensus on the "ideal" school. As one put it: "we had many different types of people with many different cultures and many different backgrounds and many different educational backgrounds. So the formation of the ideal took a little while" (Interview 7).

Another individual who had grown up in the city described the difficulty as being that many of the Board founders were from outside of the city, and they were "presenting different ideas and different processes to educate children" that he did not necessarily believe would work in the city. He described their ideas as being "pie in the sky" (Interview 6). Others also confirmed that "narrowing down what an ideal school would look like was a huge challenge" (Interview 7). As one person elaborated:

> What it would be, how we would utilize the resources around us, how we would choose to instruct the children, really philosophical issues a lot of them came into play. There were a lot of arguments and disagreements before we all came to consensus about what we want. (Interview 7)

Likewise, the founders did not agree on the curriculum. As one interviewee explained:

> For me, one of the biggest obstacles was getting everyone on board with the bilingual program. I immediately knew this was what I wanted to have in the school. (Interview 5)

This contradicts assumptions that founders may be driven by a common desire to establish a particular type of curriculum, which was also our assumption when we began the study.

Navigating the political environment within the district was complex and also presented a number of challenges. First, the application process was highly politicized. As one founder told us:

> [W]e were very aware that in those days this process of getting a charter ... wasn't necessarily just going to be on the merits of the application itself. It was going to be a highly politicized process that if there was a charter application being submitted by the wife of a city council member or the wife of a sitting state senator you can be fairly sure that the application was going to be approved regardless of what was in it. (Interview 1)

At one point the group applied for and received a planning grant, with which they were able to hire a consultant who knew the education landscape and who helped them write the charter school application. That consultant told them "it doesn't matter how beautiful your dreams are if you don't work politics in the city" (Interview 1). In short, the likelihood of getting a new charter approved apparently had less to do with the merits of the school design, and more to do with what type of political connections they had.

Second, the district as authorizer was concerned about the impact of charter schools. Though the state had passed the charter school law that allowed individual entities to apply for charters to open schools, the district – as the authorizer – was skeptical. As one interviewee explained: "The school board I think at the time and probably still to some degree and not without reason, perceived charter schools as a threat" (Interview 3). This was bothersome because the founders, most of whom considered themselves liberals, found themselves on the opposite side of the political fence from many of their friends. One person described having very mixed feelings about proposing a charter school at all. As he stated:

> I felt almost like I was betraying the [city] public school system ... between trying to fix a system that was broken as a civic minded person from [this city], or listening to external voices of concern. I also had concern about taking money away from an already sinking public school system in [this city], of not trying to address the concerns ... And what that would present as challenges to those people who were left in that system, the [city's] public school system. (Interview 6)

Third, while the group considered themselves diverse and representative of a community, when they applied to the city's school board for approval of their charter application, they were declined initially. As one individual explained this:

> I think the school board saw us as kind of this group of white people who were trying to create a school for white people and had no idea what the challenges were in the city, and that we were naïve ... we were asked the question what will you do when your student body doesn't look just like you do? So that there was sort of this attitude, like you are this group of white people and you are trying to educate African American, or other minorities, and you don't know what you're doing, you don't know what you're getting yourself into, which was true in terms of the composition of who we were, but certainly wasn't true in terms of what we wanted, expected, or hoped. Certainly we understood what we were doing, we were trying to create a school for everyone. But that I think was an obstacle for us, and I think was one of the main reasons we were turned down. (Interview 3)

Another similarly explained that the lack of racial mix of the Founders was an obstacle in getting their charter approved:

> We were mostly white, mostly affluent. We did have some minority people involved, but just the nature where we got together [at the park], those were just the people [who] got together. Later on we became much [more] diverse, but I think the initial founders' group was not. (Interview 3)

Thus, despite the democratic idealism shared by the Founders and enthusiasm for creating a 'good' public school for everyone, the Board remained skeptical of their intentions.

Furthermore, the district – as authorizer – was dynamic. Before the charter applications were approved, School Board membership had changed, and the new Board was perceived as not positive toward charter schools, and even as seeing charter schools as a threat (Interview 3). Whether it was because of the changes to the Board or for other reasons, the Board missed their own deadline for when decisions about new charters were to be made. However, with a lawyer among them, the group knew they could immediately appeal to the state for a decision, which they received. Still, the application, like so many others, was denied. They eventually appealed the decision and ultimately were approved based on a technicality—that the Board had initially missed their own deadline for making approvals. It was a time consuming process that also impacted their ability to get the school up and running before the start of the school year.

As one founder reflected:

> I guess those legal challenges and the political challenges at the time were almost insurmountable. I can imagine that a lot of groups ... if we hadn't had a pretty amazingly talented lawyer on our group who did all that work pro bono, if we would have to hire someone, there is no way we would have had the money to hire a lawyer to navigate that. (Interview 1)

Finding and financing a suitable location also turned out to be an obstacle for multiple reasons. Founders told us that "finding a kid-friendly elementary school location is difficult" (Interview 4). Some opposition came because people thought certain areas were unsafe, and they needed to find a space where parents would be willing to send their children. However, real estate (i.e., procuring an appropriate building for a school) is a big challenge for charter schools mainly because charter school law does not provide funding to procure real estate, and there is only "a teeny bit of money that the state passed that allows for the support of leases—it's very minimal and it's a long process" (Interview 4). Thus, money to finance real estate often comes from private sources.

Yet securing private financing in this case depended upon having an approved charter – something that, for the founders, was delayed by their appeal. As one interviewee described:

> [T]here was no money to buy a building or anything until you started receiving funds, so, and you couldn't contract or get anything until you knew if you are approved. Because we appealed we actually didn't get our charter approved until July of 2000, so there was no way we could open in September of 2001 ... we still were scrambling at the end. (Interview 2)

Enablers

The biggest enabler was the charter law. The charter law provided the mechanism through which the group would start a school that would be public. Without the charter law, the only way for the group to create a school would have been to create a private school. Interviewees stressed that they were in no position to start a private school and that the appeal of starting a charter school was that it would be a public school.

Another big enabler was the planning grant. The planning grant was around $25,000, a percentage of which paid for a consultant who helped write the planning grant, and, once the grant was received, guided the process for submitting the charter application. The planning grant also allowed the group to travel to other states in order to observe programs with the features they were considering.

The background of the consultant was also an enabler. The consultant had experience in and ties to the district, which gave him insight into what would be novel in the district as well as where and how to make political connections.

Another major enabler was the group's own cultural and social capital. Members brought law degrees, education degrees, knowledge of curriculum-related topics, experience as teachers, and one member brought experience with curriculum at a charter school in another state. The group also had the skill to do research and market themselves, and they had access to the necessary equipment and materials. For example, the group had access to legal databases and the internet at a time when those resources were only available to a select group of professionals.

Likewise, the group had connections to lawyers, politicians, district insiders, etc. These connections allowed the group to negotiate the complex legal and political landscape and save money. As one interviewee explained when they were starting to renovate the future school building:

> Because some of our backers were politicians who were very closely tied to labor unions ... we had to worry about whether we are going to use all labor union work, or could we get a better deal if we didn't, but would that piss off some of the politicians who were supporting us? It was a little complicated, but we were able to get that done, without ruffling anybody's feathers, and without having to pay through the nose for the renovation. (Interview 5)

DISCUSSION AND CONCLUSION

As described, the founders were a group of predominantly white and affluent young people with children entering or about to enter the education pipeline. They had negative perceptions of their neighborhood schools but also saw themselves as supporters of public schools. Fuller (2000) asks whether charter schools advance people's faith in public schools, or whether they erode the ideals of the common school by taking people out of traditional public schools? The Founders in this story wanted to stay in the city and keep others like them from moving to the suburbs in search of better public schools.

The founders were also challenged by a number of circumstances. Specifically, while they agreed they wanted to start a "good" school, they did not agree on what the curriculum for a "good" school would be. Much of their disagreement was on whether full immersion would work for all students. Also, they were predominantly white and affluent. While this contributed to their social and cultural capital, it hindered them before the school board, which perceived them as not reflective of the city's student body, and therefore uninformed (or ill-informed) about the needs of children in the city. This is paradoxical, as community based schools are by definition created by and for the communities they serve. In this case, the founders wanted to create a public school for all, representing a broad democratic vision; however, the profile of most of the founders did not resemble the broader population of the city. Furthermore, they perceived themselves as liberal supporters of public education and found the charter school law to enable them to start a school and support it as public. However, they learned over time that they were perceived by some of their peers as being on the other side of the fence from public school supporters. In addition, they recognized that establishing a charter school would inevitably take children who chose to attend it (and the accompanying financing) out of traditional public schools—presenting a dilemma in their support for public education. They also realized in retrospect that many of their city's public schools were much better than they had known at the time that they opened their school, which also contradicts their vision of themselves as supporters of public education.

What enabled their success was a charter school law that presented itself at the right time, as well as their social and cultural capital. Specifically, the charter school law was passed at a time when this group of people had a common interest in seeking to provide what they believed would be a better public school than the ones available to them and their neighbors. They obtained and strategically used a $25,000 planning grant to pay for a consultant who was well-connected in the district and to travel to schools for curriculum ideas. They also had access to the technology and materials available to the members who were also professionals. Additionally, they had on their team the legal knowledge and talent to translate an authorizer's failed timeline and denial into successful appeal.

Thus the group persevered despite challenges, and ultimately relied on its enablers to ensure success. They were motivated to start a charter school at the right time and for what they perceived to be the right reasons. In the end, they accomplished their goal to provide another public school option for the city's children.

The findings contribute to a growing body of research on community-based charter schools and the decentralization of education policy (Astiz et al. 2002) that has resulted in the emergence of school spaces where alternatives to mainstream public schooling are increasingly found. The founders took advantage of a law that allowed a group of community members united only by motivation to start a public charter school in the city. Without the charter school law, the founders would not have started a school at all. They used the charter school law because it allowed them to do what they wanted, not because they were pro-school choice or even pro-charter. In this way, charter school policy can in fact be seen as a successful means for promoting democratization and local community control.

On the other hand, the founders were able to overcome a number of challenges that might have prevented others from proceeding. The most significant of these was the fateful timeline and denial of the charter by the district, followed by a successful appeal obtained by the lawyer member pro bono. What we learn from this example is that even with policy that is open to anyone, there are obvious constraints on who can be successful. While the policy provided opportunity for all, ultimate success was dependent upon the cultural and social capital of the founders. Likewise, while the group was initially questioned on its white elitism, the social and cultural capital that came with it ultimately enabled them to open the school. Thus, while charter school policy is often touted as a way to provide local families and citizens with increased forms of access, voice and influence in the education system, through increased "choice," in fact it is likely that such a policy only allows increased 'choice' for some.

The Civil Rights Project at Harvard University (2010) states that "choice programs can either offer quality educational options with racially and economically diverse schooling to children who otherwise have few opportunities, or choice programs can actually increase stratification and inequality depending on how they are designed." The School of this study eventually became considered as among the best in the city and because of demand now has a lottery process to get in. With fewer than ten new seats available for first grade children each year (due to sibling preferences), this school becomes an available option only for some. While the Founders remain proud of the quality school they had a voice in shaping, their vision to create a school that would provide a 'good' education for everyone has in reality become a good school for everyone who can get in.

REFERENCES

Astiz, M. Fernanda, Alexander Wiseman, & David Baker. (2002). "Slouching towards Decentralization: Consequences of Globalization for Curricular Control in National Education Systems." *Comparative Education Review, 46*(1), 66–88.

Center for Education Reform. (2014, December). *Survey of America's Charter Schools 2014*. Retrieved from https://www.edreform.com/2014/01/survey-of-americas-charter-schools/

Center for Research on Education Outcomes (CREDO). (2017). *Charter Management Organizations*. Retrieved from http://credo.stanford.edu/pdfs/CMO%20FINAL.pdf

Center for Research on Education Outcomes (CREDO). (2015). *Urban Charter School Study*. Retrieved from http://urbancharters.stanford.edu/summary.php

Center for Research on Education Outcomes (CREDO). (2013). *National Charter School Study*. Retrieved from http://credo.stanford.edu/documents/NCSS%202013%20Final%20Draft.pdf

Cowen, Joshua M., David J Fleming, & Anat Goten, (2008). "Measuring the Motivation to Charter: An Examination of School Sponsors in Texas." *Journal of School Choice, 2*(2), 128–154.

Creswell, John. (2013). *Qualitative Inquiry & Research Design: Choosing Among Five Approaches* (3rd ed.). London: Sage Publications.

Education Commission of the States, (2016, January). *Charter Schools – Does the State Provide Direct Facilities Funding or Other Facilities Assistance to Charter Schools?* Retrieved from http://ecs.force.com/mbdata/mbquest2rte?rep=CS152324

Ericson, John, & Debra Silverman. (2001). *Challenge and Opportunity: The Impact of Charter Schools on School Districts*. Retrieved from http://www2.ed.gov/rschstat/eval/choice/chart_index.html?exp=0

Gill, Brian, Laura S. Hamilton, J. R. Lockwood, Julie A. Marsh, Ron Zimmer, Deanna Hill, &

Shana Pribesh. (2004). *A Decade of Entrepreneurship in Education: A Look at Edison Schools' Improvement Strategies and Their Effect on Student Achievement.* Santa Barbara, CA: RAND Corporation.

Green, Preston C., Bruce D. Baker, & Joseph Oluwole. (2015). "The Legal Status of Charter Schools in State Statutory Law." *University of Massachusetts Law Review, 10,* 240–276. Retrieved from https://ssrn.com/abstract=2560896

Fuller, Bruce, ed. (2000). *Inside Charter Schools: The Paradox of Radical Decentralization.* Cambridge, MA: Harvard University Press.

Kahlenberg, Richard D., & Halley Potter. (2014). *A Smarter Charter: Finding What Works for Charter Schools and Education.* New York: Teachers College Press.

Mathematica. (2010a). *Student Characteristics and Achievement in 22 KIPP Middle Schools.* Retrieved from http://www.kipp.org/mathematica/print/1

Mathematica. (2010b). *The Evaluation of Charter School Impacts.* Retrieved from http://ies.ed.gov/ncee/pubs/20104029/pdf/20104029.pdf

Merriam, Sharan. (2009). *Qualitative Research: A Guide to Design and Implementation.* San Francisco, CA: Jossey-Bass.

Miron, Gary, & Christopher Nelson. (2002). *What's Public about Charter Schools? Lessons Learned about Choice and Accountability.* Thousand Oaks, CA: Corwin Press, Inc.

Miron, Gary, Jessica Urschel, William J. Mathis, & Elana Tornquist. (2010). *Schools without Diversity: Education Management Organizations, Charter Schools, and the Demographic Stratification.* Available online at: http://nepc.colorado.edu/publication/schools-without-diversity.

National Alliance for Public Charter Schools. (2016). *Estimated Public Charter School Enrollment 2016–2017.* Retrieved from http://www.publiccharters.org/wp-content/uploads/2017/01/EER_Report_V5.pdf

National Association of Charter School Authorizers. (2015). *State of Charter Authorizing 2015 Report.* Retrieved from http://www.qualitycharters.org/research-policies/archive/state-of-charter-authorizing-2015/

Ravitch, Diane. (2016). *The Death and Life of the Great American School System: How Testing and Choice Are Undermining Education.* Philadelphia, PA: Basic Books.

Rofes, Eric, & Lisa Stulenberg. (2004). *The Emancipatory Promise of Charter Schools: Toward a Progressive Politics of School Choice.* Albany, NY: State University of New York.

Saltman, Kenneth J. (2010). *Urban School Decentralization and the Growth of Portfolio Districts.* Boulder and Tempe: Education and the Public Interest Center & Education Policy Research Unit. Retrieved from http://epicpolicy.org/publication/portfolio-districts.

The Civil Rights Project at Harvard University. (2010). *Choice without Equity: Charter School Segregation and the Need for Civil Rights Standards.* Retrieved from https://www.civilrightsproject.ucla.edu/research/k-12-education/integration-and-diversity/choice-without-equity-2009-report

Yin, Robert K. (2014). *Case Study Research: Design and Methods.* London: Sage Publications.

NOTE

1. This research was made in possible in part by a Faculty Research Grant from Drexel University's School of Education. The authors are grateful for the support, and for the help of the research assistants who transcribed the interviews but wished not to be identified by name.

REBECCA CLOTHEY

9. AN ALTERNATIVE EDUCATION MODEL IN URUMQI

In a classroom in a private English language training center in the south of Urumqi, the capital city of China's northwestern Xinjiang Uyghur Autonomous Region, a child raised his hand and asked a question. In classrooms throughout the world, this is not unusual. However, what is unusual for this location is that the child asked his question in Mandarin. Certainly, as Mandarin (i.e., *Putonghua*) is the lingua franca of China, and Xinjiang Uyghur Autonomous Region is recognized as a part of the People's Republic of China, one might not be surprised to hear Mandarin spoken there. Yet, the students in this particular English class are Uyghur, one of China's 55 officially recognized ethnic minority groups, and their mother tongue is Uyghur, a Turkic language that utilizes an Arabic script. It is therefore notable that the student is using his second language, Mandarin, to ask a question to his teacher, a native Uyghur language speaker. This scenario reflects a concern among many Uyghurs that their language and culture are being eroded by a decrease in Uyghur language instruction in formal schooling, in favor of an increased emphasis on Mandarin (Dwyer 2005; Strawbridge 2008; Smith Finley 2013; Clothey 2016).

This chapter considers a set of language schools founded, managed and run by Uyghur educators and entrepreneurs and supported by the Uyghur community. As such, they are identified in this chapter as 'community schools.' Uyghurs are a majority ethnic group within Xinjiang Autonomous Region in northwest China. However, they are a Muslim ethno-linguistic minority group across China, where Han Chinese are the dominant ethnic group and Mandarin is the language of instruction.

While the case of the schools in this chapter is somewhat unique, a decentralization of education policy in China that follows worldwide trends (e.g. Astiz et al. 2002; Carnoy and Rhoten 2002) has resulted in the emergence of a school space where alternatives to mainstream public schooling can now be found. This chapter examines the unique facets of these schools by exploring the context in which these English Language Training Centers have emerged and the ways in which Uyghur educators and entrepreneurs have capitalized on the decentralization of the public sector to support Uyghur employment, community development, and cultural transmission.

Much of the scholarship on ethnic minority education in China proposes that state-sponsored education has a negative impact on the ethnic identities of minority students (e.g., Grose 2010; Hu 2012; Clothey and Koku 2016). Diya Hu (2012) finds that modern schooling in ethnic minority regions of China has to some extent alienated the educated from their own history and tradition rather than facilitated the transmission of their ethnic minority culture. As she conveys, those cultural aspects that are not integrated into the formal school curriculum and thus approved institutionally are devalued by the 'cultural capital' of the formal school curriculum (Hu 2012). Studies also show that curricular and media representations of ethnic minorities in China tend to be through a Han perspective, and convey ethnic stereotypes (Grose 2010; Zhao and Postiglione 2010; Feyel 2015). However, what is not frequently considered in the literature is that those ideologies that derive from the state and are disseminated within state schools may not necessarily persist outside of the classroom, where state ideology might be challenged (Grose 2010; Clothey and Koku 2016). In fact, minority groups may find alternative methods through which to facilitate cultural transmission, if traditional methods are hindered (Mchtirajan and Reisenzein 2014). Communities may also appropriate policy to serve their own cultural transmission aims (see e.g. Heidemann 2014). In this chapter, I examine a set of privately managed schools representing a process of policy-appropriation by an ethnic minority group to serve their cultural transmission aims. These schools are community-based in the sense that they are run by members of one community, in this case, the Uyghur ethnic group in Urumqi, and they are specifically designed to meet the economic and cultural needs of that same community within the political context in which they are situated.

The discussion is based on fieldwork conducted in Urumqi during the fall of 2013, during which time I was a visiting scholar at a university in Urumqi, and the summer of 2015, during which time I returned to Urumqi for follow-up research.[1] Data for this chapter is drawn from in-depth interviews conducted with Uyghur managers, owners of English training centers, and teachers as well as classroom observations at training centers while I was in Urumqi. To supplement the data and triangulate information generated through the interviews and observations, document analyses were also conducted of relevant Chinese national and Xinjiang provincial government education policy documents, as well as promotional brochures and curriculum materials from Uyghur-run English language training centers. Due to rapidly changing policies in Xinjiang, the findings described here are particular only to the time period prior to 2015.

The chapter will first provide an overview of the social and policy context within which these training centers emerged; it will then describe the unique features of these training centers. The discussion concludes that these centers provide employment opportunities for Uyghurs who might otherwise be marginalized from the mainstream Chinese economic system of Xinjiang, as well as arguably facilitate cultural transmission and maintenance. However, they also reproduce and maintain Xinjiang's ethnic segregation, thus making China's goal of ethnic integration ever elusive.

BACKGROUND

Uyghurs, Urbanization and Migration in Xinjiang

Xinjiang Uyghur Autonomous Region is located in China's far northwest and its capital city, Urumqi, is more than 3,100 kilometers west of Beijing. Government supported economic development and migration, which has contributed to Urumqi's growth as an urban center within Xinjiang, are among the factors leading to the emergence of Uyghur-run English Language Training Centers in Urumqi.

In order to bridge economic disparities between prosperous eastern and underdeveloped western China and facilitate some economic development, in 2000 the country undertook a 'Western Development Program' (*xibu da kaifa*), in which government funding is allocated to western areas of China. As part of the western development program, the government has made considerable investment in Xinjiang's infrastructure, creating jobs and as a result also attracting migrants (Howell and Fan 2011). In fact, Nicholas Bequelin (2000) describes the migration of Han Chinese settlers into Xinjiang as an intentional Chinese government effort to advance development, reduce ethnic separatism, and promote stability, thereby better integrating Xinjiang with the rest of China.

As a result of migration and also a relatively high birth rate among ethnic minorities, the region's population has grown rapidly in recent decades, and also significantly changed the ethnic composition of Xinjiang's overall population (Bequelin 2000). Whereas in 1945, Han people comprised only 6.2 percent of Xinjiang's total population compared with 82.7 percent of Uyghurs, today the Han population encompasses 38.06 percent of Xinjiang's overall population, compared with 47.30 percent of Uyghurs (Bequelin 2004; Leibold and Deng 2016). In 2010, the number of Han and Uyghurs in Xinjiang was, respectively, approximately 8.4 million and 10 million (Xinjiang Statistical Yearbook 2010).

However, despite the relative diversity, the region's population tends to be ethnically segregated, and there continues to be economic disparity across regions. Approximately 90 percent of the rural population live in southern Xinjiang, where 73 percent of Uyghurs in Xinjiang also reside. Furthermore, the GDP is higher in almost every district in which the Han population is larger than the Uyghur population. Therefore, Uyghurs in Xinjiang are more likely to come from rural areas, and are more likely to be poor than are Han (Chaudhuri 2010).

Urumqi is the largest city of Xinjiang and its capital, as well as a hub between China and Central Asia. As such the city is uniquely positioned within Xinjiang to promote international business opportunities and forge ties with other nationalities across the borders. Consequently, Urumqi attracts a large number of migrants of different ethnicities and origins, both from within Xinjiang and other parts of China, and it is also diverse compared to some other areas of Xinjiang (Howell and Fan 2011). Foreign language skills in Urumqi are therefore a valuable asset. Approximately 72.5 percent of Urumqi's population of 2.88 million people is Han, while Uyghurs are 12.8 percent (Xinjiang Statistical Yearbook 2010). However as elsewhere in Xinjiang, the city tends to be ethnically segregated, with Uyghurs living predominantly south of the city's 'south gate' (南门) and Han Chinese living north of it. In fact, James Leibold and Danielle Xiaodan Deng (2016) claim that Uyghurs are one of the most segregated ethnic minority communities in the world.

There is also a relatively high rate of unemployment among Uyghurs in the formal economy, as compared with Han people in Xinjiang (Bequelin 2000; Ma 2009; Grose 2010; Smith Finley 2013). Some scholars suggest that unemployment of Uyghurs is due to their low proficiency in Mandarin Chinese (i.e., *Putonghua*) as compared with the Han, who speak Mandarin natively (e.g., Howell 2013; Ma 2009). However, others propose that the unemployment is due at least in part to discriminatory policies (Bequelin 2000; Grose 2010) and the influx of Han migrants competing for the available jobs (Beller-Hann 2002; Howell 2013). Certainly the surge of Han settlers into Xinjiang has increased the necessity for Mandarin language skills in the formal economy. At the same time, the perceived inability of Uyghurs to find employment within the formal economy creates a demand for alternative means of earning a living.

Education Policy and Uyghurs in Xinjiang

Just as using Uyghur language has been identified as a challenge for Uyghurs trying to find employment, it has also been noted as a challenge for educating Uyghur students (see e.g., Chen 2008; Ma 2009; Clothey 2016). Uyghur and Mandarin are from two different language families and are not mutually intelligible. However, currently most schools throughout China, even in ethnically and linguistically diverse areas, use Mandarin (i.e., *Putonghua*) as their primary medium of instruction. Although minority languages of China are protected by the Chinese constitution, the government and commerce of China primarily functions in Mandarin and the majority of government-run agencies (e.g., schools, universities, banks, etc.) within Xinjiang therefore also privilege Mandarin (Clothey 2016).

Language policy choices in education are important, as they help shape the patterns of language use among children (Kymlicka and Patten 2003). Since 2004, there has been an increased emphasis on Mandarin language instruction in Xinjiang at the expense of Uyghur. The stated aim is to help linguistic minority students improve their grasp of Mandarin and thus their potential job prospects (Liang and Zhang 2007).[2] However, maintaining minority culture and language while also integrating Uyghur students into a mainstream Mandarin Chinese language system is a continuing challenge (Beckett and MacPherson 2005; Dwyer 2005; Strawbridge 2008; Leibold and Chen 2014; Tsung 2014).

Moreover, English has also become more valued throughout China as a bridge to the global economy (Sunuodula 2015). English classes have gradually replaced minority language classes in the curriculum for Han students in Xinjiang. However, for linguistic minority students who must spend time in school learning Mandarin as a second language, the opportunities to learn foreign languages have been limited. In addition, most national English language curriculum materials in China are written in Mandarin and English and do not utilize minority languages (Chen 2010; Sunuodula and Feng 2012; Tsung 2014). Hence, in many cases learning English through formal schooling in China depends on first developing strong Mandarin language skills.

Some scholars have thus suggested that as English language education expands in China, inequities between minority people and the majority Han also widens (Beckett & MacPherson 2005; Sunuodula and Feng 2011).

DECENTRALIZATION AND POLICY FOR THE OPENING OF NON-STATE RUN SCHOOLS

Neo-liberal policies, in which state withdrawal from the public sphere is promoted in favor of privatization and localization, spread worldwide through the 1980s and 1990s (Astiz et al. 2002). China similarly began to introduce market forces and devolve centralized government control into the planned economy in the late 1970s (Mok 2003; Clothey 2012), encouraging private investment and foreign trade, and promoting new opportunities for private businesses to open. At the same time, increased foreign investment also led to the notion that English was important. A reform in educational structure since the mid-1980s enables the legal possibility to open *minban* (non-state) schools in China, resulting in the emergence of different types of schools, and which cater to different needs of Chinese citizens. *Minban* schools include self-learning schools, training schools, supplementary learning schools, and continuing learning colleges initiated by people from local communities (Mok 2006).

Across China, non-state non-degree granting schools (also referred to as 'training centers') have opened to offer services such as TOEFL, GMAT or GRE prep, computer training, foreign language education, etc. The law thus enabled an increase in the options available for studying English language outside of the state-run school system, as more than 50,000 companies and individuals set up private English language training centers across China to meet the high demand, which is now a $4.8-billion dollar industry (Deloitte 2012).

The regulations for opening and operating training centers vary according to province and district. In Urumqi, the "Urumqi Non-State (民办) Non-Academic Education Schools Implementation Rules," published in 2007, provide specific guidelines for obtaining a license to open a center there. Since this time, in Urumqi, the options for learning English privately have ranged from classes offered at branches of nationally recognized franchise centers (e.g., 'English First', 'New Oriental,' and 'Crazy English'), to smaller, lesser-known centers (e.g., 'Pumpkin English'). However, except for those classes taught by foreigners, these branches generally offer English classes using Mandarin as the medium of instruction. For this reason, some Uyghur entrepreneurs and educators in Urumqi recognized an opportunity to offer foreign language courses using *Uyghur* as the medium of instruction, and they began opening privately-run English language centers soon after the non-state education law was passed. Thus, the demand for foreign language and the opportunity to teach it in the mother tongue converged with the policy shift. Below is a description of some of the unique features of these Uyghur run English language training centers and why they are significant. The examples provided are described as an aggregate of several centers, in order to maintain the anonymity of the individuals involved in running them.

UYGHUR RUN ENGLISH TRAINING CENTERS IN URUMQI

Clientele

All of the 'training centers' run by and for Uyghurs are located south of Urumqi's south gate. Because most Uyghurs (and few, if any Han) live south of Urumqi's south gate, this location is significant for attracting Uyghur clientele. However, with a great deal of competing centers in Urumqi, it is necessary for centers to actively recruit students. Though the larger centers have more resources to put toward publicity, all of the centers that I explored actively used social media, particularly WeChat (威信), a popular Chinese mobile text and voice messaging communication service, to publicize their courses. Whereas the Urumqi-based branches of the larger nationally recognized centers advertise their courses in Mandarin with some English, the local Uyghur-run centers also used Uyghur language (Interview 10/23/2013). In fact, the use of Uyghur language for advertising at any of the Uyghur-run Centers clearly indicates that they are catering to a Uyghur clientele, as Uyghur is a language not widely spoken among non-Uyghurs.

All centers advertise and recruit from a similar potential pool of students among the Uyghur population. Classes might consist of children whose parents wish them to get supplemental English language classes on weekends, or college students who need to pass exams, or migrants to Urumqi from other parts of Xinjiang, who see English as a way to expand employment options.

The centers not only cater specifically to Uyghur clientele but also employ Uyghurs. Unlike the Urumqi-based branches of nationally recognized centers, most frequently, the majority of teachers employed by the local Uyghur-run centers are also Uyghur. The legally registered training centers, which have more resources, are also able to hire a small number of foreigners.

Current policy requires that education entities hire teachers under 2 year contracts. Thus, larger centers pay teachers' monthly salaries according to the dictates of a legal employment contract. Having more resources, such centers are also able to employ some native English speaking staff. Despite this, the majority hire mostly Uyghur teachers and administrative staff with only a very small percentage of foreign teachers. This is in part due to the higher cost of hiring foreign nationals and also the challenges of recruiting qualified foreign teachers to Urumqi. Though occasionally Han people are also hired as employees, it is often in the capacity of lawyers to interpret and negotiate government policy or occasionally to teach Chinese.

Smaller centers have fewer resources and are not always able to hire staff on a contractual basis, but they also have fewer employees. Instead, these centers often have more flexible approaches to staffing and salaries. They may pay teachers an hourly fee, per the number of students they teach, share profits, or some combination. For example, in the per pupil model, teachers recruit their own students and are paid a percentage of the profits per student in each class taught. The remainder is paid to the center owner. This approach motivates teachers to recruit students for the center, but also allows teachers to keep their classes small if they so desire (Interview 11/12/2013). In other cases, individual teachers may pay a permit owner to use their space but then keep the revenue earned from the student tuition themselves.

Teachers who work at the centers report several benefits as compared with working for state-run schools. First, they report that their incomes are higher than what they might be paid were they teaching within one of Xinjiang's public schools (Interviews 6/25/2015 and 6/29/2015). This is especially true in larger centers where full-time employment and a steady contract are offered. However, because of the per pupil payment approach elsewhere, some teachers are also able to work at the centers part-time while also maintaining other full-time jobs, or to teach at more than one locale. Some centers also allow teachers to make their own teaching schedules. Teachers reported an appreciation for the flexibility and the additional income that working in a training center afforded.

In addition, class sizes tend to be smaller than those in public schools. Teachers who had worked in the public schools prior to employment at a training center noted having 50–60 students in their English classes in public schools, as opposed to 20 or less at the training centers (Interviews 10/11/2013 and 6/25/2015). Training center classes that I observed had no more than 12 students. Some training centers also offer "VIP" one-on-one classes, which are usually for higher paying clientele. Furthermore, as training center courses are optional and require tuition fees, students usually attend because they want to learn. Training center teachers also noted this as a big difference from the public schools. One person I interviewed left her full-time position as an English teacher in a public school in Urumqi to teach at a private, Uyghur-run English Training Center because of the better conditions. As she explained: "I had 60 students in my classes at the No. [X] Middle School. It didn't matter if some of them had studied English before; I still had to start with A, B, C because that was in the textbook. And the students didn't care about learning English. They didn't pay any attention. They just slept in class. I asked them why they don't care. They said they don't need English for the [high school entrance] exam" (Interview 6/23/2015). In fact, one training center teacher I spoke with interviewed all of his students before accepting them into his classes. He did not accept any student who did not seem genuinely interested in learning English (Interview 6/23/2015).

In sum, the centers allow for attractive employment options not available through the formal Chinese-run economy, for both the staff that is hired to teach in the centers, and the people who manage and run them. It is worth noting, however, that the salaries afforded at Uyghur-run English training centers may be lower than those at the private Chinese-run English language training centers. A question might therefore be whether Uyghur English teachers would prefer to teach at Chinese-run

English training centers if they were given the opportunity. However, such an opportunity would require teaching in Mandarin. The informal economy emerges when there are fewer employment opportunities in the formal sector (see, e.g., Park and Cai 2011). Thus these English language training centers provide employment alternatives for Uyghurs in Urumqi.

Curriculum

Because the training centers are privately operated and they are not degree issuing, they can be somewhat flexible with their curriculum. However, textbook options are limited to what can be found within Xinjiang. Some centers allow teachers to select their own textbooks for their courses, rather than designate an assigned text.

As the centers must compete for students, they must also differentiate themselves through unique curricula offerings. The owner and operator of one larger center single-handedly wrote and published five volumes of English language textbooks, levels 1–5, used in all of that center's courses. These textbooks were written in English and Uyghur, and drew from material that is culturally relevant to the Uyghur students. The books also used phrases and sounds familiar to Uyghurs to make English sounds more accessible to beginners (Interview 10/19/2013).

An example from an early lesson of the first book helps Uyghur students to practice reading English words. In the lesson, students are given a clue and then asked to identify the person to whom the clue refers. A sample clue is thus:

Read and choose the name of this famous star:

This singer isn't Turkish. She's Uyghur. Her parents are from Kazakhstan. She's a singer and an actress. Her songs aren't all in English. They're in Uyghur, Russian, Kazakh, and English. Who is she?

Jennifer Lopez. B. Sean Stone. C. Dilnaz Ahmadieva. D. Russell Crowe.

(Center A English Textbook, Book 1, Unit 3)

It is likely that even without much knowledge of Uyghur culture, a westerner could easily identify the correct answer, Dilnaz Ahmadieva, who is a Uyghur singer and actress from Kazakhstan. Joanne Smith Finley and Xiaowei Zang (2015) describe how Uyghurs in Urumqi align themselves to the Pan-Turkic world by listening to Central Asian and Turkish music and buying Turkish brands, while simultaneously stressing distance from Beijing by ignoring Chinese pop culture and products. This is illustrated in the fact that no Chinese cultural figures are mentioned in the examples, despite Uyghurs being surrounded daily by Han Chinese culture.

Other excerpts from the textbooks also reflect how the curriculum is relevant to not only the Uyghur perception of pan-Turkism but also pan-Islamic identities. For example, the excerpts below refer to a popular Muslim singer from England, and a Turkish actor, respectively.

Reading. Listen and Practice.

Sami Yusuf is a British singer, song-writer, composer, producer and musician. He is 33 years old. He is very popular among young Muslims around the world. His third official album, "Wherever You Are" is very famous. (Center A Textbook, Book 1 Unit 4, Lesson 8)

Reading: Born in 1979. Listen and Practice.

Born in 1979, Murat Yildirim was a Turkish actor. He is from Konya, Turkey. He is Turkish. He is 34 years old. His TV series, "*Fırtına,*" (A Storm), "*Aşk ve Ceza"* (Love and Punishment) and "*Suskunlar"* (Sleepers) are very popular. (Center A Textbook, Book 1, Unit 5, Lesson 9)

As these excerpts show, the course materials are designed to be culturally relevant. This differentiates them from materials used at the Urumqi-based branches of nationally-recognized English training centers, which use a standardized curriculum, written in Mandarin and designed for Han Chinese students.

Up until 2017, the textbooks described above also had accompanying .mp3 files available for free download at the center's website. For those who wished to further explore the English language, the center's website also offered online English language lectures, and English videos and music, with some Uyghur narration added. Daily English idioms (with Uyghur explanation) were also available by subscription via the center's website or social media.[3] Students could thus access these English language-learning materials without Mandarin fluency, which they would need in other English classes in China.

Even in courses using English textbooks with Mandarin translations, however, there were other features that differentiated them from the Chinese-run English centers during the period of time that I explored them. For example, classes were conducted primarily using Uyghur language except at more advanced levels, where more English was used. Nevertheless, during my classroom observations of English classes at the Training Centers, I observed that no matter in which language the textbook was written or the class was conducted, Uyghur children often took notes using Chinese characters. This supports concerns of Uyghur parents who have noticed that with the decrease in Uyghur language instruction in state-run schools in favor of an increased emphasis on learning Mandarin that Uyghur children are often no longer able to read and write in their mother tongue (Dwyer 2005; Strawbridge 2008; Smith Finley 2013; Clothey and Koku 2016). Thus, my observation that students took notes using Chinese characters was a likely reflection of the students' greater comfort level using Mandarin in academic settings. In spite of this, the teachers I observed *required* students to ask their questions using either English or Uyghur, not Mandarin (Field notes, October 2013; Interview, October 2013). In fact, at least one Uyghur-run English language training center was well known among local Uyghurs for their explicit policy of using only Uyghur or English in all of their classes.

Community Resource Centers

In addition to offering English classes, some of the larger centers in Urumqi also served as community centers, offering various entertainment and other activities for the local Uyghur community. In fact, supporting and serving the Uyghur community was a common motivation stated by all of the center owners and managers that I spoke with for opening and working in the training centers in the first place.

One person who opened a training center started out by offering free English courses to make them available for people who could not afford to pay. He said he was motivated to educate people in his community. In his words: "People ask me why I don't leave this place. They say there is nothing but dirt here. I say to them: 'why not try to make this dirt cleaner?' I want to improve this place" (Clothey 2016, p. 136).

Another individual who opened a center articulated his specific aspiration to preserve the Uyghur language through his center because he had observed that Uyghurs were no longer learning the language through formal schooling. However, as he explained, though he started out offering Uyghur classes, officials asked him to discontinue doing this soon after ethnic riots in Urumqi in 2009. He then started offering English language classes, using Uyghur as the language of instruction (Interview Nov. 2013).

These language training centers also served as community centers by hosting parties to celebrate Uyghur holidays and talent shows, supporting local cultural talent with performances by Uyghur dancers or musicians and thus promoting pride in Uyghur culture.

Some centers also held a monthly lecture series by local Uyghurs who had gone abroad. According to one manager, the goal for these lectures was to promote studying abroad among the Uyghur community learning foreign languages, thereby building capacity. As he said, "These lectures provide information [Uyghurs] don't know how to find" (Interview December 8, 2013). Some centers also held fundraising events within the Uyghur community to help other less fortunate Uyghurs. For example, a large one was held shortly after an earthquake in southern Xinjiang where the center manager organized it because he felt he had a responsibility to help people from his community (Interview notes 12/8/2013).

Similarly, an English language teacher who started out working in a center before branching off on her own explained her motivation: "I wanted to open a training center to help Uyghurs learn their own language, because too many Uyghur children are learning only Chinese [i.e., Mandarin] and their parents do not have time to teach them Uyghur" (Clothey 2016, p. 136). Her goal was to eventually also offer classes in English about Uyghur culture, to help preserve the culture while also teaching English language. She also expressed a responsibility to help her community. As she put it, "we can do something for ourselves to make this place better. If we teach the children well, maybe they can do something to make this place better" (Clothey 2016, p. 136).

Some centers also add on other services as needed by the community. These may include, for example, Mandarin language classes, computer training classes, and other vocational classes on demand.

DISCUSSION AND CONCLUSION

With Urumqi's rapid growth and the accompanying increase in migration of various ethnic groups and particularly Han people, Mandarin has become a more valued commodity within the formal economy. As non-Han, non-native speakers of Mandarin, Uyghurs are thus finding it more difficult to compete for formal employment opportunities. At the same time, many Uyghurs also perceive that their own language and cultural traditions are being further marginalized by current education policies. In this climate, the emergence of Uyghur-run English language training centers serves several purposes: (1) It provides an alternative employment route for educated Uyghurs outside of the formal economy, and (2) it provides a mechanism through which language and cultural maintenance can occur.

It is not coincidental that a Uyghur market for private English language learning emerged in Urumqi, which is Xinjiang's largest and capital city, a city of migrants, and a potential hub to forge international business opportunities across China's borders. These Uyghur-run language centers would not have as much potential to succeed in areas outside of Xinjiang where there are fewer Uyghurs to attract as clients, or even in other parts of Xinjiang where there might not be as much demand for foreign language skills.

The centers hire Uyghurs, providing alternative employment opportunities in Urumqi for Uyghurs to those available through the formal economy. Non-state run training centers have facilitated the emergence of an employment niche for Uyghurs that is outside of the public sector, and Uyghurs are less dependent on having strong Mandarin skills to participate than they would likely be in the public sector. This finding is supported by scholarship that proposes that learning English can promote empowerment within minority communities, rather than perpetuate further inequality (e.g., Vaish 2005; Zhao 2010; Sunuodula and Feng 2011; Sunuodula 2015). It is also similar to findings by Jennifer Lee (2002) that ethnic minority businesses provide alternative employment opportunities to immigrants, even if there are limited options in the general economy.

In addition, despite increasingly limited opportunities within mainstream public schools to study Uyghur language formally, the implementation of the non-state non-degree education policy in China has enabled Uyghurs to find another means for maintaining language facility by opening privately operated *English* training centers, using Uyghur as the medium of instruction.

One might ask, if Uyghurs are keen to promote Uyghur language learning, then why not open a *Uyghur* language training center? As described, it is likely that Uyghur entrepreneurs avoid opening "Uyghur language training centers" to avoid political problems. However, it is also true that there is more of a market among

Urumqi Uyghurs for learning English, as many Uyghurs see learning the language as a way to level the playing field with Han people, for whom English is also a foreign language (Sunuodola 2015). Furthermore, some of the English training centers do in fact also offer Uyghur classes, though these tend to be less popular.

While the centers described here do not specifically specialize in teaching Uyghur, their use of Uyghur to teach an English language curriculum and to advertise services ensures a Uyghur clientele and Uyghur employees. It also affords Uyghurs the possibility of learning English without first developing Mandarin fluency – an option that is not available in the public school system or in the larger Chinese-run nationally recognized English training center branches in Urumqi. Uyghur students who choose to enroll in the Uyghur-run centers for classes do so *because* they are Uyghur-run and they offer a curriculum with Uyghur instruction.

At some centers Uyghur language use is explicitly promoted as a tool to teach English, while in other cases teachers make policies requiring students to use Uyghur and not Mandarin in their own classrooms. In addition, many of the larger training centers serve as community centers that provide entertainment and additional services specifically for local Uyghurs. Thus, to some extent these centers may facilitate Uyghur language maintenance, and further cultural preservation aims (see e.g., Vaish 2005; Baker 2011; Mchtirjan and Reisenzein 2014; Clothey 2016). As Colin Baker (2011) observes, networked small and medium-sized businesses developed by language minorities are essential for preserving local languages.

In many cases, the owners of such centers are also well-known and well-respected within the Uyghur community prior to opening their center; this also attracts Uyghur students. Examples include a center operated by a popular Uyghur musician, a center operated by a Uyghur newscaster, and a center operated by a Uyghur who placed in a nationally televised English-speaking contest.

Nevertheless, in December 2013, the government of Urumqi announced that they were temporarily suspending the approval procedures of non-state schools in order to get rid of "several unqualified institutes" that had gone around legal procedures ("Temporary," December 5, 2013, para. 1). Indeed, in the summer of 2015 I returned to Urumqi and discovered that some of the training centers that I had explored in fall of 2013 were no longer in operation. However, some of the smaller centers, run out of private homes and offices, were. Yet, as recently as 2018 I was informed by insiders that most of the existing officially registered Uyghur run English language training centers had also closed down due to the more restrictive political environment in Xinjiang currently. While the current number of entities known by locals as 'training centers' is difficult to estimate, it is probable that this avenue of potential alternative employment for Uyghurs has been narrowed considerably.

At their peak, these centers contributed to a Uyghur-run and supported economic system that was almost completely separate from that of the public sector run by the Chinese state. They were similarly on the fringes of the Chinese-dominated private sector (Harlan and Webber 2012). Thus, such Centers provided opportunities for Uyghurs who might otherwise be marginalized from the mainstream Chinese economic system of Xinjiang, as well as arguably facilitated cultural transmission and maintenance. While these schools remained private and non-degree granting, they represented the only means for the local community within a non-democratic political structure to have voice in the implementation of their educational curriculum. In this sense, decentralization and market reforms in China allowed for democratic processes in educational control, albeit subtle and outside the mainstream public system.

On the other hand, they also presented a policy dilemma for the Chinese government, as these training centers also reproduced and maintained Xinjiang's ethnic segregation. Segregation can help protect ethnic minority cultures, but it can also marginalize such communities from mainstream society (Leibold and Deng 2016). Despite this fact, narrowing the possibilities for opening these types of centers as has occurred in recent years may serve to further marginalize and frustrate Uyghurs, many of whom are already disappointed in the Chinese government. Thus it is paradoxical that decentralization may provide Uyghurs more opportunities for a voice in education, while at the same time potentially further serving to marginalize them.

REFERENCES

Astiz, M. Fernanda, Alexander Wiseman, & David P. Baker. (2002). "Slouching towards Decentralization: Consequences of Globalization for Curricular Control in National Education Systems." *Comparative Education Review, 46*(1), 66–88.

Baker, Colin. (2011). *Foundations of Bilingual Education and Bilingualism* (5th ed.). Clevedon: Multilingual Matters.

Beckett, Gulbahar H., & Seonaigh MacPherson. (2005). "Researching the Impact of English on Minority and Indigenous Languages in Non-Western Contexts." *TESOL Quarterly, 39*(2), 299–307.

Bequelin, Nicolas. (2000, July). "Xinjiang in the Nineties." *The China Journal, 44*, 65–90.

Beller-Hann, Ildiko. (2002). "Temperamental Neighbors: Uyghur-Han Relations in Xinjiang, Northwest China." In Gunther Schlee, ed., *Imagined Differences: Hatred and Construction of Identity* (pp. 57–81). London: Palgrave Macmillan.

Bequelin, Nicolas. (2004, June). "Staged Development in Xinjiang." *The China Quarterly, 178*, 358–378.

Bonacich, Edna, & John Modell. (1980). *The Economic Basis of Ethnic Solidarity: Small Business in the Japanese American Community*. Berkeley, CA: University of California Press.

Carnoy, Martin, & Diana Rhoten. (2002). "What does Globalization Mean for Educational Change? A Comparative Approach." *Comparative Education Review, 46*(1), 1–9.

Chaudhuri, Debasish. (2010). "Minority Economy in Xinjiang – A Source of Uyghur Resentment." *China Report, 46*(1), 9–27. doi:10.1177/000944551004600102

Chen, Yangbin. (2008). *Muslim Uyghur Students in a Chinese Boarding school: Social Recapitalization as a Response to Ethnic Integration*. Lanham, MD: Lexington Books.

Chen, Yangbin. (2010). "Boarding School for Uyghur Students: Speaking Uyghur as Bonding Social Capital." *Diaspora, Indigenous, and Minority Education: Studies of Migration, Integration, Equity, and Cultural Survival, 4*(1), 4–16.

Clothey, Rebecca. (2012). "Globalization, Decentralization And Equity: Post-Secondary English Language Policy in China." In Clementina Acedo, Don Adams, & Simona Popa, eds., *Quality and Qualities: Tensions between Global and Local in Education Reforms. Comparative and International Education: A Diversity of Voices Series* (pp. 163–182). Rotterdam, The Netherlands: Sense Publishers.

Clothey, Rebecca. (2016). "Community Cultural Wealth: Uyghurs, Social Networks, and Education." *Diaspora, Indigenous and Minority Education: Studies of Migration, Integration, Equity, and Cultural Survival, 10*(3), 127–140. doi:10.1080/15595692.2015.1111205

Clothey, Rebecca, & Elena McKinlay. (2012). "A Space for the Possible: Globalization and English Language Learning for Tibetan Students in China." *Asian Highlands Perspectives, 21*, 7–32.

Clothey, Rebecca, & Emmanuel Koku. (2016). "Oppositional Consciousness, Cultural Preservation, and Everyday Resistance on the Uyghur Internet." *Asian Ethnicity, 18*(3), 351–370. doi:10.1080/14631369.2016.1158636

Deloitte. (2012). *Reflections on the Development of the Private Education Industry in China*. Retrieved December 16, 2017, from https://www2.deloitte.com/content/dam/Deloitte/cn/Documents/technology-media-telecommunications/deloitte-cn-tmt-reflectiondevelopment-private-edu-ind-en-160412.pdf

Dwyer, Arienne. (2005). *The Xinjiang Conflict: Uyghur Identity, Language Policy, and Political Discourse*. Washington, DC: East-West Center.

Feyel, Janina. (2015). "Representations of Uyghurs in Chinese History Textbooks." In Joanne Smith Finley & Xiaowei Zang, eds., *Language, Education and Uyghur Identity in Urban Xinjiang* (pp. 114–132). New York, NY: Routledge.

Grose, Timothy. (2010). "The Xinjiang Class: Education, Integration, and the Uyghurs." *Journal of Muslim Minority Affairs, 30*(1), 97–109.

Harlan, Tyler, & Michael Webber. (2012). "New Corporate Uyghur Entrepreneurs in Urumqi, China." *Central Asian Survey, 31*(2), 175–191.

Heidemann, Kai. (2014). "In the Name of Language: Language Revitalization, Strategic Solidarities, and State Power in the French Basque Country." *Language, Identity and Education, 13*(1), 53–69.

Howell, Anthony. (2013). "Chinese Minority Income Disparity in Urumqi: An Analysis of Han-Uyghur Labour Market Outcomes in the Formal and Informal Economies." *China: An International Journal, 11*(3), 1–23.

Howell, Anthony, & C. Cindy Fan. (2011). "Migration and Inequality in Xinjiang: A Survey of Han and Uyghur Migrants in Urumqi." *Eurasian Geography and Economics, 52*(1), 119–139.

Hu, Diya. (2013). "Cultural Endangerment and Education: Educational Analysis on the Change of Cultural Transmission of Dongba Dance of Naxi People in Lijiang, Yunnan, China." *Frontiers of Education in China, 7*(2), 169–194.

Kymlicka, Will, & Alan Patten, eds. (2003). *Language Rights and Political Theory*. New York, NY: Oxford University Press.

Lee, Jennifer. (2002). *Civility in the City: Blacks, Jews, and Koreans in Urban America*. Cambridge, MA: Harvard University Press.

Leibold, James, & Danielle Xiaodan Deng. (2016). "Segregated Diversity: Uyghur Residential Patterns in Xinjiang, China." In Anna Hayes & Michael Clarke, eds., *Inside Xinjiang: Space, Place and Power in China's Muslim Far Northwest* (pp. 122–148). London: Routledge.

Leibold, James, & Yangbin Chen. (2014). *Minority Education in China: Balancing Unity and Diversity in an Era of Critical Pluralism*. Hong Kong: Hong Kong University Press.

Liang, Y., and J. Zhang. (2007). "Xinjiang Shaoshu Minzu Shuangyu Jiaoshi Peixun Tanwei" [Bilingual Teacher Training Among Minority Teachers in Xinjiang]. *Journal of Xinjiang Normal University, 28*(3), 128–131.

Ma, Rong. (2009). "The Development of Minority Education and the Practice of Bilingual Education in Xinjiang Uyghur Autonomous Region." *Frontiers of Education in China, 4*(2), 188–251.

Mchitarjan, Irina, & Rainer Reisenzein. (2014). "Towards a Theory of Cultural Transmission in Minorities." *Ethnicities, 14*(2), 181–207.

Min, Pyong Gap. (2008). *Ethnic Solidarity for Economic Survival: Korean Green Grocers in New York City*. New York, NY: Russell Sage Foundation.

Mok, Ka Ho. (2006). *Education Reform and Education Policy in East Asia*. New York, NY: Routledge.

Mok, Ka Ho. (2010). *The Search for New Governance of Higher Education in Asia*. New York, NY: Palgrave Macmillan.

Non-State Education Promotion Law of the People's Republic of China. Retrieved from http://www.pkulaw.cn/fulltext_form.aspx?Db=chl&Gid=44356

Park, Albert, & Fang Cai. (2011). "The Informalization of the Chinese Labor Market." In Sarosh Kuruvilla, Ching Kwan Lee, & Mary E. Gallagher, eds., *From Iron Rice Bowl to Informalization Book: Markets, Workers, and the State in a Changing China* (pp. 17–35). Ithaca, NY: Cornell University Press.

Smith Finley, Joanne. (2014). *The Art of Symbolic Resistance: Uyghur Identities and Uyghur-Han Relations in contemporary Xinjiang*. Leiden: Brill Publications.

Smith Finley, Joanne, & Xiaowei Zang. (2015). "Language, Education and Uyghur Identity: An Introduction Essay." In Joanne Smith Finley & Xiaowei Zang, eds., *Language, Education and Uyghur Identity in Urban Xinjiang* (pp. 1–33). New York, NY: Routledge.

Strawbridge, David. (2008). *The Challenges of Bilingual Education in the Xinjiang Uyghur Autonomous Region People's Republic of China*. London: Save the Children. Retrieved from http://www.seameo.org/_ ld2008/doucments/presentation_document/strawbridge_xinjiang_challenges_of_bilingual_education.pdf

Sunuodula, Mamtimyn. (2015). "Second/Third Language Learning and Uyghur Identity: Language in Education for Uyghurs in Urban Xinjiang." In Joanne Smith Finley & Xiaowei Zang, eds., *Language, Education and Uyghur Identity in Urban Xinjiang* (pp. 95–113). New York, NY: Routledge.

Sunuodula, Mamtimyn, & Anwei Feng. (2011). "Learning a Third Language by Uyghur Students in Xinjiang: A Blessing in Disguise?" In Anwei Feng, ed., *English Language in Education and Societies Across Greater China* (pp. 260–283). Bristol: Multilingual Matters Ltd.

Tsung, Linda. (2014). "Trilingual Education and School Practice in Xinjiang." In James Leibold & Yangbin Chen, eds., *Minority Education in China: Balancing Unity and Diversity in an Era of Critical Pluralism* (pp. 161–186). Hong Kong: Hong Kong University Press.

Urumqi City Communist Party Office and Urumqi City Department of Education. (2007, September 24). *Urumqi Private Non-Academic Education Schools Implementation Rules* (乌鲁木齐民办非学历教育机构管理实施细则). Retrieved from http://wenku.baidu.com/link?url=QvnguGVGj3pdNGjHCenxpE8DyQnZaCdsX1mXLGTmV63rMpThq62kml2VPruV3L0Llbws7dVRM41ILpFhg12MxsJHuubx4dV--Q329cv7oRm

Urumqi City Temporarily Suspending the Approval Procedure of Non-State Schools (乌鲁木齐市暂停民办教育机构审批). (2013, May 12). *Tianshan Wang*. Retrieved from http://news.ts.cn/content/2013-12/05/content_9027596.htm

Vaish, Viniti. (2005). "A Peripherist View of English as a Language of Decolonization in Post-Colonial India." *Language Policy, 4*, 187–206.

Xinjiang Statistical Yearbook. (2010). Beijing: China Statistics Press.

Zhao, Zhenzhou. (2010). "Trilingual Education for Ethnic Minorities: Toward Empowerment?" *Chinese Education and Society, 43*(1), 70–81.

Zhao, Zhenzhou, & Gerard A. Postiglione. (2010). "Representations of Ethnic Minorities in China's University Media." *Discourse: Studies in the Cultural Politics of Education, 31*(3), 31–34.

NOTES

1. This research was made possible in part by a Faculty Research Grant from Drexel University's School of Education. The author is grateful for the support, and would also like to acknowledge the Uyghur research assistants who helped analyze the policy documents as part of this study. Their names are not mentioned (at their own request) due to political sensitivities.
2. See Tsung (2014) for a thorough description of the different bilingual education programs in Xinjiang.
3. The website was taken down in 2017 by the owner due to the changing political climate in Xinjiang.

WEILING DENG

10. SCHOOL OF FEMINISM IN BEIJING

Embodied Resistance and "Weak" Education in Twenty-First-Century China

INTRODUCTION

Toward the end of August in 2013, an apartment near the east second ring road of Beijing was filled with about thirty excited young Chinese women in their twenties, happily celebrating their graduation from The School of Feminism. While they had only been classmates for the past eight Saturdays, their learning process and friendship felt like something they had rarely experienced. One alumna said it was "the freest school" she had ever attended where there was "a completely safe space of discussion." Another added that the School was "the most interesting, imaginative, and subversive" one that she had come into, "or that had come into her."[1] A third one pointed out that they "got to do things together." Many others praised the brainstorming, discussing, and debating hours they spent together, which immersed them in a democratic and diverse manifestation of thoughts, broke through the usual pattern of standardized or binary thinking, and contributed to the mutual trust that fostered ensuing activism (One Yuan Commune's[2] blog).

Though not a school in the 'formal' sense, the School of Feminism in Beijing (SFB) provided an alternative route of knowledge production by forming a counter space that criticized the objectification of the female body, and in so doing tackled two interrelated types of patriarchal oppression: domination (the power of ruling by possessing higher positions) and differentiation (the power of alienation and debilitation by constructing an exotic, unusual category of people). With a flattened or 'horizontal' structure of teaching-learning and a commitment to resisting the embodied subjectification of male dominance, the FSB sought to utilize a space of decentralization in order to create a non-profit community-based educational initiative rooted in feminist activism.

The time span of the School's operation from 2013 to 2015 is noteworthy. These three years created a niche for the School's decentralizing characteristic to stand out prominently, one that emerged out of two parallel phenomena: the steadily declining liberal atmosphere in China's politics that marks determined recentralization of power to the government and the rapidly growing fashion of feminist vocabulary that walks hand in hand with neoliberalism. Just in the moment before authoritarian governance fastened its ideological and resource control and before "progressive neoliberalism" (Fraser 2017) comfortably landed in China's non-conforming identity movement, the spark of decentralized and democratic education was found in the SFB. While the revitalized authoritarianism in China is easy to understand – the determined call to follow the new political core of the Communist Party can be seen in the changes in textbooks, the removal of migrants from metropolitan areas, and the strict surveillance of liberal dissidents and so on – the rise of identity politics that fragments, rather than cements, the already vulnerable civil society, is yet to be widely regarded as a threat to both feminist activism in particular and education in general. Besides fragmentation, the colonial and racial problems of uncritically transplanting feminist/identity politics to China from the West are hardly addressed. But elucidating these problems is not the mission of this chapter. Instead, I go back to the years from 2013 to 2015 to examine the evidence of decentralized pedagogy in this important educational site of a grassroots Chinese feminist movement.

It is within these particular spatial and temporal contexts that this chapter will discuss in detail the two dimensions of decentralization of education that the SFB showcased: making new things happen (eventful as methodology) and making subjectification happen (emancipatory as politics). The methodological and political features were co-existent and mutually reliant in the SFB before it was shut down under political pressure after the third summer session in 2015.

I begin by introducing the origin of the SFB as a product of the transnational women's movement. The United Nations' Fourth World Conference on Women (FWCW) activated a limited but negotiable space of civil society in China where women's organizations excelled in community service. In the meantime, the women's movement in the Third World called for decolonialized transformation to help economically, racially, and culturally marginalized women to become true beneficiaries of the course of gender equality. Second, I return to the School alumnae's reflections and analyze their insufficiently articulated sense of success in this unique learning opportunity. Last, I maintain that the Feminist School had a true political function in that it possessed the ability to invite participants to collaboratively generate a new everydayness separate from and resistant to that dominated by the state and patriarchal popular culture (Lanza 2010).

BACKGROUND

The School of Feminism in Beijing (SFB) was not a school in the narrow sense: providing a fixed area for teaching, hiring lecturers through complex administrative procedure, or training for job-oriented purpose. Instead, its classes could be held anywhere: a living room, a coffee shop, an art gallery, or a park. As a volunteer-run event, it did not have sponsorship or a grant. Its income completely depended on the thirty students' tuition, which was one hundred yuan each (about fifteen US dollars). All the income went to two ends: the rental fee of the room for the meeting and travel compensation for guest speakers, whereas lecturers from Beijing taught for free. All who volunteered or were invited to teach were experts of gender studies or on women's movements. They shared the experience of attending the FWCW in Beijing in 1995, a monumental event that made the Chinese government agree to open the society to non-governmental organizations (NGOs). The conference was seen as the government's expediency to reopen the country to the rest of the world after the 1989 crackdown on students' protest. The severely damaged Chinese civil society could take advantage of this conference to regain liveliness.

After the conference, the women who later became the founders of the SFB left their governmental jobs for a more autonomous atmosphere in NGOs. NGOs were thought to be a "grey space" by some scholars because although they were under the government's watch, the boundary of control was ambiguous and negotiable (Zhao 2016). Foreign funds began to pour in to support local civil rights activists and their research and service to ordinary and marginalized people. NGOs that served women and LGBTQ groups had been a highlight and held a remarkable portion among all themes. As freelancer Zhao Sile (2016) summarized in her news article for *Oriental Net*:

> They mushroomed in Chinese society after the FWCW, playing a dual role of lobbying within the governmental institution and serving communities. As the state changed leaders and socio-political environment altered, some NGOs lost their influence and even ceased to exist, while others developed activist working tactics, cultivated feminist activists and had the individuals and organizations grow up together. The latter then gained certain level of capacity of designing their own agendas independent from the government. (p. 1, author's translation)

The SFB was an incubator of the latter type of activism. Beijing was the second city after Seoul to open a feminist school following the agenda named Network of Glocal Activism (NGA). Clearly reflected in the blend word "glocal," the mission of NGA had been to creatively understand and tackle the consequences and ongoing challenges of globalization, while keeping an eye on its impact on the local (usually the city) level. Meanwhile, because of globalization, the complexity of local/city-level problems could not be solved in isolation from other regions, which required collaboration across geographical and cultural borders. NGA's principle of operation was threefold, represented in three colors: red (Marxism, labor movement), green (ecology, environmental movement), and purple (feminism, women's movement) (*Network for Glocal Activism/School of Feminism for Glocal Activist Handbook*). But under this umbrella framework, the local experience of the women's movement was the actual highlight. The SFB's lecturer on feminism and culture, Dr. Li Jinzhao, explained that South Korea's labor union was an effective organization and could provide a solid ground for the Seoul School to recruit a lot of female staff, making the intersection of gender equality and labor their focus. But China was different: its labor union was not independent from the government. Therefore, the Beijing School was largely open to female *students*, either still in college and graduate school, or freshly graduated. According to the memoir of the One Yuan Commune in its blog post, the applicant's identification with feminism and the civil women's movement, as well as the willingness to be engaged in activism, would give her/him a high chance to be admitted.

In the first two years, namely 2013 and 2014, the class was open in July and participants met on every Saturday for eight weeks in a row. In the first meeting, students brainstormed several topics that they hoped to discuss in the following weeks and finalized the curriculum for that particular class. In general, these topics were framed under the most practically urgent struggles that Chinese women had been undergoing, such as misogynist shaming in school and workplace, domestic violence, sexual harassment in public places, the tension between development and gender, and the difficulty of creating a subcultural space for women in capitalist societies. The lecturers prepared their own materials to share but would make changes according to students' requests. However, due to increased pressure on organizing any form of activism in China, the 2015 summer session necessarily became an underground activity. The recruitment of students was moved from online public notification to word of mouth. The meeting place went as far as a remote resort in between a rural area and Beijing city. Furthermore, the duration of class was reduced from eight weekend days to five days in a row.

As the political environment in China becomes more stringent and hegemonic, it is crucial that any resistant experimentation be documented, remembered, and thoroughly studied. It has to be sufficiently and repeatedly accentuated that fewer people will fit in and benefit from the centralization of all sources. Women and ethnic minorities are placed on the disadvantaged side of commercial competition; the poor, the disabled, and the sick are having a harder time surviving at the bottom of the capitalist, neoliberalist, and bureaucratic hierarchy. The disappearance of dissenting voices, words, and arts has accelerated at a surprising speed. And at the same time, names of people, places, events, and matter fade from being sensible, affective, and inspiring. Therefore, in the age of coerced and/or voluntary forgetting, to curate and articulate a past civil rights action is essentially helpful to keep the soil of (future) actions fertile. As an event happening in a place and time in which feminist activism was still tolerated, the SFB that centered on the reconnection between the human mind and body, and between an individual and places, events, and matter must be re-presented to the present time and made inherently meaningful. As an NGO "radically … outside" (Biesta 2014, p. 6) the dominant educational system, the School used its marginal and precarious position to pursue education as an emancipatory practice.

THE BODY AND GROUND-UP EMANCIPATORY EDUCATION

In conventional pedagogy and student research, the individual waits to be positioned in certain places within the social structure to perform whatever characteristics and responsibilities are deposited in those places as marked by gender, class, race, and so on (Albrecht-Crane and Slack 2003; Lanza 2010). But individuals with subjectivity will not only fall out of the fixed categories, they should also be encouraged to recognize the power of the body as a generator of life and liveliness, as a co-creator of specific relations and affective moves that constitute the uniqueness of the person's subjectivity (Albrecht-Crane and Slack 2003, p. 194; Biesta 2014, p. 21).

Amongst the many action-oriented learning plans that the SFB carried out, this research found that the body – or more tangibly, "my body" – was situated at the center of all the educational means and ends. While formal schooling conditioned students to understand the body as something closed, embarrassing, and restraining, the feminist philosophy undergirding the SFB straightforwardly reached for a radical practice to unlearn the conventional meanings imposed on the body and instead view it as generative, admirable, and emancipatory. The contrast between the conventional and radical conceptualization of the body pinpoints the fact that learning, which inevitably involves the body as a means of participation, was never value-neutral. Although creative pedagogy and outdoor activities have been stressed by various stakeholders claiming some kind of educational expertise, it is the realization of the non-neutral value a body may carry that determines how far certain pedagogical practice will go on the road toward emancipation. Simply taking students out of classroom to know that there exists an "outer" world is not enough to mentally break down the four walls of the classroom. To imprint in mind that there is a binary between "real" and "textbook" worlds is rather an ironic idea, since the binary will keep segmenting the learner's worldview and will form a stereotypical pattern of thinking that things have to be categorized to be understandable (Orr 1994). In this sense, what was remarkable in the School's feminist pedagogy by reconnecting and regenerating knowledge with the body was the breakdown of the binary between the received concepts of real and scholastic worlds, of the dependence on fixed category to comprehend society, and of the classroom walls from within.

The body of a woman is too often misrepresented as a trigger of mystification, abhorrence, unorthodoxy, and vicious lust. For female students in their formative years of growth, the social environment teaches them to be embarrassed by the incongruency between the timing of the female body and that of careerist mobility. The embarrassment, if such preaching continues, asks for discipline, punishment, distrust, and thus self-distance from the possibility of autonomy. The consequence does not only fall on women, young and old. It falls on the entire population immersed in the misogynist and disembodied axiom of accomplishment. The result is conspicuous, appalling, and sickening. In occasions where students are asked to relate their pathway to the current interest of study, a clear masochist tone sprawls across the explanation, as if the personal can only be proved and shown through the nearly unbearable suffering of hard time, as if only the conquest over an embarrassed and embarrassing past could win the hearts of the audience.

The tint that every step is so carefully planned and walked on the pavement to success, as is exhibited in each description of the "personal" purpose of study, is and always has to be dramatized by the wounded and disciplined body. This collection of unanimously drafted dramas fits so well in neoliberal rhetoric, both unrooted from local knowledge of the particular, in favor of an inflamed feeling of belonging to the global, the infinite, and the invincible. In this case, the centralization and de-democratization of education do not have to be implemented through force, but rather, as Nancy Fraser (2017b) potently argued, citing Gramsci, through "consent." Generations of learners are left defenseless to governmentality in the form of consent after having been converted to technicians of only specialized and fragmented knowledge. For technicians, education is apolitical and is a channel through which they submit personhood and intelligence to the dream of irregulated augmentation of wealth and ego. Education as such forgets to ask what consequences it would bring if nothing more than a short-term high score is desired. There are barely fifty years since China last learned a terrible lesson with the unintended but unavoidable consequences of massive production of technicians. The danger of accumulating knowledge without foreseeing and being responsible of its impact should not be discarded so hastily (Orr 1994, p. 56). But the speed of forgetting is indeed accelerated by neoliberalism's landing in China, reconfiguring individuals into undistinctive and entrepreneurial homo oeconomicus (Brown 2015). Learning with the purpose of trading knowledge for power and mobility submits to the truly powerful, rather than restores within each embodied subject, the agency of making a more equal world.

To resist the trend of being easily submissive and manipulable, education should teach about the small instead of the big, the particular instead of the metanarrative, vulnerability and limitation instead of impeccability and infinity, responsibility and humility instead of unruly ambition and the tyranny of expertise. These goals cannot be achieved without an emphasis on the body, or on "my body" that puts even one more layer of self-consciousness and criticism of fantasy to the politics of body (Rich 1986, p. 215). Genuinely looking inward to emotion and valuing difference, "my body's" resilience in its own good may well irritate the authority that relies on the elimination of the personal. An actively learning body does not need an institution to define which knowledge is valid and salient, which place is effective and legitimate for the very action of learning, or which person plays the role of the master of knowledge. Against the theology of mobility written in the most secularized careerism, a revitalized feeling of the liveliness of the body evokes a sense of sacredness of knowing that is an end in itself. While a physical body may not be free from authoritarianism, nor the body of a school free from a specific site strictly watched by the authority, the body as a continuous means of communication and self-reassurance is in itself a site to experiment emancipatory education.

The following reflection that a former auditing student at the School of Feminism in Beijing had (see One Yuan Commune's blog), illuminates this idea of emancipation. In the reflection, the student admitted that the only feeling she had after attending the first class at the School of Feminism was nothing but great shock and confusion. She was shocked by those youth colleagues' fearless expression of the necessity to do justice to women's rights, where their fearlessness seemed a mixture of courage and superiority to her. An uncertain position to the fellow feminist activists puzzled her until she gradually participated in the actions organized by this and other feminist communities. She later learned that one of her classmates in the SFB was a college girl who walked 1,500 miles from Beijing to Guangzhou (the capital of Guangdong province), a remarkable act fighting both sexual harassment and the protective, and sexist, warning that women ought not to travel alone. Then she went to the screening of *The Ways of Vagina* [阴道之道], a localized, college-student-adapted version of Eve Ensler's drama, *The Vagina Monologues*. Weeks later, she found herself listening to a feminist radio station regularly and recommending this radio station to others. Where this transformation from an offhand observer to an engaged participant led her was the materiality of educational outcome in the form of a sincere expression of rights.

This result was beyond her expectation, given that she entered the School with discernible suspicion and discomfort. The situation of mentality where the learner sets foot – can be a controversial land of pedagogical foresight just because it is uncertain and desired. Whose desire is this? How can it be adjusted to the possibility of consistent transformation?

The auditing student's transformation clearly satisfied her, at least at the moment she wrote her reflection. The transformative experience of screening *The Ways of Vagina* can be seen as a new relationship between her and the stories on the screen, as a confrontation between her past and present in the unfolding of historical episodes, and as an entanglement between the agencies of her own body and others'. Elizabeth Ellsworth had a good explanation of the affect that emerged out of film screening. She said:

> Visual experience of watching a film entails not only representation. It has a material nature that involves biological and molecular events taking place in the body of the viewer and in the physical and imagined space between the viewer and the film. Affect and sensation are material and part of that engagement. (Ellsworth 2005, p. 4)

FEMINIST EDUCATION: POLITICS, EVERYDAYNESS, AND RESISTANCE

According to Gert Biesta (2014), education is strong because it polices, not liberates and permits growth. "Strong" education sees domination as the incentive of reproducing and reinforcing the existing socioeconomic hierarchy. In contrast, "weak" education warns against domination and emphasizes difference as ontologically meaningful to a person. The two principles of education battle over the eradication and protection of difference. Schools distinguish themselves as schools by constructing teaching modules for students to measure them against and emulate, as is indicated by the phrase "learning from." But the SFB was different in that it followed the reverse logic, "being taught," where learning solely concerned the student and the student was open to all possibilities of gradually coming to a different stage of knowing.

When the body demands a break from a "strong" education, it violates the state's project of development and competition. However small, the violation, once expressed, destructs the myth that a "strong" education can lead to the emancipation of the "weak" and subsequently will bring the dissent into trouble. A dry pursuit of "strong" education, either in a morally ascetic socialist society where production is vitally costly (like in China starting in the twentieth century) or in a capitalist society where morality is dismantled overall (like the neoliberal model China is trying to copy), education as a means of creation and reproduction is in nature a problem (Orr 1994). In the combined legacy of socialist revolution and capitalist corruption, finding a proper and agentive position for the (female) body is (un)surprisingly risky. But it is in this risk where the value of embodied feminist activism deposits the least contaminated educational principle.

Constructing around a blog comment that read "using the body as a form of protest is the last self-help tool of the vulnerable," feminist activist and scholar Zeng Jinyan (2014) depicted and discussed the difficulties and high risks of working for a civil rights movement in China. Thanks to telecommunication technologies and social media, the only tactic that one could use to mobilize ordinary people's reactions and that cannot be taken away by the authority is the combination of the body and subjectivity. The authority can make the material body disappear, but not the body's inherently pedagogical agency. Therefore, the body is independent of centralizing demands of the state. The activism-oriented SFB was established to teach young Chinese women the creativity and agency of the body. To be clear, the SFB did not mean to tell the students to risk their safety for risk's own sake; on the contrary, its existence and mission were to lower the cost of survival by destigmatizing "at-risk" people and the symbolic and material usage of the female body. Instead, the SFB taught that education would cease to be creative and inspirational if it did not take the risk to attend to the infinity of the body's physical and potentially political movements.

Movements are political in their agendas to shift the current structure of interest, but are not necessarily always allowing each participant to be equally and reasonably heard. For instance, the socialist movement that took place in mid-twentieth century China politicized male workers, peasants, and women in the augmentation of a unified subaltern narrative. While these subalterns were put to the forefront of historical revolution, their voices were represented and remained ambiguous and unheard. As a monolith, official vocabulary of the anti-hegemonic movement took over the diverse expressions of everyday subordination and became a mandatory learning of the people. The acquisition of politically aggressive language resulted not in solving life problems, but in instigating and centralizing the destructive power of anger. Historian Gail Hershatter (1997) accurately argued that "the people's" voices were appropriated to *make* the vulnerable and angry masses criticize the oppression that had not been articulated before (Hershatter 1997, p. 22). Hershatter continued to warn that:

> The ability to articulate that rage creates palpable political forces that are easy to applaud. Nevertheless, at best the official language of revolt is homogenizing,

unilinear, flattening in its inattentiveness to any categories other than those of the official class structure. At its worst, as in Cultural Revolution-era historiography, it is overblown, with resistance inflated to the point of heroic caricature or downright falsified. (Hershatter 1997, p. 23)

While Hershatter spoke of historians' responsibility to keep the specificity and historicity of the subaltern's voice from being stifled in the recorded history, her reminder is effective and sharp to educators who hope to bring marginalized voices toward the center.

It is ironically exemplary that in Hershatter's (1997) study of Chinese prostitutes in post-1949 Shanghai, when a government official in charge of "redeeming" the fallen women to communist righteousness, he only found that "not a single one of them thought that the Communist Party had come to save her" (Hershatter 1997, p. 23). This example explains very well why Chinese women's liberation was not completed when the revolutionary political party took office. The communist emancipation agenda, operationalized in totalizing and belligerent language, ignored complexity and derided the subtleness of everyday life. Education embedded in and promoting this agenda failed to develop its emancipatory function, instead encouraging enragement. The devastating result provoked interpersonal hostility and suspicion, and also compelled destruction of endeared objects (letters, photos, souvenirs, and so on) that would preserve "bourgeois" memories, leaving a hole of affection and trust to be refilled.

A social policy and management PhD student at the SFB described herself as physically "exhausted and hungry" after intensive and genuine learning of theories and brainstorming, but the result of this practice also energized her profoundly (One Yuan Commune blog). The sensitivity of feminist thinking constantly refreshed her cognition and demanded self-reflexivity in becoming a greater person. She hoped that "all feminists scattered in different places and struggling in pursuit" of knowledge and solidarity would have the chance to participate in the School of Feminism, to enlighten each other's life and know that the steps to progress needed the sight of connected lives.

Similarly, one of her classmates stated that she "finally felt the kind of sisterhood described in Euro-American feminist works" (*ibid*). There was a time lapse, which was at least months-long, between reading about sisterhood and actualizing it. What triggered the actualization of sisterhood was the experience of doing things together with like-minded feminist classmates – reading, discussing, brainstorming, debating, and going on fieldtrips. Essential to these collective activities was that each piece of experience was regarded as an "event" in which the subject was gradually becoming what she had not been, and the progression coincided with the theme of the SFB: to challenge the fundamentalist and binary pattern of judging. It is only in this way that the individual is independently politicized, brought from the margin to the ownership of embodied knowledge. And together with her colleagues who have had the same patient experience of growth, it opens the possibility of developing "the personal is political" know-how into a feminist movement.

Remaining centrifugal from state politics is key to keeping this movement reflexive and dynamic. The SFB's contribution to the contemporary Chinese feminist movement was that it used the politics of feminism not only to set up a safe space of storytelling and criticism, but also "to produce a space in which a new everyday can be experienced, new relationships formed, and alternative lives can be lived" (Lanza 2010, p. 7). It made the apartment-turned classroom a space where politics happens "in moments that are seemingly insignificant or mundane" (Albrecht-Crane and Slack 2003, p. 191), "in the most unpromising places, in what we tend to feel is without history – in sentiments, love, conscience, instincts" (Foucault 1977, pp. 139–140). A student from the 2014 cohort recalled her surprise upon entering the classroom:

> I shaved my head and was bald, and was expecting people's curious looks at me like everywhere else. But there were no judgmental words! I was warmly greeted, and no one asked about my hairstyle. That moment sparkled my life. I have always been a strange person from a very poor countryside but I love people. I was class monitor in my college because I took care of everyone, cleaned our dorm like a mother.

She laughed at herself choosing the phrase "like a mother" to indicate the mistake of gender stereotype.

> But once I confessed that I was lesbian, our dorm room was immediately frozen. My roommates stopped appreciating my caring work. I hurt them, but also felt hurt. Spring felt like winter, until summer came and I was introduced to the School of Feminism by Jinzhao. I would have gone deeper into depression and solitude had I not known her or the School.

Later, she collected the courage gained at the SFB to work as an assistant for Kim Lee. Lee, an American woman, became famous after she spoke against the domestic violence of her then husband Li Yang, who was a household name in China for learning English by yelling inspirational phrases (Lim 2013). Li Yang's "Crazy English" brand successfully kept pace with a masculine rise (雄起) of China in the world order that was stirred up by the imminent Olympic Games. Kim Lee's winning a lawsuit against her husband inspired the student to think that life was promising. But the vision of a happy future was abruptly cut short with the detainment of five Chinese feminists who protested against sexual harassment on public transportation on March 7, 2015. The negative impact of this incident, later known as "The Feminist Five," was so huge that it sent her to an asylum for depression and sent the third and last summer session of the SFB to a remote resort in suburban Beijing, sixty miles away from the apartment classroom.

CONCLUSION

In many ways, the SFB was not a "school." It existed outside the entire Chinese educational system and did not participate in any form of competitive test. It not only permitted, but also encouraged the involvement of an affective body in the classroom, sharply contrasting with conventional pedagogy that detaches body and emotion from the learning subject and at the same time requires the submission of body and mind to the authority of knowledge – the teacher. Instead, the SFB provoked radical and affective thinking and speech as a method to turn on the creative capacity in students.

All the hardship of establishing and operating the SFB in the summers from 2013 to 2015 meant to create a counter space that sheltered, though temporarily, its students from the pressure of living in a sexist, capitalist, and post-socialist Chinese society. From the constraint of learning in the School in terms of space and time derived an unlimited educational project that encouraged learners to keep the power of knowledge production. This project worked against the regulation of behavior, sexual orientation, academic performance, personality, and career goal, as does the mainstream, market-driven educational principle to fantasize a strong, efficient, and flawless learning outcome.

The SFB classroom was subversive, for which it was praised by its alumnae, and decentralized in that it acknowledged and made familiar the primal forces of social production. In this light, the SFB's coerced closure was a direct result of it being a decentralized educational laboratory in both pedagogical and political aspects. It provoked the fear of people by falling outside of the comfort zone of knowing and doing (Deleuze and Guattari 1987, p. 227). Feminist incubators like the demised SFB are still trying today to find a way through the crackdown on the agency of the divergent.

Through embodied acts, the SFB trained students to think of the dominant power behind the binaries that had been translated into their daily environment – family, classroom, factory, media, and so forth, and consequently raised the students' awareness of what Foucault (1982) called "the government of individualization" (Foucault 1982, p. 781). In doing so, the feminist pedagogy destabilized the binaries of class, man and woman, adult and child, and teacher and student, which had been institutionalized to code, organize, and regulate social activities. It is the simultaneously political/subjective and methodological/material praxis of resistance in which the SFB's momentum as a democratic and decentralized educational model was developed and carried on. This momentum did not cease to exist when the School was closed; rather, it will keep inspiring feminist actions in China.

REFERENCES

Albrecht-Crane, Christa, & Jennifer Daryl Slack. (2003). "Toward a Pedagogy of Affect." In Jennifer Daryl Slack, ed., *Animations (of Deleuze and Guattari)* (pp. 191–216). New York, NY: Peter Lang.

Biesta, Gert J. J. (2014). *The Beautiful Risk of Education.* Boulder, CO: Paradigm Publishers.

Brown, Wendy. (2015). *Undoing the Demos: Neoliberalism's Stealth Revolution.* New York, NY: Zone Books.

Deleuze, Gilles, & Felix Guattari. (1987). *A Thousand Plateaus: Capitalism and Schizophrenia* (Brian Massumi, Trans.). Minneapolis, MN: University of Minnesota Press.

Ellsworth, Elizabeth. (2005). *Places of Learning: Media, Architecture, Pedagogy.* New York, NY: Routledge.

Foucault, Michel. (1977). "Nietzsche, Genealogy, History." In D. F. Bouchard, ed., *Language, Counter-Memory, Practice: Selected Essays and Interviews* (pp. 139–164). Ithaca, NY: Cornell University Press.

Foucault, Michel. (1982). "The Subject and Power." *Critical Inquiry, 8*(4), 777–795.

Fraser, Nancy. (2017a, January 2). "The End of Progressive Neoliberalism." *Dissent Magazine*. Retrieved December 20, 2017, from https://www.dissentmagazine.org/online_articles/progressive-neoliberalism-reactionary-populism-nancy-fraser

Fraser, Nancy. (2017b, January 2). "Against progressive neoliberalism, a new progressive populism." *Dissent Magazine*. Retrieved December 20, 2017, from https://www.dissentmagazine.org/online_articles/nancy-fraser-against-progressive-neoliberalism-progressive-populism

Hershatter, Gail. (1997). *Dangerous Pleasures: Prostitution and Modernity in Twentieth-Century Shanghai*. Berkeley, CA: University of California Press.

Hickey-Moody, Anna, & Tara Page. (2016). "Introduction: Making, Matter and Pedagogy." In Anna Hickey-Moody & Tara Page, eds., *Arts, Pedagogy and Cultural Resistance: New Materialism* (pp. 1–20). London: Rowman & Littlefield.

Lanza, Fabio. (2010). *Behind the Gate: Inventing Students in Beijing*. New York, NY: Columbia University Press.

Lim, Louisa. (2013). American woman gives domestic abuse a face, and voice, in China. *NPR*. Retrieved July 4, 2017, from http://www.npr.org/2013/02/07/171316582/american-woman-gives-domestic-abuse-a-face-and-voice-in-china

Network of Glocal Activism (NGA). (n.d.). *Network for Glocal Activism/School of Feminism for Glocal Activist Handbook*. Seoul, Korea: Network for Glocal Activism.

One Yuan Commune. (2014, June 16). (9:43 p.m.). 爱上唯一的女权主义学校——女权主义学校第二期招生简章 [Love the Only Feminist School – Second Session's Admissions Guide of the School of Feminism]. *The Sina Blog*. Retrieved from http://weibo.com/p/1001603722204759112653

Orr, David W. (1994). *Earth in Mind: On Education, Environment, and the Human Prospect*. Washington, DC: Island Press.

Rich, Adrienne. (1986). *Blood, Bread, and Poetry: Selected Prose, 1979–1985*. New York, NY: W. W. Norton & Company.

Rowe, Stan. (1990). *Home Place: Essays on Ecology*. Edmonton, AB: NeWest Press.

Zeng, Jinyan. (2014). "The Politics of Emotion in Grassroots Feminist Protests: A Case Study of Xiaoming Ai's Nude Breasts Photography Protest Online." *Georgetown Journal of International Affairs, 15*(1), 41–52.

Zhao, Sile. (2016, April 30). "Farewell, Grey Space." *Oriental Net*. Retrieved June 29, 2017, http://hk.on.cc/cn/bkn/cnt/commentary/20160430/bkncn-20160430000319080-0430_05411_001_cn.html

---

NOTES

1. This mentee said in a mockingly sexualized way about her relationship with education, from which we could see that the School of Feminism had been a space safe enough to know and talk about body and sex, and to reconstruct personal relationship with the larger world in a more sensible and sensational manner. It also reflects that the previous education she had had was comparable to an unpleasant sexual relationship where she virtually took a passive position.
2. One Yuan Commune was an NGO that used to have a wide range of community service, including but not limited to gender issue. Its year-round activities were virtually supported through fundraising, one yuan after another. Its name accurately reflected the difficulty of raising money for non-profit activities, but also urban youths' willingness to remain activist, grassroots, communitarian, and hopeful.

INDEX

A
Activism, 14, 75, 92, 145–148, 152
Agricultural work/agricultural reforms, 13, 20, 22, 23
American Federation of Teachers (AFT), 117
Argentina, 1, 6, 31–39, 41, 45, 46
　crisis, 31–39, 41–44, 46
Authoritarianism, 34, 67–69, 146, 150

B
Beijing, 8, 130, 136, 145–155
Bilingual education, 121, 143
Brazil, 1, 6, 12–14, 16, 17, 21, 27
Brazilian Landless Workers Movement (MST), 6, 11–27, 29, 30
Brazilian Socialist Party, 11
Buenos Aires, 31–37, 40, 41, 46
Bush schools. *See* village schools

C
Centralization, 65–70, 148, 150
Charter Management Organization (CMO), 119
Charter schools, x, 8, 115–127
China, xvii, 1, 3, 8, 129–133, 137, 139, 141, 145–148, 150, 152, 154, 155
Civil rights, xi, 73, 115, 118, 127, 147, 148, 152
Civil society, 7, 15, 16, 18, 27, 31, 41, 43, 97, 103–111, 146, 147
Classism, 87
Communism, 69, 71, 74
Community schools, ix, x, xi, xvii, 7, 8, 83–88, 93, 97–111, 117, 129
Community-based education, ix, 1, 2, 7, 8, 34, 78, 81, 99, 145

Community-based management, xvii, 47–60
Community education associations, 51
Community participation, 3, 6, 7, 25, 33, 37, 39, 42, 48, 49, 51, 53–56, 59, 89, 97, 98, 100, 103, 108–110
Cooperativism, 17, 50, 110
Corporal punishment. *See* violence
Cultural transmission, 8, 129, 130, 141

D
Decentralization, ix, xvii, 1–8, 12, 14–16, 18, 28, 31, 38, 40, 45, 47–49, 60, 65–81, 83, 91, 97–100, 103, 109, 111, 117, 126, 129, 133, 141, 145, 146
Democratization, 1–8, 14, 20, 31–45, 47, 51, 60, 98, 99, 108, 111, 126, 150
Disabilities, 86
Discrimination, 7, 71, 73, 74, 76, 80, 85

E
Education authorizer, 118, 119, 123, 124, 126
Education Management Organization (EMO), 119
El Salvador, 1, 7, 47, 50, 51, 53, 58, 60, 63
Employment, xviii, 8, 26, 71, 75, 79, 102, 106, 129, 139, 132, 134, 136, 139, 140
Empowerment, 5, 7, 18, 33, 37, 60, 75, 139
English, 46, 67, 78, 82, 106, 129, 130–140, 154
Escuelas de Gestion Social/Cooperativa, 32–35, 40, 42, 44, 45
Ethnographic methods, xviii, 67, 75

F

Farabundo Martí Liberation Front (El Salvador), 50, 52, 54, 60, 63
Financing. 35, 91–93, 97, 98, 103, 107, 111, 124, 126. *See also* Resources
Foreign language, xvii, 121, 131–133, 138–140

G

Globalization, xvii, 147
Glocal, 147
Grassroots, ix, x, xvii, 16, 23, 26–28, 31, 33–36, 40–45, 97, 100–110, 146, 156

H

HIV/AIDS, 83, 84, 104, 108
Horizontalism, 33, 42
Hungary, xviii, 1, 7, 65–82

I

Illiteracy, 17, 101
Inclusion, ix, 4, 27, 71, 86–88, 93, 107
Inequality/inequity, 5, 7, 12, 16, 21, 31–34, 88, 40, 41, 76, 79, 80, 81, 88, 89, 98, 102, 111, 118, 127, 139
International non-governmental organizations (INGOs), 83, 91–93

K

Kirchner government (Argentina), 35, 43, 44, 46

L

Language immersion, 121
Leadership/leaders, xviii, 2, 12–15, 17, 19, 20, 22–27, 40, 42, 43, 59, 85, 86, 88–91, 108, 147
LGBTQ, 147

M

Mandarin, 129, 132–134, 136–140
Menem government (Argentina), 38

Minorities, 1, 71, 75, 123, 130, 131, 140, 148
Minority education, 65–81, 129
Minority Rights, 71, 111
Mother tongue, 129, 133, 137
Missionary schools

N

Neoliberalism, ix, x, xvii, 18, 36, 44, 92, 145, 146, 150
Non-governmental organizations (NGOs), 105, 147
  Save the Children, 98
Non-profit organization(s), 119

O

Oppression, xi, 63, 76, 88, 90, 145, 152
Opportunity structures, 31

P

Participatory governance, 12, 15–18, 26–28
Patriarchy, 145, 146
Policy making, 3, 4, 35, 39, 41, 85, 92
Politics, xvii, xviii, 3–5, 8, 12, 14, 18, 20, 41, 42, 44, 46, 47, 67, 83–85, 91–93, 122, 145, 146, 150–154
Primary schools, 74, 75, 77, 97–99, 101, 103, 104
Privatization, ix, x, 4, 7, 37–42, 49, 85, 92, 93, 104, 111, 117, 133
Protest, 6, 23, 25, 27, 31–45, 65, 66, 147, 152
Public education. *See* Public Schools
Public schools, xi, 6, 8, 11, 14–17, 19–24, 27–29, 38–40, 45, 51, 53, 56, 57, 60, 76, 86, 89, 91, 115–121, 123, 125, 126, 129, 135, 139, 140
Public sector/private sector, 1, 39, 43, 83, 92, 115, 129, 139, 140

R

Racism, 73, 87
Resources, ix, x, 5, 8, 16, 20, 21, 37, 48, 52, 54, 55, 57, 59, 60, 65, 71, 72, 74, 75, 77, 78, 84, 88, 90–93, 101, 102, 105–107, 109–111, 122, 125, 134, 138, 145. *See also* Financing
Rhodesia, 100
Roma/'gypsy', xviii, 7, 66, 67, 70–82
Rural schools, 17, 21, 75, 104

S

School choice, 117, 126
School of Feminism, 145–156
Segregation, 5, 7, 8, 37, 66, 70, 72–75, 80, 84, 130, 141
Social movements, x, xi, xvii, xviii, 6, 11–28, 31, 33–36, 38, 42–44
Soviet/Sovietism, 66–69, 71, 82
Spanish, 51, 115
Structural adjustment, 37, 97, 100, 103, 110, 113
Sub-Saharan Africa, 99

T

Tanzania, 1, 8, 83–93
Teachers, 1, 2, 4, 7, 11–15, 18–27, 33, 34, 37–39, 41, 42, 47–49, 51, 52, 54–60, 65, 67, 68, 70, 72, 76, 78–80, 82, 84–90, 93, 97, 98, 101–103, 105–111, 117, 119, 121, 125, 129, 130, 134–138, 140, 155
Teacher training, 14, 15, 20–23, 26, 35, 85, 103, 106

Teaching profession, 29, 84, 85
Technocratic governance, 48
TOEFL, 133

U

UNESCO, xix, 17, 18
UNICEF, 17, 18, 49, 104–106
United National Independence Party (UNIP), 101
United States, ix–xi, 1, 8, 49, 82, 115–127
US Agency for International Development, 49, 107
Uyghur, 8, 129–141, 143

V

Vendor Operated Schools (VOS), 119
Village schools, 66, 74–80, 90, 101. *See also* Bush schools
Violence, 35, 39, 69, 81, 86, 87, 148, 154

W

Women's movement, 146–148
World Bank, x, 7, 17, 37, 49, 50, 52, 56, 58, 63, 92, 97, 102, 109

Y

Youth, xvii, xviii, 7, 12–14, 17, 19, 21, 27, 37, 66, 71, 74–79, 150, 156

Z

Zambia, xvii, 1, 7, 97–105, 107, 109–111

Printed in the United States
By Bookmasters